MODERNISM, IRELAND AND THE EROTICS OF MEMORY

NICHOLAS ANDREW MILLER

Loyola College in Maryland

PUBLISHED BY THE PRESS SYNDICATE OF THE UNIVERSITY OF CAMBRIDGE
The Pitt Building, Trumpington Street, Cambridge, United Kingdom

CAMBRIDGE UNIVERSITY PRESS
The Edinburgh Building, Cambridge CB2 2RU, UK
40 West 20th Street, New York, NY 10011-4211, USA
477 Williamstown Road, Port Melbourne, VIC 3207, Australia
Ruiz de Alarcón 13, 28014 Madrid, Spain
Dock House, The Waterfront, Cape Town 8001, South Africa

http://www.cambridge.org

First published 2002

Printed in the United Kingdom at the University Press, Cambridge

Typeface Baskerville Monotype 11/12.5 pt   *System* LATEX 2ε   [TB]

A catalogue record for this book is available from the British Library

Library of Congress Cataloguing in Publication data
Miller, Nicholas Andrew.
Modernism, Ireland and the erotics of memory / Nicholas Andrew Miller.
p.   cm.
Includes bibliographical references and index.
ISBN 0 521 81583 5
1. English literature – Irish authors – History and criticism.
2. Modernism (Literature) – Ireland.   3. Historical films – Ireland – History and criticism.
4. Ireland – Civilization – 20th century.   5. Literature and history – Ireland.
6. Motion pictures – Ireland.   7. Memory in literature.   I. Title.
PR8722.M6 M55   2002
820.9'112'09417–dc21   2002017501

ISBN 0 521 81583 5 hardback

For my wife, Alyssa
In dreams begins responsibility.

Contents

Illustrations

Acknowledgments

We all unite thoughtfully in rendering gratias.
James Joyce
Finnegans Wake

The writing of this book has been sustained by the patience, honesty, and generosity of a great many people. It is a simple and material fact that it would not exist were it not for their numerous intellectual, emotional, and spiritual gifts to me. Beyond the margins of these pages, however, it is for their wise companionship through myriad small acts of investigation, choice-making, and acceptance, for their collective instruction in what really amounts to a kind of practical faith, that I am most deeply grateful.

My greatest thanks are due Vicki Mahaffey, whose graduate seminar on Joyce swiftly and convincingly ended my flirtation with a career in Renaissance Studies, and who oversaw this project in its earliest incarnation as a dissertation in the Program in Comparative Literature and Literary Theory at the University of Pennsylvania. For her generosity as a teacher and friend, for her willing acceptance of commitment's arduous demands, and for her wisdom in knowing that honesty and intellectual resistance are forms of support indispensable to every writer, I am profoundly thankful. The ideas explored in the pages that follow owe more to her incomparable example as a reader and a thinker than their expression perhaps betrays.

The support of my extraordinary colleagues in the English Department at Loyola College in Maryland, and the example of intellectual integrity and commitment they daily provide, have provided inspiration when it was most sorely wanted. In particular, the guidance and diplomacy of my department chair, Paul Lukacs, have been invaluable in helping me navigate the stresses of teaching and academic service while completing the difficult, concluding stages of research and writing. I want especially to thank Brennan O'Donnell who, with insight and

ix

unfailing good humor, diagnosed crucial problems and their solutions in two versions of the introduction. I am indebted to him and to my fellow Joycean, Mark Osteen, for their supportive, critical engagement with my work, as well as for their scholarly examples.

Other parts of the manuscript, in various stages, benefited from the careful and insightful readings given them by Jean-Michel Rabaté, Arkady Plotnitsky, Joseph Valente, Craig Saper, and David Herman. Brian Murray fashioned needed improvements in Part I with a skill-fully applied editorial scalpel; Janet Headley offered patient guidance through successive drafts of the first and fourth chapters; Genevieve Rafferty transcribed much of the bibliography; Fr. Michael Braden, S. J., and Daniel Schlapbach invested time and technical expertise in tracking down appropriate illustrations. The Center for the Humanities at Loyola College provided grant money through two successive summers during one of which I completed research at the Irish Film Centre and at the National Library in Dublin. I am indebted to Liam Wiley, formerly of the IFC for his encyclopedic knowledge of the Archive and of Irish film generally. Sunniva O'Flynn, director of the Archive, has been extraordi-narily generous with the Centre's resources and supportive of my work in general.

Special words of gratitude are due Sean Flanigan, a true lover of ideas and a great friend, for generous and encouraging comments on the manuscript, for persistence in flagging down infelicities of expression I had overlooked, and for work on the index that can only be described as heroic. For these many contributions, but especially for sharing with me the joys and challenges of the work, I am extremely grateful. I am also fortunate in my enduring friendships with Jonathan Hess, Marian Eide, and Barbara Lonnquist, all of whom shared enthusiasm and perspective, as called for, at key junctures. To my film and literature students at Loyola College I want to express my appreciation for insisting that complex ideas be expressed clearly and for reminding me in material and human terms why those ideas matter in the first place.

In my continuing explorations of memory, I have been privileged to encounter certain fellow travelers whose courage and honesty I will truly never be able to repay. Although they are far too numerous to mention by name, I wish to thank them, as deeply as it is possible to do, for their guidance in helping me to understand memory-work as a human and spiritual process through which we let go of the past without, however, ever shutting the door on it. I am profoundly grateful to my parents, Lucien and Bonnie Miller, for their love, support, and faith in me, to George and Rose Fieo whose generosity and humor have lightened the load considerably, and to Claudia Fieo, whose extraordinary artistic vision has allowed me to hope that readers will judge my book by its cover.

Finally, and most of all, I want to acknowledge a gratitude that is indeed inexpressible to my sons, Aidan and James, and to my wife, Alyssa Fieo, for their love and for the joy of their presence. It is they who have felt most keenly the "endnessnessessity" of "this letter self-penned to one's other, this never-perfect ever-planned." It is also they whose support has been most pure, abundant, available, and freely shared.

All history is local: modernism and the question of memory in a global Ireland

> To give an accurate description of what has never occurred is . . . the proper occupation of the historian.
>
> Oscar Wilde
> *The Critic as Artist*

It may no longer be possible to speak and write of "Ireland." Amid the vast cultural and economic shifts of the last decade, the Irish Republic has emerged as something unfamiliar: an international economic power asserting its political will on the European continent, marketing its own culture through a powerful indigenous film and media industry, and staking its claim to a high-tech manufacturing future powered by multinational corporate investment. It makes far more sense to speak now of a "global Ireland" as the country has become, for the first time in its history, a destination of choice not only for tourists but for job-seekers, investors, and international businesses selling everything from microchips to ketchup. The old familiar touchstones of Irish experience and identity have come to seem oddly dislocated in this context. It is not simply that "Kerry Gold" and other registered trademarks have displaced St. Patrick, shamrocks, and the color green as authentic signifiers of Irishness. After centuries spent in embattled pursuit of independence in its many elusive forms – economic prosperity, political autonomy, religious and geographic unification, historical atonement – Irish culture has quite suddenly begun to shed its identification with struggle as its principal and defining characteristic.

Observers weary of wandering the barbed and tangled thickets of the country's long colonial and post-colonial past have, quite logically, leapt at the chance finally to announce that at long last Ireland is coming into its own. Witness *Irish Times* journalist Fintan O'Toole's assertion that in the mid-1990s, "arguably for the first time in recorded Irish history, it became possible to understand the Republic of Ireland without reference to Britain. It was no longer possible to blame British colonialism,

I

the nightmare of a benighted past, for the country's problems. It was no longer possible to envisage Irishness as merely the other side of Britishness."[1] For O'Toole, the actuality of Ireland's economic independence effects, de facto, a significant and measurable degree of autonomy in the political sphere. As an emerging economic power, Ireland loses the yoke of British oppression (along with the ability to blame Britain for its troubles), and shoulders responsibility for its own new global self-conception. England, for its part, is reduced to "an inconsequential and edgy presence on the margins" (O'Toole, *Ex-Isle*, 12) as Irishness, given sufficient economic clout, can now finally begin positively to define itself in its own terms. No longer, O'Toole asserts, in the shadow of its historically more powerful and richer neighbor, Ireland has ceased, in an imaginative sense, "to be an island off Britain. After centuries of sending its people into exile, it [has become] itself an ex-isle" (O'Toole, *Ex-Isle*, 11).

O'Toole's island-no-longer metaphor registers the magnitude of contemporary Ireland's imaginative removal from Britain in geographic terms. At the same time, the "ex" of "ex-isle" places the greatest emphasis on Ireland's historical removal from its own former self, and thus reopens what is in fact a quite familiar, age-old rift in Irish identity, that between the past and the present. In the rush to claim the present as that time in which the true voice of Irishness may finally speak, the past becomes a distinct and contrary position, that time of Ireland's sacred but benighted struggle. Proclaiming Ireland's new existence as an "ex-isle" betrays a hope that if economic independence has not fully succeeded in healing partition's legacy of violence, it has secured for contemporary Ireland something even greater: independence from its own past.[2]

O'Toole is well aware, of course, of the irony implicit in the notion that Ireland might ever by "no longer" what it was. The country's long history of cultural, political, economic, and legal subjugation at the hands of Britain has produced the past as the only territory to which the Irish could reasonably lay claim. Thus, in Ireland the effort to know history has frequently aligned itself with a discourse of political essentialism in which it is not the past but Irishness itself that hangs in the balance. What has seemed indisputable to observers of modern Irish culture and politics is that in Ireland's case the past has been all too insistent, all too present an influence. In his classic investigation of Irish historical imagining, *States of Mind*, Oliver MacDonagh comments wryly on British Prime Minister Lloyd George's discovery that "while the English do not remember any history, the Irish forget none." After meeting with Eamon de Valera on

July 14, 1921 to negotiate a peace treaty between Ireland and Great
Britain, Lloyd George reportedly said, "I listened to a long lecture on
the wrong done to Ireland ... [by] Cromwell, and when[ever] I tried to
bring him [de Valera] to the present day, back he went to Cromwell
again."[3]

"To remember everything," suggests Hugh, the polyglot hedge-school
master in Brian Friel's play, *Translations*, "is a form of madness," and many
observers have seen fit to locate Ireland's defining cultural pathology in
the notoriously long memory of its people.[4] As David Lloyd has recently
remarked, "We Irish have often enough been accused of indulging an
obsession with the past."[5] From a certain point of view, the charge may
seem true enough: while conventional wisdom holds that "those who do
not know the past are destined to repeat it," in Ireland's case, knowing
history has seemed to ensure nothing so well as the continuation of age-
old patterns of violent rebellion, internal betrayal, and political failure.
From one failed rebellion at Kinsale in 1603 to another at Dublin Castle
in 1641, to yet another in Wexford in 1798, to still another in Dublin
in the spring of 1916, so much of Irish history has seemed to unspool
according to some fatally deterministic law of sameness – and defeat.

In fact, the impression of repetition in Irish history is less an indicator of
actual historical patterns than of the dominance of a preferred narrative
in which the future continuously holds the promise of newness. The
story of Ireland, suggests Roy Foster (borrowing a phrase from Michel
de Certeau), is conventionally "linked to the expectation that something
alien to the present will or must occur" – that a future departure from the
pattern will finally allow Ireland to "come into its own." In these terms,
O'Toole's characterization of Ireland as an "ex-isle" participates in what
Foster has argued is in fact a venerable Irish historiographical tradition,
the search for Irish history's proper ending.[6] The importance within this
tradition of specifying, even speculatively, a future moment in which the
past will be left behind suggests that what has always been at stake in the
telling of Ireland's "story" is nothing less than the country's modernity. In
conventional usage, after all, to be "modern" is to be current, up-to-date,
forward-looking: in a word, *new*. Indeed, "modernity" seems to imply a
certain distance from the past as its defining condition. As David Lloyd
eloquently puts it:

The accusation [of Irish historical obsession] is usually made in the name of a
modernity defined not so much by the erasure of the past as by the discrimination
of those elements of the past which can be incorporated in a progressive narrative from those which must be relegated to the meaningless detritus of history.

But, as [Walter] Benjamin well understood, such "historicism" entails a drastic reduction of the field of possibilities for the sake of a singular verisimilitude called "progress" and "development." To capitulate to such historicism, rather than continually opening the historical narrative to undeveloped possibilities, is to accept the reductive logic of domination. (Lloyd, *Anomalous States*, 10)

In other words, the potential risk in characterizing contemporary Ireland's new birth as a nation – its modernity – as a departure from historical pattern is not that the past will be forgotten, but that it will be relativized. In the new Ireland, history's once blinding insistence in the present is dimmed by the floodlights of real economic power. Phrases like "Ireland for the Irish" and *Sinn Féin, Sinn Féin Amhain* [Ourselves, Ourselves Alone] continue to resonate, but do so in an unaccustomed, apolitical register. The past, so long an instrument of cultural confinement is at last de-barbed and placed, unthreatening, like a sort of cultural trophy or curiosity on the shelf of history. Here is the actual flip-side of historical obsession: not denial of the past, but disinterested reverence for it; not a fearful sense that history might be ignored, but a relieved one that it has been at long last safely discontinued.

My point here is not to claim that economic opportunity is somehow on balance a liability for Ireland, or that participation in global trade compromises the authenticity of its culture. Even less is it to complain, along the lines of the old joke, that in Ireland nostalgia is not what it used to be. What is important is to recognize to what extent optimism about Ireland's financial independence affirms disconnection from the past as both an instrument and, indeed, a desired outcome of Ireland's contemporary autonomy. O'Toole's formulation releases Ireland from its political dependencies only to reassert its modernity in opposition to what it once was. When in the name of historical progress and development Ireland is reconfigured as an "ex-isle" belatedly cut off from its own past, history is promptly reconfirmed as the perpetual nightmare from which Ireland is trying to awake.

MODERNISM AND THE EXILE OF MEMORY

In a curious way, Ireland's current effort at re-imagining itself parallels its political and cultural transformation in the early decades of the twentieth century. Then, as now, the struggle to become modern linked the definition and achievement of Irish independence to a separation, or moving on, from the past. During the thirty years between Parnell's death in 1891 and the signing of the Anglo-Irish Treaty in 1921, the romantic values of the late nineteenth-century Irish literary and cultural renaissance provided a convenient foil for a twentieth-century Ireland striving to claim its independence as a modern state. At the same time, the loss of Parnell's coalition-building abilities as a political leader led, as has often been noted, to a return to factionalism and violent methods for political change, leading up to the Easter Rising in 1916 and its aftermath, the War of Independence.[7] At both ends of the twentieth century, modern Ireland's collective task has been not simply to rethink the terms and conditions of Irishness, but to reconfigure their relation to a past that, despite being finished, refuses to be left behind. Ireland's struggle to become modern expresses what is, at its root, a crisis of historical imagination.

It was the transformation not of Irishness, but of Irish historical imagination that T. S. Eliot cited in what has become a seminal statement on "modernism" in the aesthetic sphere. In his famous review of *Ulysses*, Eliot accorded the newness of Joyce's writing "the importance of a scientific discovery," and placed its significance on a level with Einstein's theory of relativity.[8] Joyce's use of the "mythic method," a technique Eliot said originated in the work of another Irishman, William Butler Yeats, had fundamentally transformed the landscape of literature, and the way we read, for all time. Eliot's assessment of the mythic method went well beyond the description of a formally innovative technique to link modernism as such specifically to the project of remembering differently. The mythic method, Eliot suggested, consists in a kind of radical affirmation of the past's currency in the imaginative description of present experience: "In manipulating a continuous parallel between contemporaneity and antiquity," Eliot wrote, "Mr. Joyce is pursuing . . . [what] is simply a way of controlling, of ordering, of giving a shape and a significance to the immense panorama of futility and anarchy which is contemporary history" (Eliot, "*Ulysses*, Order, and Myth," 177). Joyce, Eliot insisted, found and transformed his "living material" by opening it to a vibrant and insistent past, the "modernity" of Homer's *Odyssey* read as a structural foil for middle-class life in early twentieth-century Dublin. In a similar way, the "newness" of Yeats's writing affirmed the radical currency or "modernity" of Irish myth. In their use of this method, literary art was transformed; the novel revealed itself as a dead form and was at the same time reborn, phoenix-like, in its modernity as *novel* once more.

Despite his description of the "mythic method" as a technique aris-
ing out of a deep appreciation for the past's perpetual currency, Eliot's
emphasis on Joyce and Yeats as formal innovators gave rise to a powerful
and enduring critical misprision regarding both the condition of modernity as such and, especially, its articulations through aesthetic discourses
of modernism. Within certain strains of literary and cultural criticism,
"modernism" has come to be synonymous with a willful, even adolescent,
ignorance of historical continuity in the pursuit of formal and stylistic
innovation for its own sake. If the expression of modernity seems to require new languages and forms, it has also come to imply a problematic
process of self-fashioning based on disconnection from the past.

Traditionally, this view of modernism is linked with the historical emergence of the New Criticism in the 1930s and 1940s. Certainly, the New
Critical assertion that the literary work is an autonomous object, distinct from its determination both by authorial intention and by context,
rhymes well with the assessment of modernism as a project of "making
it new" always at the past's expense.[9] Moreover, this view is articulated
most clearly in work by the direct heirs to the New Critical tradition,
American scholars such as Irving Howe who, writing in the 1960s, argued that "the modernist sensibility posits a blockage, if not an end, to
history...A frightening discontinuity between the traditional past and
the shaken present."[10] Such assertions depend for their force on a largely
imposed and artificial view of modernism as a discrete movement or period; in other words, on the monolithic unity of a "modernist sensibility."

My goal in proposing a reassessment of modernism here is not to cross
swords with the historically distant proponents of a critical tradition the
limitations of which have long since emerged. What I wish to point out
is that the framing of modernism in its distinction from the past forms a
key part of a larger critical strategy, one that is accepted across otherwise
conflicting spheres of ideological, political, and intellectual preference.
The notion of a modernist "sensibility" persists, for instance, in some of
the structuralism and post-structuralism of the 1970s and 1980s, a period
when Paul de Man could write of the defining modernist desire "to
wipe out whatever came earlier."[11] Similarly, amid the various "returns"
to context and history advocated by post-colonial and cultural critics
in the 1990s, the characterization of modernism as a hopelessly dated
movement founded on a willed condition of historical disconnection
has gained its widest acceptance.[12] In a very different context, and with
different implications, the same view informs the linking of modernist
aesthetics with fascism, a critical tradition that spans all of these decades,

from Frank Kermode's *The Sense of an Ending* in the mid-1960s to Charles Ferrall's recent book, *Modernist Writing and Reactionary Politics*.[13]

In much of twentieth-century critical discourse, the expression of modernity and "newness" in the aesthetic or cultural spheres has become linked to an alleged "denial" of – or at the very least, separateness from – history. At the same time, it is a more or less established fact that the canonical milestones of modernist aesthetics everywhere belie this critique and its simplistic pairing of innovation with historical disconnection. Eliot's own pastiche of textual fragments in *The Waste Land*, for example, certainly embodies a new approach to epic form. That formal novelty, however, is rooted not in the denial of previous forms, but in an acknowledgment of the past's continued insistence in the present. As the poet put it in "Tradition and the Individual Talent," the one thing indispensable to the true artist of contemporaneity is a profound "historical sense," a "perception, not only of the pastness of the past, but of its presence."[14] Eliot's contention is convincingly borne out by the very artists literary criticism has canonized as definitively "modernist." From Joyce to Yeats to Conrad, from Barnes to Stein to Woolf, what unites the extraordinary diversity of modernist writing is the vitality (or as Marjorie Perloff has put it, the *eros*) with which its creators handle history.[15] In light of such work, modernism's alleged "denial" of history appears to be something of a critical shibboleth, a charge that has served the purposes of some professional critics but holds up only as long as the works themselves are selectively ignored.

What the traditional critique of modernism and the assessment of Ireland's modernity have both managed to bypass is precisely the question of memory. Exiled from their examination of "newness" is modernity's ongoing formal and cultural expression through individual and collective acts of historical imagination. Such acts of remembering constitute what is in fact modernity's – and modernism's – proper and defining praxis. "Modernism," in these terms, is not a monolithic or unified aesthetic strategy for denying the past, but rather the expression of every present culture's material experience of the past's insistence. What modernism leaves behind are strategies for engaging the past that render history factually dead; what modernism in all periods and forms "makes new" is nothing other than memory – the active, variable, ambivalent process that continuously opens up the narrative of history to new possibilities of vitality and relevance.

Put a different way, what I am suggesting is that modernism as such consists in the dynamic reconfiguration of the present's relationship with the past, and that in that reconfiguration memory itself operates as a process not of the past's recovery exclusively, but also of self-fashioning in the present. Insofar as modernism articulates a new fashioning of self, it relies on a dynamic and varied practice of memory as the mechanism by which we not only know the past, but in that knowing also construct ourselves as stable subjects.

Here it becomes possible to formulate a powerful and far-reaching distinction between the aims and implications of "history," on one hand, and "memory," on the other. In its conventional conception, the historian's task consists in bringing to light what definitively occurred, explaining causes and effects and, in general, giving the past the narrative form in which it can be known: "history." The narrator of such a discourse, the historian or rememberer, is quite clearly one conceived primarily, even exclusively, in his or her capacity to know. While disposing the past for knowledge is the announced goal of historical inquiry, its effect is the production – and more or less constant reproduction – of human beings as knowers of the past. Indeed, history so conceived is meaningless unless human beings are presumed exclusively as rational subjects whose stability is commensurate with their capacity to know.

Memory's goal, on the other hand, is never a comprehensive and final knowledge of the past or its preservation, but a process of continuous renegotiation of selfhood in relation to that past. In acts of memory, forgetting must be acknowledged as an instrumental aspect of remembering rather than its opposite; gaps make their positive contribution to the forms and images and stories through which the past "occurs" to the present. Indeed, memory in general is a process directed not primarily toward grasping an accurate or adequate knowledge of the past – what really "occurred" then – but toward allowing to occur now precisely those pasts, those histories, that have never occurred to the historical imagination of the present. As Oscar Wilde insisted, "To give an accurate description of what has never occurred is . . . the proper occupation" of those who remember.

IRELAND'S EX-CENTRIC DISCOURSES OF MEMORY

Approaching modernism as a varied and variable discourse of memory places criticism's primary investigative emphasis on an activity of remembering as it is carried out under material and historical conditions by human beings in the present. Such an approach represents a significant displacement of critical attention away from the easy distinction between an unfolding present and a factual, completed past, and thus from modernity itself as a state or condition of radical historical disconnection. Reconfiguring modernism's relationship with memory in this way returns us to the site of the past's only real actuality in the present, that of its localization in the memory-work of human beings who remember – and forget. Modernity consists in nothing other than this continuous renegotiation of memory, the material and vital activity in which all history, even that of a "global Ireland," becomes particular, specific, and actual. In memory – to paraphrase a famous Irish-American, Tip O'Neill – all history is local.

Highlighting the role of the human subject in forging Ireland's relationship to its past underscores the difficulty of the question of Irish autonomy and independence with which I began. In a modernity centered on newness, where does it become possible to locate anything that might be called an authentic discourse of Irish memory? In a global culture that relativizes traditional signifiers of Irishness, where might we locate Ireland's "own" discourses, its newly established languages of cultural authenticity? The post-colonial critique of Irish culture has produced a rich and complex consideration of such discourses, centering on a recognition that as a nation Ireland has been defined from the "outside" for most of its existence.[16] The work of American Joyce scholar Vince Cheng, to cite one prominent example, responds to a common recognition of the critical tendency to situate Ireland, throughout its history, in relation to England, America, continental Europe, and a host of other "Others." In such a perspective, Irish experience needs to be released from observation from without; its authentic discourses of self need to be heard from and spoken to "on their own terms." As Cheng puts it, "*who* gets to speak for Irishness?"[17]

My difficulty with such approaches is that they frequently preserve by clandestine means the power of the "Other" to frame Irish authenticities.[18] That is, they see themselves as framing a theory or a practice that will somehow "allow" the heretofore silent voices of indigenous experience to speak their own truth. Irishness, it is hoped, can then begin positively to define itself in its own terms – the terms of "Irishness." The not-so-hidden tautology here signals an ironic return to the familiar, repetitive process of an Irish history centered, self-consciously, on isolation and opposition in the articulation of its "own" voice: "Ireland for the Irish" and *Sinn Féin, Sinn Féin Amhain.*[19]

The emergence of a "global Ireland" suggests the possibility of locating Irish authenticity differently. After centuries of poverty, it is indeed striking that Ireland should attain, relatively suddenly, a significant degree of real economic independence. O'Toole's point in formulating contemporary Ireland's status as an "ex-isle," however, is not simply that Ireland is wealthy, but that wealth has become one of the actual historical conditions of "Irishness" in the contemporary world. Capital, and the international commerce that is creating it, has become, of all things, an authentic discourse of Irishness. In this case, coming into its "own" has meant for Ireland a wholesale redefinition of the terms of its identity and a de-centering of traditionally privileged centers of Irishness. Globalization is routing the process of Irish self-fashioning through vocabularies of culture and experience that have traditionally been defined as non-Irish. The customary distinctions between what is external and internal to Irish experience and culture are becoming blurred. As Irishness speaks increasingly in and through "Other" discourses, Irish identity is becoming itself profoundly "ex-centric."

Of course, the instant we credit a contemporary process of globalization for producing this de-centering or ex-centering of Irish identity, we remember that Irish culture has always been "global" in precisely this sense. Historically, *Sinn Féin, Sinn Féin Amhain* is a politically pedigreed rallying cry for Irish nationalists, but it belies the myriad ways Irish experience can be, and indeed has always been, articulated through discourses that do not issue exclusively from privileged centers of Irish cultural authenticity; as a phrase qualifying a putatively authentic discourse of Irishness, "Ourselves Alone" has always ignored the specific complexities both of foreign determinants within Irish culture and of Irish influences on the rest of the world.[20] Every culture uses languages and discourses that it has inherited, adopted, purchased, or borrowed. With respect to those discourses, none of us thinks and acts within his or her "own" culture from a position of mastery or authenticity. Indeed, the very notion of one's "own" discourse is a political and cultural ideal, but seldom if ever a practical reality: "And haven't you your own language to keep in touch with – Irish?" asks the nationalist Molly Ivors in Joyce's "The Dead." "Well," replies Gabriel, "if it comes to that, you know, Irish is not my language."[21]

The "exogamy" of Irish culture is one of Brien Friel's principal themes in *Translations*. The play's central dramatic action concerns the nineteenth-century British Ordnance Survey which, while mapping Ireland for taxation purposes, anglicized Irish place names in order to "standardize" them: "What the hell," one character comments. "It's only a name. It's the same me isn't it?" (Friel, *Translations*, 38). Through Jimmy Jack Cassie's final, cautionary speech to Maire, who is in love with the British Lieutenant Yolland, Friel acknowledges the danger in crossing cultural boundaries: "Do you know the Greek word *endogamein*?

It means to marry within the tribe. And the word *exogamein* means to marry outside the tribe. And you don't cross those borders casually – both sides get very angry" (Friel, *Translations*, 82). Yet the play's complaint against British political and linguistic hegemony is complicated by Jimmy's own easy use of another foreign language: Greek. Indeed, in the characters of Jimmy and Hugh, Friel grounds Irishness in the historicity of a rural people who are not only fluent in Latin and Greek, but to whom "it is perfectly normal to speak these tongues" (Friel, *Translations*, 8). Even as it condemns political and linguistic colonization, the play affirms Irish culture's emergence at the intersection of internal and external discourses. As Wilde argued in a different context, "People . . . go through their lives in a sort of coarse comfort . . . without ever realising that they are . . . thinking other people's thoughts . . . and never being themselves for a single moment."[22] The words we speak are always *other* words; the knowledges of Ireland we share are always riven through with shards of histories, cultures, methodologies, and technologies that are profoundly external, or "ex-centric."

The crucial point to be made in the present context is that Ireland's discourses of memory are also and have always been "ex-centric" discourses. The forging of Ireland's cultural and political identity in relation to its past has always been rooted in other, foreign technologies and languages of memory. Like all cultural generalizations, the notion that historical obsession is Ireland's special "anomaly" (to adopt Lloyd's useful term), says a great deal more about the investments observers make in Irish culture than it does about that culture itself. If reverence for the past seems something more than a liability for Irish culture, it may be due to observers' own investments in Ireland's remaining eternally and perversely caught between the immovable objects of its own collective memory and the unstoppable force of historical "progress." In a culturally reductive way, an obsessive memory may well be one of those things "We Outsiders" need "We Irish" to have – like wit or whiskey – in order to make sense of what seems otherwise a profound and confounding strangeness. Seeing the Irish as a people unable to look back without staring is intellectually convenient not least because it bypasses a crucial examination of what is meant by "looking back" in the first place. One way to begin to understand the presence of the past in Irish experience without resorting to cultural essentialism, then, is to examine memory itself as a cultural function.

A focus on "ex-centric" discourses of Irish memory enables a powerful and far-reaching reinvestigation of Irish memory where more conventionally "Irish" texts cannot. The latter speak necessarily from within

Irish culture and tradition, and so are constrained either to rely on or to react against those cultural values of Irishness that have been sentimentalized or essentialized as "authentic." The notion of ex-centric cultural discourses of memory opens the study of Irishness to a range of influences and articulations, localized in technological discourses (the cinema), interpretive discourses (psychoanalysis), representational discourses (memorials and monuments), methodological discourses (literary criticism), and so on. Languages such as these are "ex-centric" in the sense that they are external to that comparatively narrow range of discourses conventionally linked with Ireland. On the other hand, they frame and inform observations of Irish culture both from within and without to an extent that is observable and important.

My exploration of Irish memory in what follows is centered on the impact such external discourses have had both on Irish culture and on its perceptions; on the ways in which Irishness is articulated and modulated in them especially during the country's political reconfiguration at the beginning of the last century. The ex-centric perspectives on Irishness I pursue here all attempt to reveal those functions of memory that operate within Irish culture, but remain occluded, or are even deliberately disallowed, when the question is framed in the register of Ireland's isolation and right to self-possession. Ex-centric perspectives are necessary because without them, scholarship about Ireland continues to barter in tautologies without apprehending the actual historical complexity and elasticity of cultural identity. To seek a discretely and authentically Irish discourse of Irishness is, as this book attempts to demonstrate, not only intellectually reductive but historically inaccurate.

THE OCCURRENCE OF THE PAST

The principal purpose of this book, then, is to explore memory, both in the Irish context and in general, as the unfolding process through which the past continuously "occurs," for the first time, to the present. Looking back is always a "local" endeavor, an attempt by human rememberers to make the past present, to allow what might have occurred in history but never yet occurred in the present's continuous conversation with the past, to occur now, imaginatively, through stories, images, language, and other discursive means. It is worth noting explicitly what will be obvious from this description: namely, that the conception of memory with which I am working is rooted, at both personal and collective levels, in the concrete and complex existence of individuals who, on a continuing basis, remember and forget the past, and who do so through a diversity of authentic discourses. What has motivated the writing of this book is not so much an interest in the theory of memory for its own sake – even though this is, in many aspects, a work of theory – as in the kinds of human subjects different theories of historical engagement imply, rely on, and presume to exist.

My investigation proceeds in two complementary but distinct sections. Part I, "The erotics of memory," explores the theoretical dimensions of memory's cultural function in general by examining the processes of textualization, narrative and otherwise, through which memory recovers the past. Part II, "The spectacles of history," pursues a series of case studies in modern Irish historical imagination, each centering on the authenticity of the Irish past as revealed through "ex-centric" discourses of memory.

Part I begins with an investigation of one of the most powerful cultural instruments of the past's "occurrence" in the present, the public memorial. By giving the past its textual, legible form as inscription, conventional memorials – like all forms of history writing – bury its actuality in language, re-covering it anew. Viewers who cede this textualizing and narrativizing function to the memorial itself obviate their own active memory-work in the present, and thus accept the memorial's disposition of the past as complete and distant. A specific alternative exists in the modernist "counter-memorials" of German-Jewish Holocaust memorialist Jochen Gerz. Gerz's installations routinely render the memorial inscription itself inaccessible to the viewer, thus placing responsibility for the past's duration squarely in the active and transformative memory-work of individuals in the present.

Gerz's emphasis on remembering as a process of investment in self-formation sets the stage for Chapter Two's more general intellectual history of modernism and memory. Turning to a seminally modern text, Dante's *Divine Comedy*, the chapter examines the image of the pilgrim Dante crossing Lethe, the classical river of forgetfulness, at the conclusion of the *Purgatorio*. An icon of modern memory, this figure embodies a model of the human rememberer as a rational knower of history, a being who stabilizes the past, and his own presence in distinction from it, by giving it the form of a finished narrative. It is on this exclusively rational model of subjectivity that historical criticism has come to rely. Despite a powerful twentieth-century critique of the knowing subject's status, carried out both in the literary sphere and in the fields of the "human sciences" (psychoanalysis, linguistics, anthropology, philosophy,

sociology), criticism's current investments in historical or contextual perspectives have remained insufficiently examined. In particular, I contend
that a broad-based "return" to historical issues in critical practice in the
last twenty years has enabled the authority of the rational subject, constituted in a defining disconnection from the past, to reassert itself in veiled
form.

Once again, modernism is the source of a dynamic alternative to
this model of historical engagement in which memory is constituted as
a discourse, exclusively, of knowing. The psychoanalysis of Freud, and
after him Lacan, I argue, describes historically specific techniques of
memory that emerged, not coincidentally, in the context of modernism's
struggles to configure new forms of historical imagination in the wake of
nineteenth-century positivist historicism. The importance of the psychoanalytic model here lies in its powerful repositioning of memory as a
discourse not of knowledge alone but also of "erotics," a discourse that
implies the existence of subjects constituted not only in their capacity to
know but also to desire.

While Freud is generally credited with the "discovery" of the unconscious, I maintain that what is radically new – indeed, "modern" – about
psychoanalysis is its apprehension of the subject in its relation to history.
The key structure in this psychoanalytic approach to the historical subject is not the unconscious but the symptom. Psychoanalysis regards
the symptom as the mark of a history necessarily retained, if not necessarily remembered, and thus as the sign that history persists at the
level of the human subject's identity – although not in a form accessible
to knowledge. Through the symptom, psychoanalysis apprehends the
human subject as, essentially, a configuration of desire. Put another way,
in the neurotic symptom, psychoanalysis apprehends the erotic subject:
the human being configured within its erotic (as opposed to its rational)
relation to its own past.

Like Gerz's counter-memorials, psychoanalysis frames the question of
remembering differently, first by placing equal emphasis on the impact
of forgetting and remembering (forgetting the past is an equally powerful
means by which our perceptions of the past are formed), and second by
revealing the operations of subjective desire that animate the memory-
work of subjects in the present. In its apprehension of the symptom,
psychoanalysis theorizes what is essentially an alternative model for textualizing and reading the past. Part I concludes with an elaboration of this
model in the cinematic and literary spheres, examining a "symptomatic"
reading of Joyce's "The Dead" undertaken by Roberto Rossellini in his

remarkable film, *Viaggio in Italia*. A species of anti-adaptation, Rossellini's film refuses to present Joyce's text in any literal sense, allowing it instead to "occur" for the first time through a practice of symptomatic memory-work. Foregrounding its own symptomatic desire in relation to Joyce, Rossellini's film offers an exceptional example of interpretive reading as an "erotics of memory."

Part II extends this exploration of memory as an "erotics" by focusing on specific examples of ex-centric discourses of memory within Irish modernism. Conceived as an "erotics," historical discourse acknowledges the present's engagement of the past as an exchange, a conversation in which the spectacle of history influences acts of memory in the present, just as those acts of memory construct the past's "occurrences." More importantly, an erotics of memory reveals the drive to know as connected to a desire for subjective and cultural stability and control in the present, a desire that is constantly both satisfied and necessarily deferred in particular acts of memory. Memory normally functions as a primary mechanism by which we not only know the past, but also deny its power to disturb in order to construct ourselves as stable subjects.

The historical imagination of modern Ireland eloquently and movingly demonstrates this relationship between the construction of stable cultural and political identities in the present and the designation of the past as revered but finally distant and non-threatening. Chapter Four opens with a historical reevaluation of Ireland's political and cultural transformation in the early decades of the twentieth century. A central but overlooked role in this transformation was played by the arrival of the cinema, a new and foreign technology of memory that focused largely upon historical narratives. Focusing on the 1916 screening of D. W. Griffith's *The Birth of a Nation* in Dublin, my investigation explores the cinema's entry into the gap in Irish historical imagining first carved out by Parnell's death, and argues that its supplanting of a pre-modern historical self-fashioning had lasting and negative political effects for twentieth-century Ireland.

A profoundly ex-centric discourse of Irish memory, the early cinema could and did evoke highly personal identifications in local audiences; indeed, it quite literally enabled the spectacle of Ireland's past to "occur" in a new way, and thus became the site of new, modern constructions of specifically Irish memory. Images of the "screen-Irish" have clearly impacted Irish culture and continue to do so. Yet exclusive attention to them through a cultural critique that would call for an oppositional cinema, one that would be somehow uniquely and authentically "Irish,"

tends to avoid the issue of film's actual historical impact as a new technology. In its earliest form, the cinema entered Irish culture as a medium
that, because it was shared collectively and concretely in local performances, necessarily altered the very imaginative forms through which
Irish citizens could conceive of their own past.

This historical material on early cinema and Irish politics constitutes
the groundwork for a new exploration, in the fifth chapter, of Yeats's
poetic handling of history. The now traditional sense that Yeats transformed himself imaginatively from the "last romantic" to a lyric artist of
rage, joy, and uncompromising power benefits, I argue, from a reading
of his poetry in relation to the transformation of Irish culture effected
by mechanical reproduction. While Yeats had no specific interest in film
as a cultural medium, awareness of the cinema's ambiguous impact on
Irish culture and memory is necessary for an understanding of his de-
ceptively simple lyricism. Focusing on the poet's life-long interest in the
mythic hero Cuchulain, I argue that while Yeats initially treats the figure
as a memorial construct, it emerges in his middle and later poetry as
a counter-memorial, an index of the past's persistent presence and an
occasion for Irish memory-work.

The final chapter offers an extended elaboration of a transformative
"erotics of memory" in the aesthetic sphere, reassessing Joyce's *Finnegans
Wake* as a history text. I argue that in his last and most challenging work,
Joyce undertakes a radical historiography which, unlike most histories,
demands that its reader acknowledge his or her own motivations for remembering the narrative histories that emerge from it. In Joyce's text,
the status of the historical event is contingent not merely on its representation by a historian (Joyce), but on the many different connections and
disconnections, alternatively pursued, ignored, felt, noticed, and missed
by a reader of history, the reader of *Finnegans Wake*. In essence, the *Wake*
demands a difficult and often ambiguous investment of memory-work
from its reader. As a historiographical text, it presumes no proprietary
authority over history's truth value, but only the instrumental role of
a reader's unconscious motivations in framing histories that are fundamentally connective rather than discursive, affective rather than mimetic,
living rather than dead. Using the language of the text itself, we might
say that the wake of Finnegan marks the point at which history ceases
to be a funeral and becomes a "funferal" ["fun for all"], the waking of
everybody's (Finnegan's, Ireland's, our own) erotic relation to history.[23]

The series of ex-centric discourses of Irish memory that I am opening here is obviously potentially infinite, and the reader will doubtless

think of more examples. The point is that as discourses of Irishness, such languages never aspire to or claim final mastery of their object. There is no sense in which the cinema or psychoanalysis can finally capture and exhibit a definitive description of Irishness, any more than can a Holocaust memorial in Germany. What I am suggesting is that Irish experience receives its many articulations as cultural commodity, as intellectual conundrum, as emotional or psychological state, and so on, through external discourses as well as through those voices and texts conventionally designated as "authentic." The conditions of Irishness are thus both more concrete and more dynamic than a single methodological perspective – a sociological description, say, or a post-colonial critique – can afford to allow. It is in the diversity of perspectives and shifting vocabularies of ex-centric discourses that Irishness, like the past itself, continuously and repeatedly "occurs."

PART I

The erotics of memory

CHAPTER I

Lethal histories: memory-work and the text of the past

> A historical phenomenon, known clearly and completely and
> resolved into a phenomenon of knowledge, is, for him who has
> perceived it, dead.
>
> Friedrich Nietzsche
> "On the Uses and Disadvantages of History for Life"

In the dark, early morning hours of a spring night in 1990, a group
of unlikely urban guerrillas entered the public square that fronts the
Saarbrücker Schloss, a historic castle in the city of Saarbrücken,
Germany. There they began digging up and removing a small number of the cobblestones with which the square is paved, concealing their
work from the daytime gaze of palace guards and police by placing false,
"dummy" stones in each of the resulting holes. Their work completed,
the thieves deposited the stolen cobblestones at their base of operations in
a nearby school and parted company, returning to their respective homes
to sleep. The perpetrators of this odd theft, or exchange, of municipal
property were art students, members of visiting professor Jochen Gerz's
seminar on memorial design at the local art academy, the Hochshule
der Bildenden Künste; their nocturnal sojourn into the square was only
the first of many in what was to become an extraordinary collective undertaking: the clandestine design and installation of a public memorial
dedicated to the victims of Germany's wartime past.

The stimulus for the unusual project had been provided by the history of the Saarbrücker Schloss itself. Originally built as a home for
German royalty, the palace functioned during World War II as a Gestapo
headquarters. Currently, the building houses the offices of the regional
government, while the space once occupied by the Gestapo has been
converted into a museum of local history, the Regionalgeschichtliches
Museum Saarbrücken. Within this latter wing, in a space directly below the square itself, curators have preserved a tiny room, six meters
square, which served during the war as a detention cell for prisoners

awaiting interrogation. The walls of this cell are covered with graffiti left by the occupants – men and women, Russians, Poles, Ukrainians, Italians, French; as many as sixteen held at once, and for months at a time – in which they recorded their names, places and dates of birth, and dates of incarceration.[1]

Having visited the museum soon after his arrival in Saarbrücken, Gerz, a Berlin-born conceptual artist whose work has dealt repeatedly and brilliantly with the problematics of history and memory, initially conceived of the monument project as a kind of counterpoint to the cell's own space of inscription. In the artist's own words, the work would carry out "an act of recollection, comparable to the decision to preserve the names scribbled on the cell wall in the basement of the castle" (Gibson, "Clandestine Warning"). Taking their cue from the names listed on the room's walls, Gerz and his students spent more than a year in dialogue with the leaders of Germany's Jewish communities, enlisting their help in discovering the forgotten names of German Jewish cemeteries in use during the war.

The exhaustive list that resulted became the core of the memorial project, and the focus of its engagement with history. As the borrowed cobblestones arrived in the studio, each was to receive a name from the list, along with the date of transmission, carved into its surface. Once inscribed, the stones would be restored, once again under cover of night, to their respective positions in the square. Carved into the surface of the square's cobblestones, the names would serve to remind the citizens of Saarbrücken – and visitors in general – of the city's wartime past; eternally insistent, the memorial would impress upon a forgetful present the urgent necessity of memory.

Proceeding at a rate of twelve to sixteen stones per night, the sixteen artists continued their operation for well over a year, until more than a quarter of the square's eight thousand stones had been thus removed, inscribed, and reinterred. The project was unknown to local officials until the summer of 1991, when Gerz, running short of funds, was forced to contact Oskar Lafontaine, minister-president of the Saarland and vice president of the German Social Democratic Party, to request support. Fortified by Lafontaine's grant of 10,000 Deutschemarks (about $6,300 in 1991), Gerz presented the project before the Stadtverband, a municipal voting body, at the end of August, ultimately winning a vote of official approval.[2] In May of 1993, the nearly completed installation was officially dedicated as a space of public remembrance under the title, *2,146 Stones – Monument against Racism*.[3] In a final gesture of recognition, officials placed a plaque nearby, identifying the monument for visitors and announcing its invitation to memory.

That Gerz received government sanction and funding for his clandestine and illegal use of public space is perhaps surprising. What is more shocking is that the square's official transformation into a space of public memory took place despite a singular and astonishing fact: the "monument against racism" itself is entirely invisible. The names, so painstakingly researched and carved, cannot be read; the square and its cobblestones appear today exactly as they did before work on the project began. Indeed, the mark of the work's official recognition, the plaque which proclaims its very existence, is itself the only visible trace of the monument-makers' guerrilla artistry. Through an extraordinary and paradoxical detail of the memorial's design, the artists effectively guaranteed their work's indefinite resistance to all recognition, official or otherwise: in restoring the inscribed stones to their places in the square, Gerz and his students deliberately replaced them name-side-down.

INELUCTABLE MODALITY OF THE MEMORIAL

Strolling on Sandymount Strand in the "Proteus" episode of *Ulysses*, Stephen Dedalus ruminates on the irreducibly textual nature of visual perception: "Ineluctable modality of the visible: at least that if no more, thought through my eyes. Signatures of all things I am here to read, seaspawn and seawrack, the nearing tide, that rusty boot. Snotgreen, bluesilver, rust: coloured signs."[4] On the visual plane, the furniture of the world disposes itself as a series of not merely visible but *legible* objects, "signatures" to be deciphered and understood. The modality of the visible is ineluctably textual: to see is to read.

On the plane of historical perception, the faculty of memory effects a similar textualization of its object, the past. Like so much seaspawn and seawrack, the jetsam of history appears before the historical gaze as a collection of signatures – events, people, lives, stories – that are at once irreducibly contextual (that is, situated within and among cultures, societies, institutions, ideologies, and so on) and irreducibly textual (that is, susceptible of being read and understood in the present as history). Among the normative mechanisms of historical perception, one of the most effective instruments of this textualization of the past is the public memorial. While the term "memorial" encompasses myriad strategies for the formal encounter with the past as well as for political uses and abuses of it, and while in practice the memorial site can be a space for either mourning or celebration, the function of indexing and textual-izing history is coterminous with the very concept of memorialization. Regardless of differences in aesthetic or ideological vocabulary, all memo-rials are, at the most basic level, textual markers: sites for the reading of history. Indexical signifiers of the past, memorials bring past objects or events into their discursive presence as history, a presence in which they are resolved and identified in the form of legible texts.[5]

In the course of his extensive work on Holocaust memory, James Young has observed that the formal gesture toward the past embodied in the very concept of memorialization carries out a kind of fetishization of history, and with it, paradoxically, an atrophying of memory itself.[6] Without denying the importance of the debate over how precisely to represent particular aspects of the past, Young points out repeatedly that every historiographical gesture – both the "scientific" and the "artistic"; both the "truthful" presentation of artifacts and the ideologically moti-vated "revisionist" interpretation of such artifacts – every such gesture threatens always to direct attention toward the objective status of the event and its proof, and away, therefore, from the ongoing (and indeed, historical) activity that Young calls "memory-work." While human access to the past is necessarily dynamic (a reflection of the irreducibly fragmen-tary and shifting nature of memory), memorials of all kinds risk displacing the constantly mutating historical perception of individuals with a more or less static notion of "memory," an objectified version of history for which the physicality of the memorial itself stands. The protean insta-bility of the historical object fades before the memorial's authoritative stance as textual marker, its confinement of historical perception to the modality of the en-graved.

Such a displacement is clearly at work, Young suggests, in museum-type memorials such as those at Auschwitz in Poland and the United States Holocaust Memorial and Museum in Washington. The illusion of witnessing the past is given a prominent role at such sites, where authentic artifacts such as the shoes, eyeglasses, or hair of victims are displayed as the surviving fragments of historical catastrophe. Without parting company with those who maintain the importance of preserving the past and our access to it – those who subscribe to a "never forget" imperative – Young pauses long enough to ask what, precisely, the sight of such objects awakens in viewers. His answer allows for both intel-lectual responses (enhanced historical knowledge, a sense of evidence) and emotional ones (revulsion, grief, pity, fear). At the same time, Young moves beyond assessing the relative appropriateness of such responses to highlight their underlying passivity with respect to the historical Real, a past which produced the artifacts themselves (Young, *Texture*, 132).

At such sites, Young contends, the effort toward historical perception that is the sole and individual responsibility of viewers becomes unnecessary; it has been effectively completed in advance by the material presence of the memorial itself. Young's point is not that the Holocaust memorial literally and materially takes the place of the past event in the minds of viewers – that it replaces the past with a present text – but rather that it obviates viewers' own "memory-work," that active construction and destruction of the past that continuously produces the text of history. For Young, the Holocaust memorial tends to obscure the dynamic process of both memory and forgetting that is the Holocaust's only contemporary reality: what is lost in the act of memorialization is "not the event itself, but *memory* of the event" (Young, *Texture*, 344).

In granting this reprieve from the work of memory, memorials succeed, Young has suggested, in delivering a message in which viewers are perhaps far more heavily invested than they are in the acquisition of so-called "pure" historical knowledge: namely, that the history they reference is comfortably discontinuous with the viewers' own. The disposition of the past as legible object, carried out in the name of remembrance, is a particularly effective means of distancing present rememberers from the past in which such objects accrue their historical meaning. Knowledge of the Holocaust becomes the very mechanism by which its historical reality is kept comfortably distant: Auschwitz happened, certainly, but to someone somewhere else, in a time that is safely finished. The subject and object of historical knowledge have, in this context, entered a neat, relational economy of exchange that supports their communication only as an effect of their mutual separation.

Conventionally, the form of the memorial is what ensures this displacement of memory-work by a distant, known, objective past: "history." The material durability of inscribed stone or metal is the indicator that the past has been permanently resolved for memory; that it has been, quite literally, en-graved. Gerz's installation, on the other hand, reverses this convention, adopting the en-grav-ing of the past itself as the most prominent feature of its own discursive and material form: the salient characteristic of *2,146 Stones* is not its invisibility, but rather the act of burial by which it achieves that invisibility. The artists' decision to "re-collect" (belatedly) the names of cemeteries rather than those of individual victims of racism places interment, the ritual laying to rest of the dead, at the center of their memorial's "act of recollection." It is not the past that is the monument's principal concern, but our accustomed methods of engaging it: Gerz in fact draws a striking and unlooked-for equivalence between the recovery – literally a re-covering – of the past for knowledge and its burial, between historical knowing and historical elision, between memory and forgetting.

The need for a "faithful" remembrance of the past gives way in this instance to a more crucial acknowledgment of the denial that is at work within every act of knowing and remembering history, a function of burial that is indeed carried out by those very acts. In textualizing the past, Gerz's monument declares, historical knowledge brings the past to light only by producing a "lethal history," a story of the past that is itself the discursive form of the past's burial. History's most basic task, the representation of a fundamentally un-present-able past, has in this sense an essentially funereal, or commemorative, function. Historical writing draws the past into its discursive significance as "truth" essentially by burying it in language. The measure of normative historiography's value, in this light, lies not in its successful maintenance of a scientifically objective point of view, but rather in its enactment of a discursive burial through which the past is "disposed" (that is, both "positioned" and "discarded") as a dead body or corpus. The "accuracy" and "adequacy" of historical knowledge thus comes to be seen in direct proportion to its legibility; the writing or reading of history produces an ideal narrative to commemorate or memorialize a past that is in itself unrepresentable.

The idea that historical knowing bases its recovery of the past in an operation that also effects the past's burial returns us to the notion of memory as a sort of cultural pathology and, in particular, to the traditional resonance of that notion in the Irish context. As Stephen Dedalus well understood, Irish history gains its nightmare quality in its apparent tendency inevitably to recur. The motor driving that perceived pattern of repetition is not history itself, but a modality of memory that is deeply invested in the past's figurative burial. Yet such a modality is hardly exclusive or endemic to Irish culture. The objective status of the past within an economy of knowledge is the residual effect of ambivalent human desires both to know that past and to be done with it for good and all – to "lay it to rest." Neither of these desires is primary with respect to the other: to remember is to find the past in its disposition as dead body, and thus to bury it; to incorporate this dead, objective past is to specify its integrity and truth as an object of knowledge. The creation of "lethal histories" (textual or discursive interments of the past), is in that sense a structural necessity of historical discourse itself: the "recovery" of the past for knowledge will always gravitate toward an ambivalent process of re-presentation and re-burial because knowing the past is always a matter of specifying a thing that is inaccessible in itself.

It is to the lethal effects of this mode of historical knowing that Irish history bears particular and profound witness. Yeats's discovery, at the end of his life, of his own poetic images of the past in the guise of "circus animals" confirms, in a specific instance, memorialization's curious capacity to distance Ireland's present from its past. In his early work, Yeats had sought poetic subjects that expressed "character isolated by a deed," images that could revitalize Ireland's mythic past and make it available to the present. In "The Circus Animals' Desertion," Yeats acknowledges that what animated the figures of Oisin, Cuchulain, the Countess Cathleen, and others for him was their purity as symbols and emblems. In his poetic idealization of them, he confesses, "Players and painted stage took all my love, / And not those things that they were emblems of."[7] The tone of regret that suffuses this poem suggests the poet's belated awareness that a too-selective gaze made of these images memorial figures in James Young's sense:

> Those masterful images because complete
> Grew in pure mind but out of what began?
> A mound of refuse or the sweepings of a street,
> Old kettles, old bottles, and a broken can,
> Old iron, old bones, old rags, that raving slut
> Who keeps the till.
> (Yeats, "The Circus Animals' Desertion," 33–38)

Selected "in pure mind" as representative figures, Yeats's images of the Irish past become in the poet's canonical corpus instruments for the sentimental fetishization and elevation of history. They come to "stand for" a preferred Irishness that is ideally beautiful and therefore irreducibly distant from the complexity and perpetual changeability (David Lloyd's "undeveloped possibilities") of anything that might be called Irishness in the present. What is striking is Yeats's explicit and bitter acknowledgment that this inevitable historical separation is what in some sense motivated his celebration of such figures in the first place. Chosen for their beauty, passion, and nobility, they leave unacknowledged their own rootedness in the less presentable material and emotional realities of Irish history, what Yeats called "the foul rag and bone shop of the heart" (Yeats, "The Circus Animals' Desertion," 40).

As memorial figures, Yeats's "circus animals" render the Irish past both legible and comfortably distant, prompting for Yeats, as for Gerz, the arduous search for a new practice of memory-work: "Now that my ladder's gone / I must lie down where all the ladders start . . . " (Yeats, "The Circus Animals' Desertion," 38–39). Yeats's poem concludes without any promise of success in this endeavor to reconfigure his engagement with the Irish past; on the contrary, the idealization of history clearly remains as a persistent threat to any act of memory, poetic or otherwise, undertaken in the present.

SHUT YOUR EYES AND SEE

In contrast to Yeats's desire to forge a new, less idealized textualization of history in the "foul rag and bone shop of the heart," Gerz's approach to a reconfigured practice of memory-work seems, at first glance, to reject the necessity of textualizing history altogether. Against every cultural and aesthetic expectation, Gerz deliberately disables the textual mechanism by which historical perception engages its object. And yet *2,146 Stones* itself consists of nothing but text: names – signifiers whose connection with history is never in question – are after all at the core of the project from the beginning. The realization of the monument depended on a process of historical research – a process in which the students' training and skill as artists counted for little.[8] The artists' primary object of production, in fact, was not a work of art, but a document that was in every sense a historical text, a list of previously forgotten names that underscored precisely the past's unknowability, its inestimable yet real absence. What is striking about Gerz's installation, then, is the manner in which it accepts the function of textuality in constructing historical memory. It renders its own text invisible as a way of openly welcoming illegibility as a vital aspect of the historical text itself. The past in this case remains a text that presents itself in a non-fetishized, illegible (although not entirely unrecoverable) form. Paradoxically, *2,146 Stones* offers a memorial text that cannot be seen, only read.

Strolling on Sandymount Strand, Stephen Dedalus distills the paradox of the invisible yet legible text in an imperative that might also serve the viewer of *2,146 Stones*: "Shut your eyes and see" (Joyce, *Ulysses*, 3.9). What Stephen is able to "see" as he shuts his eyes and continues to walk is, in fact, the same physical landscape of the strand, now no longer visible but textualized through a vocabulary of sound: "Stephen closed his eyes to hear his boots crush crackling wrack and shells. . . .

Exactly: and that is the ineluctable modality of the audible . . . Crush, crack, crick, crick . . . Rhythm begins, you see. I hear" (Joyce, *Ulysses*, 3.10–23). Absent visibility, the objects of perception dispose themselves for Stephen as an auditory text, a rhythmic poem: "acatalectic tetrameter of iambs marching" (Joyce, *Ulysses*, 3.23–24).

This replacement of a visual text by an auditory one is a cue to the reader of *Ulysses* itself. Like all of Joyce's works from *Chamber Music* to *Finnegans Wake*, *Ulysses* asks its reader not only to see, but to hear the language on the page. Gerz's monument does not replace the visual text of history with an auditory one in the same sense.[9] It does, however, issue a similar directive to the visitor who would take the accessibility of memorial texts – not to mention of historiography in general – for granted. By negative demonstration, Gerz's monument underscores the fact that, normally, memorials reduce history to its most legible, decipherable form, that of an objective past. By refusing to fulfill this function, Gerz's memorial suggests the possibility of reading history otherwise.

For Gerz, the construction of *2,146 Stones* was a logical, even necessary, step in a career that has been largely dominated by the use of absence as a mode of expression. Virtually all of the artist's work engages the realms of the historical and the political through a vocabulary of silence, invisibility, erasure, or illegibility. Such a palette invariably requires the active engagement of the viewer. It is the viewer, and not the artist, who must produce the work of art. It is the viewer's capacity to know and not to know, to remember and to forget, that textualizes the viewing experience and brings into being, there in the plane of the viewer's own gaze, a legible object: the work of art – or the work of memory – itself.[10]

A singular case in point, and one that illustrates the crucial function of the viewer perhaps more clearly than does *2,146 Stones*, is Gerz's best-known work, the disappearing *Monument against Fascism* (1986) installed in a suburban business center near Hamburg. Designed in collaboration with his wife, Esther Gerz, the installation consisted of a twelve meter high by one meter square hollow pillar, covered by a veneer of soft lead. Hard metal styluses attached by cables at each corner of the base enabled visitors to inscribe their names directly on the surface of the monument. As its lower surface became saturated with the recorded markings of viewers, the monument was lowered, by degrees, into a space that had been opened in the ground beneath it. Over the course of five years, the pillar was so lowered six times, finally disappearing completely on September 27, 1991.[11] At present there is nothing but a plaque in the ground where the pillar once stood, a marker commemorating the memorial itself – its birth, life and death – in the manner of a gravestone.

The monument's disappearance in this case implicitly acknowledges that the memories worked by present viewers are impermanent, which is to say historical. The installation's radical relation to history lies in its willingness to submit memory itself to a process of decay, a process in which not only history but historiography is destined for the grave. Paradoxically, what distinguishes such a work as a memorial is the fact that it is conceived as having a life of its own, a limited span of time in which to exist, to work its textualization of history for and with the populace of the present as knowers of history. Its "life-span" complete, it will – like the events of a more distant past toward which it gestures without representation – cease to be present.[12]

Installations such as these, the disappearing pillar outside Hamburg and the illegible cobblestones in Saarbrücken, function as "counter-memorials." They gesture toward the past without revealing history so much as the volatility of history's perception, its constant tendency to decay and disappear even as it is revealed through acts of textualization in the present. In this perspective, the important factor is not the objective truth of the past, but the dynamic process of memory-work engaged in by knowing and unknowing subjects in the present. The counter-memorial's central purpose is not to represent the past; neither is it to index it through a particular stable, material, and legible gesture. What the counter-memorial makes known is its own dependence on a vital and dynamic present and on the work done in that present by living rememberers. At the counter-memorial site, then, it is the writers and readers of the present who shoulder the burden of responsibility for "adequate" and "accurate" historical representation; it is their memory-work that produces the counter-memorial's varied and ambivalent "texts" of commemoration.

In the case of the disappearing pillar, for instance, many of the visitors and tourists and accidental passers-by responded to the monument's invitation in the intended fashion by inscribing their names. But others reacted very differently, "defacing" it – ironically but perhaps not surprisingly – with scrawled swastikas or, less congruously, with declarations of adolescent love ("Hans leibe Christiane"). A few passionate observers actually shot bullets at the pillar, while a significant portion of the local population, exercising a more common form of "memory-work," ignored it altogether. The counter-memorial thus reconfigures the function of monuments in general so as to emphasize the variable and inclusive processes of text-making which they enable in the present; it is the text produced, the legible, permanent text as well as the disappearing or "invisible" one, that records the reality of the historical event. The counter-memorial bears witness to the fact that history's crucial truth lies not in a lost, objective past that must be captured and accurately rendered by the historical gaze, but in memory itself, a text which in all its protean volatility must be continually read and unread, remembered and forgotten.

If as a counter-memorial *2,146 Stones* affirms the necessity of memory-work, its particular handling of history raises some persistent and difficult questions. In view of recent efforts to revise Germany's wartime history – efforts contextualized by the resurgence of xenophobic and nationalist passions in Germany and elsewhere – the problematic political implications of a monument designed to render particular elements of Holocaust memory permanently invisible are obvious. To have so painstakingly re-captured something of this lost history, only to render it invisible rather than legible and public, seems a cynical sort of betrayal at best. What, it seems worth asking, is the point of Gerz's taking such a radical step, especially when the risk of perceived collusion with the forces of outright falsification is so great? Indeed, the monument's apparent complicity with an amnesiac historicism seems heightened by Gerz's claim that he originally conceived of the work as, literally, "an act of *recollection*, comparable to the decision to *preserve* the names scribbled on the cell wall in the basement of the castle" (Gibson, "Clandestine Warning"; emphasis added).

So far from generating a more consummately "historical" work, Gerz would appear to have borrowed the conventional public form of the memorial in order to produce through it a fundamental derailment of that form's presumed value as mediating historical text. From the perspective of normative historical discourse, such a derailment raises strong suspicions that the artist might be guilty of an elaborately quixotic – not to say pretentious – denial of history. At the very least, Gerz would seem to have appropriated the vocabulary of commemoration in order simply to proclaim the impossibility of forging any real connection with the historical past whatsoever. Indeed, the painstaking care invested by the monument builders only intensifies the irony of their work's apparently self-negating gesture. Even if the work can be said to be thoroughly "historical" in its execution and its subject matter, in what sense can it reasonably be said to "remember" the particular history of Germany's Jews – which, after all, it seems not to have memorialized, but only to have buried once again?

Gerz's penchant for the expressive dynamics of absence is rooted neither in a post-modern aesthetic sensibility nor in a professionally oppor-
tunistic fondness for aesthetic games and ruses. Rather, as Gerz himself
has insisted, the source of his artistic proclivities must be located in history, and particularly in the timing of his birth in Berlin in 1940: "The
power of absence, which some people still encounter as a religious, literary, or artistic experience, was in my case a concrete biographical fact
which might be translated as a case of being 'too late.' This may seem
absurd, but I don't think I am the only German of my generation to be
concerned with such a feeling."[13]

What Gerz was personally "too late" for was, of course, the rise of
German fascism in the 1930s, the course of Berlin's history during the
war and the effects of that history on Germany's Jewish population. It
is precisely this lateness that defines both historical experience and historical consciousness at the level of the individual subject. Gerz's having
missed a particular historical moment at which a certain kind of political
action may have been both possible and necessary highlights the fact
that, with respect to the past, all knowing is necessarily a retrospective
and therefore belated reconstruction. To the extent that any object is designated within a discourse of "history," it is so designated only from this
perspective of lateness, from the point of view of a subject that has come
into being at precisely that moment at which the object of remembrance
cannot be seen or experienced in fact.

This "lateness" informs Gerz's subjectivity as an artist at the deepest
level. It is not that his art articulates some compensatory expression of
guilt for not having "been there" when his action would have counted;
on the contrary, it directly expresses the extent to which, as a historical
subject, he (like every rememberer) is continuously "not there," and is
instead continuously "late." It is from this point of view – subjectivity
predicated on history's unrecoupable loss – that Gerz approached the
building of *2,146 Stones*. To look at this monument is to see the absence
not only of the past to which it refers, but also of any convenient means
(such as a narrative or figural representation) by which one might comfortably situate oneself as knower of that history; to experience the work's
invisibility, in other words, is to discover one's own inexorable alienation
from its most crucial function as a memorial, that of putting the past in
play discursively and rationally for knowledge. It is this deeply historical
experience of coming upon the past "too late," then, that the invisibility of Gerz's *2,146 Stones* makes concretely available and indeed, in a
metaphorical sense, "visible" to its viewer.

Gerz's installation offers itself, then, as a sort of catalyst to memory, a reminder of racism's historical reality in Saarbrücken. At the same time, the work itself refuses absolutely the role to which historical indexes of this type are typically reduced, that of embodying an adequate textual compensation for, and implicit resolution of, the past itself. This paradoxical structure is what allows the memorial to subvert the neat constitution and separation of historical identities that produces a "lethal history." As a "counter-memorial," Gerz's work registers the simple fact that remembering is a kind of work, a continuous and active engagement, and that as such it is distinct from the particular memories that may be licensed by the textualizing gesture toward history performed by a given memorial. So far from denying or relativizing historical knowledge, it is this approach that enables Gerz to engage Saarbrücken's wartime past so forcefully and so concretely.

BELATED RECOVERIES: THE RETURN TO "HISTORY" AND THE SUBJECT OF MEMORY

Gerz's counter-memorials also serve to distill and amplify a number of issues regarding the relationship between textual representation and historical knowledge that gained prominence in critical and theoretical debate during the very years in which those memorials were constructed. Within the field of literary studies in particular, concern with "the question of history" in the late 1980s and early 1990s fueled a pronounced shift in focus from textual to contextual concerns. Disaffection with the perceived failings of structuralism, deconstruction, and so-called "text-centered" methods of criticism compelled scholars to turn with increasing confidence and frequency to history as a means of grounding what has often been judged to be a more politically aware and socially responsible critical practice. As the study of literature became increasingly engaged with issues of ethics, politics, and social justice, historicism emerged as something of a panacea for what many continue to identify as literature's traditional ills: the ivory-tower isolationism and hermeticism which result from purely textual or theoretical approaches to reading. While theoretical interrogations of historicism, the status of memory, and the values and methods of historical discourse continue to be brought forward, it is clear that, practically speaking, history has also gained a discrete and positive – though enigmatic – value of its own within the debate.

In the context of this methodological shift, it might seem logical once again to dismiss Gerz's construction of an invisible memorial as an irresponsible and anachronistic act of artistic self-indulgence. From the perspective of a criticism generally convinced of modernism's fundamental complicity with theoretical "denials" of history, Gerz's project must seem a nostalgic, and ultimately pointless, cliché. Placed in a modernist aesthetic trajectory that might include works such as Kasimir Malevich's "White on White" paintings or John Cage's *Silence* recordings, Gerz's work might seem to mark the logical extreme at which the elevation of form over real experience becomes both absurd and self-defeating: precisely at the moment of art's engagement with the plane of the real (here, the history of German Jews), it promptly erases itself. In this context, *2,146 Stones* appears to justify by its own negative example the gradual but wholesale condemnation of structuralism and formalism that has accompanied the recent ascendancy of history in critical discourse. More importantly, the monument seems to lend credence to the idea that aesthetic formalism, specifically that of modernism, is necessarily compromised by an unwillingness to acknowledge art's effects in the political and social spheres.

Yet the apparent disingenuousness of Gerz's *2,146 Stones* only persists as long as it is presumed that because the past is stable and unchanging, it is also, in an ideal sense, purely and adequately legible; that the authoritative coherence and narrative stability of the memorial form merely reflects the natural stability of historical objects and events themselves. In fact memorials are, in the most generic sense, never indicators of the past as such, but always of its absence and loss. What is "textualized" in the memorial form, and in historical discourse in general, is not the positive, ontological reality of past events, but the radical unpresentability – indeed, the illegibility – of the historical. Borrowing Lyotard's diction in his concluding essay to *The Post-Modern Condition*, we might say that the memorial, generically speaking, is that which puts forward the persistence of the illegible within signification itself.[14]

Gerz's willingness to take the extraordinary and deliberate step of forfeiting entirely his work's power to signify denotes a remarkable refusal to compromise or reduce in any way the real paradox of historical perception: namely, that the effort to know the past is at once both necessary and impossible. Regarded from this angle, what *2,146 Stones* "denies" is not history, but precisely the ease with which the past tends to become fetishized within the debate over historical representation. Gerz's monument reminds its viewers that what, in fact, historical representation is typically expected to produce is concrete evidence – a textual marker – of history's restoration, atonement, and conclusion for the present.

Against a fetishizing practice within which the legibility of historical events is construed as ideally equal and adequate to their ontological reality, *2,146 Stones* insists that the incomprehensibility of history's loss be acknowledged to cohere alongside – indeed, flush with – history's textual re-presentation.

This matter of historical knowledge's fetishizing function is one that literary criticism, in its return to an overtly contextual methodology of reading, has managed largely to bypass. Like the sign erected to identify Gerz's otherwise invisible monument, the term "history" has itself come to operate within critical debate as a kind of cipher, a strangely transparent signifier that seems to designate a concrete, definable act of critical engagement with the past. Under the sign of "history," that act somehow seems familiar to all – and yet, also remains maddeningly elusive in practical terms. For most readers, the adoption of a "historical perspective" means simply that the value of history as a viable ground for reading practices in general has been presumed. Meanwhile, the radical and unrecoupable absence of the past, the persistence of history's illegibility within historical texts, is conveniently ignored.

In this context, the existence of *2,146 Stones* exposes a core assumption driving academic and theoretical discussions of memory in general, namely that history is a discourse exclusively of knowledge. "History," as it is traded about in the intellectual marketplace, coheres and has value as an object of rationality, a thing either known or unknown, a series of events either remembered or forgotten: the "question" of history inexorably concerns the attempt to know the past. It is because of this allegiance to rationality as history's ruling frame of reference that recent debates, while they have opened themselves to a vast array of concerns including not only textual, but political and social uses and abuses of the past, have also tended to confirm the authority of the rational subject at the center of historical discourse. Emphasizing the objective status of historical truth and the relative adequacy of its textual or linguistic representation, historically oriented scholars have tended to presume the discrete coherence of the subject itself as knower. The return to history has, in this sense, masked a return to a peculiarly humanistic notion of the subject as a being constituted exclusively in its capacity to know.

In a powerful way, Gerz's approach to memory as a "belated" activity reveals what has actually been at stake in criticism's pursuit of "the question of history" from the beginning. What the "late" visitor to the Saarbrücken site directly confronts is neither the past nor a representation of it, but precisely his or her own subjective status as a knower of

history. At a stroke, Gerz displaces the customary vocabulary of historical discourse – the endless march of variously "adequate" or "complete"
representations, the insistence either on historiography's scientific or aesthetic function, and so on – with the question of a subject, one for whom,
at this and every instant, history functions as a discourse of knowing. By
erasing the textual field of history's representation for the knowing subject, Gerz not only reminds us that the past's principal defining feature
is its absence, but also demonstrates that it is the institutional status
and authority of the rational subject that is history's more fundamental
mechanism of mediation.[15]

In more precise terms, what I am suggesting is that the discursive burial
of the past displaces onto an objective hermeneutic system, "history," an
interment that in fact takes place at the level of the knowing subject him-
or herself. Conventional historical discourse always posits knowledge
(a figural or narrative presentation of the past) as compensation not
only for history's crucial absence, but also for the subject's crucial lateness. While knowing buries the past as the victim of a lethal history, it
also buries the knower's own radically unpresentable subjectivity, a subjectivity incommensurate with knowledge, erecting in its place a commemorative, idealized construction: the rational, authoritative subject of
historical knowledge. The term "lethal history," then, carries the literal
connotation that it is also the knower of history who is "en-graved" within
historical discourse, or constituted there in a posture of terminal stability
as a "dead" certainty. In the act of reading monuments and other historical texts, rememberers become, in an imaginative sense, monuments in
their turn.

Among the qualities that make Yeats's late poetry so compelling is his
manifest willingness to fight – despite advancing age and creative ex-
haustion – against this interment of the subject for rationality. The opening line of "The Circus Animals' Desertion" acknowledges the poet's
blocked state – "I sought a theme and sought for it in vain / I sought it
daily for six weeks or so" (Yeats, "The Circus Animals' Desertion," 1–2) –
but turns, finally, as we have seen, to what amounts to an act of appalling
courage and faith. In Yeats's poetry, such moments are not without prece-
dent. Ten years earlier, in the extraordinarily difficult and beautiful poem,
"Among School Children," Yeats revealed a stroll through a schoolroom
as on occasion for memory-work in the present, a "questioning" of his
own past in the eyes and faces of the children before him.

Dreaming of Maud Gonne in an idealized form as "a Ledaean body"
(Yeats, "Among School Children," 9), the poet looks upon the children

and wonders "if she stood so at that age – / For even daughters of the swan can share / Something of every paddler's heritage –" (19–21). This memory-work has the unexpected effect of collapsing, for the poet, the conventional separation of present and past: "And thereupon my heart is driven wild: / She stands before me as a living child" (23–24). Yeats presents this eruption, the past's sudden and material presence in the schoolroom, as a disruption of the normative historical order in which the rememberer's rational stability is constituted as a compensation for historical loss. The poem openly questions this compensatory structure –

> What youthful mother, a shape upon her lap
> Honey of generation had betrayed,
> . . .
>
> Would think her son, did she but see that shape
> With sixty or more winters on its head,
> A compensation for the pang of his birth,
> Or the uncertainty of his setting forth?
> (Yeats, "Among School Children," 33–40)

– and casts a baleful eye on Yeats's own status as a monumentally authoritative subject-of-knowledge.

At a time when the poet had reached pinnacles of both local and international stature (he was an Irish Senator and a Nobel laureate), his bitter descriptions of himself as "a sixty-year-old smiling public man" (8) and as "a comfortable kind of old scarecrow" (32) expose the lethal consequences of historical knowing at the level of the individual subject. While Yeats's "circus animals" depict the costs of idealizing the past, "Among School Children" finally resonates as a sort of plea for the apprehension of the *self* through a different sort of memory-work, a "labour" that would be less like knowing than it is like "blossoming or dancing," and in which "body is not bruised to pleasure soul, / Nor beauty born out of its own despair, / Nor blear-eyed wisdom out of midnight oil" (Yeats, "Among School Children," 57–60). The poem's final question, "How can we know the dancer from the dance" (64) seeks, but does not define, a mode of knowing that would not produce a dead thing, the commemorative, monumental self – "a sixty-year-old smiling public man" – as its necessary compensation.

Yeats presents the knower of history in his poem, just as Gerz does in *2,146 Stones*, as a being who is not figuratively but literally "late." In placing the commemorative status of the subject who knows at the center of their "acts of recollection," Yeats and Gerz both reveal the myopic and fearful character of our customary engagements with the past. In accepting knowledge of the past in place of an awareness of history's more radical unrecoupability, we inscribe our identities as historical subjects within a fundamentally compensatory economy. To the extent that we negotiate history exclusively from the position of knowing subjects, the past becomes for us, in the most literal sense, a mere pre-text for the identities in which we are invested.

The critique of modernism's alleged "denial" of history has always presumed historical discourse's viability and truth when grounded in the authority of the knowing subject. Yet modernism emerges historically as the antithesis of critical investment in this model. Indeed, modernism as such might be fairly characterized as the site of the individual's inscription and configuration beneath the sign of history as something other than a subject of knowledge. This Other subject of history, the theoretical coordinates of which were first sketched by psychoanalysis, is one for whom the absent past insists on being written and re-written, not in the form of coherent, finished narratives, but in the very life and vital being of the individual him- or herself. Psychoanalysis apprehends a different sort of memorial subject in whom the past persists symptomatically, in forms that are by definition inaccessible to knowledge: vocal tics, physical behaviors, psychological patterns and so on. Recognizing that such symptoms are memorial texts – products of the individual's self-fashioning within a continuing process of memory-work – psychoanalysis specifies historical discourse's proper ineluctable modality, that of desire.

Before turning to a fuller exploration of a psychoanalytic "erotics of memory" – and to criticism's historical resistance to it – it is worth noting that what *2,146 Stones* makes visible is precisely the remembering subject's constitution in this paradoxical and ambivalent dynamic of desire. Radically disappointing every expectation of compensatory knowledge, the monument instead invites a spectacular range of apparently incongruous and ambivalent reactions: fascination, boredom, anger, disappointment – even (perhaps) a newly configured sense of "evidence." Put succinctly, what Gerz's monument puts in play is the quotidian and unwieldy reality of the subject's actual relation to history. The rememberer, in this case, coheres no longer within the world of ideally legible facts, the world of adequate historical knowing, but instead within an erotics of memory, the ineluctable modality of desire in which the activity of memory-work takes place.

CHAPTER 2

A Pisgah sight of history: critical authority and the promise of memory

> Concealed in the submission to the rules of a task and the regularity of objectively imposed exigencies there is a possibility for an eroticization of history – a quickening and quickened passion, I might almost say, love itself.
>
> Michel de Certeau
> *The Writing of History*

Within a normative, "common-sense" approach to the question of history, the problem of historical knowledge cannot be disengaged from the fundamentally paradoxical notion of the human subject on which it is predicated. On one hand, discursive convention links the idea of time and the bodies, consciousnesses, or "selves" which occupy it to a profoundly spatial concept of presence. Locked within their accustomed "here and now," subjects experience the passage of time, or history, as "what happens." It is time that is the prime mover in this conceptual system; the subject itself is confined, within its spatial moment of presence, as a locus of identity and sameness within the diachronic movement of time. In this sense, subjectivity is (temporally speaking) the site of a radical paralysis of consciousness: while the moment the subject occupies moves with time, subjectivity remains whole and inviolate; presence itself is nothing more nor less than the concept of a space in and beyond which the subject literally cannot move.

On the other hand, linguistic convention also suggests that historical knowledge enables, and indeed necessitates, precisely that movement of the subject that it has rendered impossible: we speak of past, present, and future as "places" that are not only discrete and contiguous, but also ideally accessible to the faculties of memory and, to a somewhat lesser extent, prognostication. Knowing the past, in this case, amounts to a kind of transmigration of the subject beyond the prison-house of presence that defines it, an entry into a historical space other than that which is the subject's own. In this sense, the very notion of historical knowledge, or of the subject as knower of history, demands an awareness of history as a conceptual space in which the movement of the subject is both radically necessary and radically impossible.[1]

Dante's *Divine Comedy*, certainly one of modernity's crucial textual touchstones, reveals in a remarkable passage the "lethal" historical condition of the human subject in quite literal terms. A curious experiential paradox signals the pilgrim's arrival in the terrestrial paradise near the conclusion of the *Purgatorio*. In the encounter with the river that marks the threshold of this arrival, the pilgrim's forward progress is at once arrested and maintained: "With feet I stayed and with my eyes I passed to the other side" ['Coi piè ristetti e con li occhi passai di là'].[2] At the close of the preceding Canto (*Purg.* XXVII.124–42), Virgil had relinquished his role as Dante's guide, and in this context, the momentary staying of feet may be reasonably taken to symbolize the pilgrim's reluctance at having to proceed for the first time without the *ingegno* and *arte* of his master. Yet the fact that this aqueous boundary actively impedes him – "when lo, a stream took from me further progress" ["ed ecco più andar mi tolse un rio"] (*Purg.* XXVIII.25) – suggests that within Dante's allegorical cosmography the river is not simply a convenient external metaphor for the pilgrim's hesitancy. Indeed, its subsequent identification in the text belies its status as a merely generic topographical barrier. The river, as both pilgrim and reader learn nearly one hundred lines after the initial encounter, is in fact Lethe, a stream whose mythic associations with memory-loss and oblivion are richly suggestive with regard to the pilgrim's simultaneous "staying" and "passing beyond."

A psychological as well as a spatial boundary, Lethe not only impedes the pilgrim's physical progress, but confines him to a position in which consciousness is framed and informed by memory, and in which experience is therefore explicitly constituted as historical. In these terms, the pilgrim here faces the prospect of a disorientation far more profound than that occasioned by his loss of Virgil as guide. Crossing Lethe would entail for him the surrender of all memory of the past, and thus an unmooring of historical consciousness as such. On the river's near side, the pilgrim remains a memoried being; the subject of a historical "sense," he occupies a moment of presence while gazing at an irreducibly distant past. This historical condition is literally one of both confinement and mobility. A self-conscious and stable locus of historical subjectivity, the pilgrim occupies a space of presence beyond which his feet cannot pass, but which his eyes, instruments of contemplation, can overleap to gain the image of Paradise on the other side. The pilgrim's act of look- ing beyond the river of forgetfulness here suggests a figuring, in spatial terms, of his ability to look "back" at history. Indeed, it is memory, and not visual acuity, that allows Dante to see the young woman whom he perceives singing and dancing on the other side of Lethe as a likeness: "You make me recall where and what Proserpina was," he says, "at the time her mother lost her, and she the spring" ["Tu mi fai rimembrar dove e qual era / Proserpina nel tempo che perdette / la madre lei, ed ella primavera"] (*Purg.* xxviii.49–51).

Dante never suggests that he thinks the young woman is Proserpina (as it turns out, she is not), but merely that she resembles her, based on his memory of Ovid's description in the *Metamorphoses*.[3] What is at stake here is not, therefore, a demonstration of the fallibility of perception, the blurring of historical "reality" by mythic "fiction." The pilgrim's seeing suggests, rather, that visual recognition is always an act of historical consciousness; present perception passes through the circuit of the past, accessing, in this case, a literary memory.[4] The crucial point is that the perceptual "movement" of this act of remembering is only possible within the system of historical consciousness in which the pilgrim is situated, paradoxically, as staying. Passage is thus intimately linked to a subjective condition of necessary immobility. After all, if the pilgrim passed bodily beyond the river (that is, with his feet), this movement of memory would no longer be possible. Of course, the reverse is also true: if the pilgrim were unable to pass beyond through an act of remembrance, his "staying" within a historical moment of self-conscious presence would be compromised.

The two experiential poles marked by the "staying" of Dante's feet and the "passing beyond" of his eyes are thus, allegorically, the two prin- cipal – and contradictory – poles between which subjectivity is inscribed as "historical." To distinguish these poles (whether rhetorically, as I am doing here, or iconically, as in Dante's poem) as separate moments of "historical" experience is, of course, merely convenient. The "passing beyond" in which memory encounters the past is indissociable from the condition of temporal paralysis which the self-conscious subject expe- riences as its own historicity. History as such is inscribed precisely in the irreducible duality of this experience; the moment of "passage" is flush with the radical impossibility of any such movement. In precise terms then, the encounter with Lethe expresses the constitutive paradox implicit in the pilgrim's condition as a "historical" subject. Historical consciousness is at once a moving beyond the static condition of the subject and a reinscription of its bounded status.

Dante's principal source for the Lethe myth was, of course, the famous sixth book of the *Aeneid*, in which Virgil recounts the hero's journey through the underworld.[5] Led by the Cumean Sybil, Aeneas enters the Elysian Fields where the souls of the dead await reincarnation to a second mortal existence on Earth. During their period of waiting, the hero learns, these souls must drink of Lethe's water, so that when reborn, they will recall nothing, either of their previous lives or of their sojourn in Hades. In displacing the river from its traditional location in the underworld, Dante maintains its liminal function while also inverting its orientation as a boundary.[6] Situated at the summit of Purgatory, the highest point on the surface of the terrestrial globe, the *Comedia*'s Lethe marks the place from which the souls of the dead finally depart from the human sphere, rather than return to it.

In these terms, the faculty of memory appears at this extreme limit of the mundane as, literally, a *super qua non* of human experience. It is the historical perspective in this sense that marks for Dante the boundary between the pilgrim's understanding and an Other (divine) order inaccessible to human rationality. Passage beyond this boundary implies not merely a disorienting – while ultimately still human – amnesia, but rather, a breach of human rationality itself. Such a breach requires, of course, that the pilgrim trade the guidance of the pagan Virgil for that of Beatrice, and with it, the comforts of human reason for the divine grace available to him only through faith.

In a similar fashion, Dante's adaptation of Aeneas' Lethean encounter marks, on a textual level, the poet's own requisite departure from Virgil as literary precursor. Just as the pilgrim substitutes faith for human reason at this point in the journey, so the poet's "passage beyond" is attended by a necessary shift in textual registers from the literary to the scriptural. Specifically, Dante's displacement of Lethe to the top of the Mount of Purgatory recontextualizes the river's liminal function within a more properly Judeo-Christian mythic tradition, namely, that of Moses' Pisgah sight of Palestine. In his staying and passing, Dante's pilgrim appears as an avatar of the Moses of *Exodus*. It is Moses, of course, whose arduous journey of deliverance culminates – at a border marked again by both a mountain and a river – in a similarly iconic moment of stasis and passage:

And I pleaded then with Yahweh. My Lord Yahweh, I said, you that have begun
to reveal your greatness and your power to your servant, you whose works and
mighty deeds no one in heaven or on earth can rival, may I not go across and see
this prosperous land beyond the Jordan, this prosperous country of hills, and
Lebanon? But because of you, Yahweh was angry with me and would take no
notice of me. "Enough!" he said "Speak to me no more of this. Climb to the
top of Pisgah; let your eyes turn towards the west, the north, the south, the east.
Look well, for across this Jordan you shall not go."[7]

For Moses, of course, the visual act of "passing beyond" into the promised
land is linked to a more terminal "staying of feet" than that experienced
by Dante. While Moses must die on the mountain top, never to enter the
earthly paradise reserved for his people by Yahweh, the pilgrim, aided
by Beatrice, will eventually undergo the requisite baptism of oblivion
in preparation for his passage through the heavenly spheres.[8] Yet, it
is in precisely this crucial respect that Dante's "historical" encounter
with Lethe most compellingly makes the reader recall where and what
Moses was at the moment of his death. In his imbrication of biblical and
classical mythic tradition, Dante links the subject's historical knowing to
its terminal boundedness as a subject, to its status and coherence figured
in terms of a certain death. Moses' example implies that the stability of
the pilgrim-hero as subject, constituted directly in the act of "seeing"
(knowing) historically, is in fact a sort of death, the same sort in fact, that
Moses himself suffers. Dante's Lethean encounter is in this sense also a
lethal one.[9]

The sort of death that Moses dies is that of the tragic hero in the strict
classical sense: it is a death that occurs only after a certain accession
to knowledge has taken place. Yet at the same time the episode under-
mines the narrative logic of the tragic paradigm. Moses' Pisgah vision
suggests that his knowing in fact coincides with his death. As in the case
of Dante's staying and passing, this coincidence implies neither temporal contiguity nor a teleological, cause–effect relation between seeing
and staying. It is only within the narrative structure of the myth that
Moses' fate can be said to accord with Yahweh's command – that he
dies, in other words, "because" or "when" he has seen the promised
land. On an allegorical level, the image of Moses suggests what is in fact
a non-dialectical convergence between knowing and death. There is no
synthetic position implied here, no "later" or "higher" state achieved,
and, accordingly, no Hegelian *Aufhebung* of initial thetical or antithetical
positions. Instead, knowledge and death remain mutually implied aspects

of a position thereby designated as that of a subject. Their relation is in this respect, strictly speaking, a non-relation; in their coincidence they do not constitute between them a logical association, whether of determinacy, opposition, or similitude. Their mutuality is not an atonement of differences, but rather their paradoxical coincidence. At the same time, if this coincidence is not a collapse or erasure of difference, neither is it merely the eternal suspension of difference in opposition: "death" as against "life"; "knowing" as against "not-knowing." Rather, the terms of this non-relation suggest a certain displacement of the structure of logical opposition itself: "death" as against, or with, its asymmetrical other, "knowledge."

Isolated from the narrative of which it is the culminating event, Moses' death coincides immediately with his knowledge of the promised land. This death is not, in that sense, an event, the end of Moses' life-story, but a position – literally, a "point of view." From the perspective of narrative, the crucial point is that Moses, leader of God's people, ceases to exist and therefore to lead: he dies. At the level of the iconic image itself, however, it is this death that positions his subjective act of seeing, constituting him as knowing subject within a space of immobility as irreducible as it is final. Moses' tomb, the writer of *Deuteronomy* notes, has never been found; no shrine or monument marks the event of his death.[10] It is rather the Pisgah vision itself that marks this event, not by placing a significant stone or an inscription, but by becoming itself the fact of burial; the moment at which Moses sees the promised land is the moment in which he is constituted as a subject in a posture of eternal interment. Neither a momentary pause ensuring the integrity of narrative continuity, nor the end of such continuity itself, Moses' death is a position of radical stasis discovered precisely within the subjective experience of process; his visual passage across the Jordan is licensed precisely by the irreducibility of his staying. In these terms, "death" is found to be at work within the act of knowing, or rather, within the constitution of the subject as, exclusively, a subject of knowledge. Meanwhile, it is the very dynamic of "knowing" itself that designates the knower as radically inert – or, a better word in the present context, interred.

Put another way, Moses' death represents a certain arrival of the subject, not at its ultimate demise – the end of "knowledge," of "consciousness," or of "life" – but rather, at its very constitution *qua* knowing subject. This arrival situates the subject in its very coherence and integrity as the embodiment of a contradictory Mosaic law, the paradoxical coupling of a "thou shalt" with a "thou shalt not." It is Dante's encounter with

Lethe that gives this Mosaic law of subjectivity its proper name: history. What is principally at stake in Dante's use of the Lethe myth is not the "natural" or "ontological" disposition of the subject in history, but rather the structural contradiction by which the subject is positioned, for rationality, as historical. This distinction is crucial, since it specifies the function of paradox, rather than that of narrative sense-making, as history's proper modality. It is only by both seeing and staying, by sustaining a contradictory posture in which motion and stasis are oddly collapsed, that the pilgrim maintains his purchase on subjectivity as a "historical" condition.

In this sense, Dante's allegory of the subject's historical condition appears to controvert history's traditional (and etymological) alliance with narrative as its proper logic and representational form. The word "history" derives from Latin, *historia*, meaning the narrative of past events. This term is itself a social adoption of Greek, ιστορια, which the *Oxford English Dictionary* defines as "a learning or knowing by inquiry, an account of one's inquiries, narrative." "History" thus appears to signify an exclusively narrative hermeneutic, one that can only admit paradox as a suspensive structure ultimately resolved and subsumed by its own great, internal logic of process. History makes proper narrational sense of stasis, immobility, interment, and death by relegating them to their proper space as events, the space of endings. It is only the lives of subjects, after all, their vitality and process, that can be the stuff of history. To insist that subjectivity admits of death (its own burial; a radical stasis) as a structural component of historicity is patently absurd; death is precisely that which never "takes place" within history, but only ever appears as history's end. Indeed, history in this sense is the very form of thought by which the interment of the subject is eternally forestalled.

Yet it must also be said that this alliance with narrative is built on structures of opposition (present/past; present/future) and of teleology (past-present-future) which only cohere, as Dante's encounter with Lethe shows, at the level of the subject itself. That is to say, history's identity with narrativity is not a "natural" condition, but proceeds from a prior identification of the subject with rationality. The earlier Greek form of ιστορια is ιστωρ, ιστορ-, meaning "knowing, learned, wise man, judge." As a hermeneutic system, then, history is predicated on the prior appearance of the subject in its exclusive disposition as rational, a stable locus of potential or actual knowing. The form of this rational constitution of the subject is that of irreducible paradox: the coincidence of passage and stasis, knowledge and interment. The "historical" subject in this sense not only continues to progress, but ceases to move as well; its grinding to a halt is internal to its very act of passage. In Dante's treatment of the Lethe episode, the pilgrim finds himself bound (constituted as a staying/passing subject) not within a condition of history, then, but within one of historical knowing. Dante's translation of Moses' "death" into the pilgrim's "staying" suggests that what is at stake here is not the end of the subject's life (history as tragic narrative) but the subject's very constitution as knower within a historical system which posits death as its own teleological, tragic moment of non-passage. What Dante's treatment renders explicit is the fact that this moment of non-passage cannot be relegated to the convenient and comfortable distance of an "end" (a distance posited immediately by the rational system in which it makes narrative sense). Rather, it is inscribed ("takes place") within the subject's very constitution as knowing, and within its very status, therefore, as a historical being. It is the pilgrim's status as a subject of knowledge that designates him, in the paradoxical structure of staying and passing, as consisting within a rational system of "history."[11]

Indeed, history, in this sense, must be designated as precisely that lethal dimension in which the subject "knowingly" subsists. Death, or rather, the interment that marks the event of a death, is the position from which the subject accedes to "history" as the form of its rational condition. Constituted as knower on a Lethean boundary between remembrance and forgetting, the subject of history is stabilized, not as the subject of a narrative which will ultimately admit death as its tragic conclusion, but as one whose passing beyond is flush with its own interment, whose culminating immobility is marked, at every point in the process, by the appearance of a static, localizable subject of knowledge.[12] Functionally indissociable from this plane of rationality and its internal contradiction, history appears in the non-relation defined at one pole by a subject both knowing and interred (one who sees but does not pass beyond), and at the other by a knowable-unknowable object ("seen" by the faculty of memory, but never reached). The subject of knowledge is only ever the subject of a lethal history.

"ALWAYS HISTORICIZE"?

The latter half of the twentieth century has of course constituted the rational subject's "lethal history" in a more literal sense as well. The progress of thought in psychoanalysis, linguistics, anthropology, philosophy, and sociology has produced a steady erosion of the knowing subject's status, and indeed, of rationality's purchase on subjectivity as such. In literary criticism and theory, this decline of the subject who knows has carried specific institutional and professional implications, since from the beginning, the image of the modern professional critic was equated with precisely that Mosaic authority who sees but does not pass beyond. The poet responsible for institutionalizing Moses' staying and passing as an iconic image of the subject of knowledge is not, of course, Dante, but Matthew Arnold. In the famous conclusion to "The Function of Criticism at the Present Time" (1864), Arnold explicitly placed a professional value on Moses' Pisgah vision of the promised land, characterizing the modern academic critic as the aesthetic realm's master and judge, but also its permanent exile:

The epochs of Aeschylus and Shakespeare make us feel their preeminence. In an epoch like those is, no doubt, the true life of literature; there is the promised land, towards which criticism can only beckon. That promised land it will not be ours to enter, and we shall die in the wilderness: but to have desired to enter it, to have saluted it from afar, is already, perhaps, the best distinction among contemporaries; it will certainly be the best title to esteem with posterity.[13]

It is difficult to imagine a more apt or compelling illustration of Arnold's ideas, or indeed, of the modern critical function he did so much to define, than this image of Moses in his posture of far-sighted confinement. Arnold's well-known definition of the critical activity as the endeavor "to see the object as in itself it really is" (Arnold, "Function," 584) posits the distance between subject and object as an irreducible condition of criticism. At the same time, it specifies a certain closing of that gap in the critic's apprehension of a truth: the knowing of the object, fully and completely, "as in itself it really is." Utterly comprehensible, entirely "known," the object of criticism nonetheless greets its knower, the critic, from the safety of a certain distance, as though sequestered precisely for knowledge and for nothing else. As a purely aesthetic object, it has no political or social aspect worthy of the critic's notice, while its historical dimension is dismissed with an ancillary acknowledgment of its origin, the accident of its birth within the field of the critic's gaze. The critic, similarly sequestered, is nothing other than the subject reserved and isolated within this act of aesthetic apprehension; the subject, in other words, disposed exclusively as knower. Arnold's critic is liberal education's ideal product, a proprietor of culture and caretaker of aesthetic tradition charged with that noblest of tasks: "to learn and propagate the best that is known and thought in the world."[14]

In spite of the pious elitism of such language, Arnold's description of the critic as iconic Moses continues to resonate in the field of literary studies. Indeed, an eerie confirmation of this image's profound influence is suggested by the mountaintop death of modern criticism's most iconic representative. The idea that Walter Benjamin resembles Arnold's Moses in some fashion is, of course, profoundly ironic, since it is Benjamin after all whose call for the "politicization of art" effectively reverses the Arnoldian emphasis on professional "disinterestedness."[15] Nonetheless, the story of Benjamin's death realizes the terms of Arnold's figural metaphor with a remarkable accuracy of detail. Attempting to flee Vichy France in 1940, Benjamin obtained a United States visa in Marseilles and traveled to Port Bou, a small town in the Franco-Spanish Pyrenees. Upon his arrival there, he learned that border officials, by orders received from the Gestapo that very day, were prohibited from honoring visas issued in Marseilles. Imagining his capture to be imminent, Benjamin committed suicide that evening, within sight, as it were, of his goal.[16]

In his late essay, "The Storyteller" (1936), Benjamin argued that "a man . . . who died at thirty-five will appear to *remembrance* at every point in his life as a man who dies at the age of thirty-five" (Benjamin, *Illuminations*, 100). This formula might be applied equally well to Benjamin's own writing, which appears, to those who would remember, as that of a man who died his particular death at his particular age. This is not to say that, in a trivial sense, one cannot read Benjamin without being reminded of the circumstances and meaning of his death, but rather that Benjamin's life, and particularly the writings produced in it, have been received institutionally as having the authority of a certain death, the authority of the professional critic.

Yet Benjamin was never an academic professional in any sense. His "career," to the extent that he had one, was, according to Hannah Arendt, at most that of a free-lance "contributor to magazines and literary sections of newspapers" (Benjamin, *Illuminations* 1; see also 22 ff.). Nonetheless, literary criticism in the twentieth century has succeeded in institutionalizing Benjamin's legacy, celebrating him as a native son and proto-professional whose work exhibits the values of creativity, incisive thought, and genius to which academics universally aspire. In Benjamin academic intellectuals seem capable of finding an idealized picture of themselves, as the portrait which graces the covers of the English-language editions of his essays, the *Illuminations* and *Reflections* volumes, attests. Inclined in a Rodinesque pose of scholarly seriousness, the author of these essays greets us as an academic authority: his is the image of the genuine and dedicated *penseur*, engaged in the quotidian and earnest task of intellectual discovery. He is, the photograph un-equivocally informs us, a true man of the academy; he is a *professional*. To an ivory tower practice which perceives itself as committed to social and political reform, yet which finds itself stymied by the mistrust and disbelief of those outside the academy, Benjamin seems to hold out the promise of criticism's relevance – and indeed, of its crucial importance. On Benjamin the mantle of scholarly elitism does not look hypocritical; applied to his practice, the title "materialist philosophy" does not appear oxymoronic.

Arnold's definition of the critical subject rose to institutional promi-nence in the early decades of the twentieth century with the dominance of the New Critical and Formalist methodologies, both of which accepted, though in varying ways, not only the object's purity within the aesthetic dimension, but also criticism's ability to perceive it in that respect "as in itself it really is." In particular, these text-centered approaches to liter-ary practice affirmed Arnold's insistence on the true critic's attitude of "disinterest" toward non-aesthetic experience generally. Arnold's notion of critical disinterest, though not unlike that which Kant stressed in considering the mind's apprehension of the beautiful, concerns a social rather than a psychological plane of experience; for Arnold, the critical perspective constitutes by definition an avoidance of textuality's politi-cal dimension, or what he calls "the practical view of things" (Arnold, "Function," 588). It is this matter of political and social disinterest, of course, that current literary practice has so soundly rejected. Against Arnold's injunction that critics engage the best of what is known and thought, and that they pay for their expertise in distance from the real world, scholars have openly abandoned disinterested authority as a value, seeking instead to establish precisely their engagement with literary ob-jects of study – with, in fact, "the practical view of things" – on many and diverse fronts.

More than any other single term, it is the dimension of historical inquiry and interpretation that has afforded literary scholarship its op-portunity to unmask both criticism's isolation and the aesthetic "purity" of its objects. In recent years, the question of historical knowledge has come to occupy a crucial position in the continuing critical and theoret-ical debates taking place in literary studies. Scholars of widely varying theoretical, political, and methodological allegiances have sought in in-creasing numbers to address in specific terms the historical contingencies not only of texts, but of their own critical and interpretive practices as well.[17] From a professional point of view, this "return to history" is typically characterized as a shift in the literary *Zeitgeist*, one of those systemic sea changes periodically wrought by an essentially cyclical or reactive process of intellectual history. Indeed, the prominence of the historical term in current literary practice does seem to balance a traditional, Arnoldian focus on the literary text as a discrete, aesthetic object. Practitioners of various forms of "new historicism" position themselves against a double tradition in this regard. On the one hand, the text-centered methodologies that are frequently associated with modernism, such as those of New Criticism, Formalism, and Structuralism, are alleged to have impoverished the literary endeavor by simply ignoring contextual issues wholesale. On the other, the post-structuralist and deconstructive strategies of reading which supposedly displaced these methodologies merely obviated questions of contingency by reconstituting such contexts as "texts" in their own right. Instead of expanding and enriching literary practice, such approaches have allegedly rendered reading a witheringly self-referential and self-satisfied activity, while elevating literary scholarship itself to a rarefied and unassailable position of mastery as the science of language's infinite play.

History, in this context, has emerged as something of a cure-all. The charge most frequently leveled at the old, text-centered methodologies, in fact, is that they "deny" history, by which is meant not only that they dismiss the importance of historical contexts, but also that they anachronistically impose contemporary concerns and perspectives on past documents and artifacts. This accusation of history's denial, carrying as it does the connotation of willful ignorance, has the advantage of communicating seemingly transparent and universal values. It would seem that history is after all ontologically undeniable; the past has been, and therefore demands that we pay it heed. Only the most benighted sort of thinker would claim that history does not "exist" or that it does not affect our lives, much less our readings of texts. Even more importantly, the patent fallaciousness of such a denial gives late twentieth-century criticism its own equally transparent moral absolute: "Always historicize!" Initially coined and elaborately celebrated by Fredric Jameson in *The Political Unconscious* as "the one absolute and we may even say 'transhistorical' imperative of all dialectical thought," this injunction explicitly posits historical inquiry as criticism's only corrective against the methodological sins of its past.[18]

Yet literary practice does more in breaking with its modernist and post-modernist past than simply disavowing a habitual disinterest in dates and contexts. The return to textuality's historical dimension announces a self-conscious and concerted effort to ground professional engagements with literature on a plane of both responsibility and relevance. The call to historicize one's readings is in fact meant to signal the complexity and dynamism of this effort; the term "history" functions as a catch-all for the multiple contextual forces that inform both the production and reception of texts. In confronting the "historical" text, readers encounter a poly-vocal, unstable literary object, one that is formed by, but that also reproduces, specific structures of ideology, culture, politics, and institutional power. It is the complex system of exchange between such texts and the various, changing contexts in which they are both written and read that current literary practice attempts to negotiate under the aegis of "history."

In light of this emphasis on history as the index of textuality's contingency and instability (rather than of its objectification in time), it is hardly surprising that literature's celebrated return to history has coincided with a return to narrative. Initiated largely by Jameson's arguments in *The Political Unconscious*, the rediscovery of history's irreducibility has been linked from the beginning to an acceptance of narrative as history's representational final instance. Narrative is seen as the only structural form that is at once both elastic and specific enough to encompass the complexities of historical knowledge. Indeed, Jameson's statement of his work's "specific critical and interpretive task" might be taken as representative of the methodological return to history as a whole: Jameson's modest goal is "to restructure the problematics of ideology, of the unconscious and of desire, of representation, of history, and of cultural production, around the all-informing process of *narrative*, which [he] take[s] to be (here using the shorthand of philosophical idealism) the central function or *instance* of the human mind" (Jameson, *Political Unconscious*, 13). In these terms, narrative is a kind of ideal representational solvent: never saturated by the histories it continually incorporates and reveals, it is the only medium through which rationality can remain eternally receptive to history's objective complexity, as well as to its diachronic instability.

It is Jameson's appeal to narrative as a specifically dialectical tool that allows him to negotiate what he calls the dilemma of historicism. "The historicizing operation," he writes, "can follow two distinct paths, which only ultimately meet in the same place: the path of the object and the

path of the subject, the historical origins of the things themselves and that
more intangible historicity of the concepts and categories by which we attempt to understand those things" (Jameson, *Political Unconscious*, 9). On
the objective side, Jameson posits an "antiquarian" practice of historical
reading which exhausts itself in the rather prosaic task of apprehending
historical allusions and resonances in texts. Such an approach presumes
an idealist (positivist) vision of history and of the historical process according to which it is possible to read texts as in themselves they really
are. On the other hand, Jameson is equally disparaging of the subjective
alternative: an anachronistic use of specific texts to support one's own
current theoretical views concerning historical or aesthetic "truths." This
second practice reduces the encounter with history to a bottomless but
predictable relativism: the function of realism in historical representation becomes that of a convenient straw man, against which the writerly,
open, playful text can be set as a utopian alternative (Jameson, *Political
Unconscious*, 18).

Only Marxist historicism, Jameson insists, resolves this dilemma by
allowing the past to speak its own "mystery" fully, and in a context (the
present) that is fundamentally alien to it. It is of course the demonstration of Marxism's priority as an interpretive paradigm that is in fact
Jameson's chief concern in *The Political Unconscious*. But this priority is
itself due to what he considers Marxism's power as a totalizing narrative
system. All other rational paradigms (psychoanalytic, ethical, and so on)
reflect responses to local ideologies and problems, and thus submit the
complexity of history to the hegemonic perspectives governed by these
specific localities. Jameson's polemic would champion the historicizing
operation as a complex effort to sustain a thoroughly dialectical process
of discovery, a process that would take for granted neither the past's objective status as truth nor the subject's perspective as isolated and knowing. Only Marxist narrative, he says, considers the factor of diachronic
change along with local, objective considerations, thus both canceling
and preserving the latter within the "untranscendable horizon" of its
own totalizing narrative hermeneutic (Jameson, *Political Unconscious*, 10).
Only Marxism demonstrates in dialectical fashion that we are all part of
one, great, unifying story (Jameson, *Political Unconscious*, 17–19).

In the early 1980s, Jameson's temerity in declaring the Marxist dialectic the only tenable means of philosophical engagement with history
gave the resurgence of narrative its needed political dimension, and thus
struck a nerve with many in the academy who had grown impatient with
their profession's perceived detachment from issues of social reform.[19]

But Jameson's appeal to the mystical powers of the Marxist paradigm is ultimately tautological: history for him is a Marxist dialectical narrative the "untranscendable horizon" of which is . . . Marxist dialectical narrative. Astonishingly, his commitment to the narrative structure of historical reality enables him to align his project with precisely those structuralist and post-structuralist intellectual traditions that are most vehemently opposed to the notion of history's essential narrativity. In particular, Jameson appropriates Althusser's rejection of the hidden narrative hegemonies of all historicisms, whether messianic (Augustine), idealist/utopian (Hegel), or cyclical (Vico), to support his own view that narrative is history's "absolute horizon." The problem, Jameson claims, is not with Althusser, but with the assimilation of his thought to a fashionable theoretical position in which "[h]istory . . . the reference to a 'context' or a 'ground' . . . is simply one more text among others" (Jameson, *Political Unconscious*, 35). While Althusser may be sympathetic to the notion of history as a text (though whether or not it is a narrative text is uncertain[20]), he does not conclude on that basis that history's referent does not "exist." Underscoring this distinction enables Jameson to restate Althusser's conclusion in a form more agreeable to him, namely as a belief that "history is *not* a text, not a narrative, master or otherwise, but that . . . it is inaccessible to us except in textual form, and that our approach to it and to the Real itself necessarily passes through its prior textualization, its narrativization in the political unconscious" (Jameson, *Political Unconscious*, 35).

This distinction between history and the text of history (a distinction between the Real and the Symbolic), is one to which Althusser would certainly be the last to object. It is Jameson's final phrase, the reference to "narrativization *in* the political unconscious," that reveals the crucial misprision that governs his project. For Jameson, the unconscious is the place in which Real history becomes Symbolic history; it is not the zone of the inaccessible, but the region in which meaning (truth) resides and is given the narrational structure through which rational subjects apprehend it. "Interpretation proper," Jameson writes, "always presupposes, if not a conception of the unconscious itself, then at least some mechanism of mystification or repression in terms of which it would make sense to seek a latent meaning behind a manifest one, or to rewrite the surface categories of a text in the stronger language of a more fundamental interpretive code" (Jameson, *Political Unconscious*, 60). This formulation is strange, since Freud stressed repeatedly in *The Interpretation of Dreams* and elsewhere that while meaning may be latent, it is not therefore "unconscious."

The unconscious cannot be construed as "a more fundamental interpretive code," because desire only attaches itself to meaning as the effect
of structures produced in the preconscious and conscious mind.[21]

Althusser's structuralist argument culminates in the dictum, "history is
a process without a *telos* or a subject," a statement which Jameson takes
(correctly) to mean that history is a non-narrative process (Jameson,
Political Unconscious, 28). Yet he then rushes to disarm the more radical
implications of this statement by suggesting first that it reveals Althusser's
belief in history's symbolic consistency, and second that it specifies that
consistency as latent. Narrative is itself the more fundamental code that is
"in" the unconscious; narrative, in other words, is the Real. The problem
with history for Althusser, however (as is indeed implied by Jameson's
reading of him), seems rather to be precisely that narrative is the human
mind's submission to an ideology of the rational subject, and not its
final instance. In that case, narrative structures of knowing, Marxist or
otherwise, inevitably return us, tautologically, to a prior understanding
of the knowing subject as narrationally rational. In this context, the
unconscious can offer no answer, no totalizing, absolute political horizon, but can only ever be a severely troubling and disturbing term. The
unconscious is only ever the radical Other of both representation and
presentation, and thus of narrative as well. That we can only talk about
it in narrative terms does not mean that it obeys exclusively narrational
logic; indeed, Freud's point in suggesting the rebus paradigm for the
structure of dream-thoughts seems to have been that that which is unconscious becomes narrational only as a result of secondary processes of
revision and translation.[22] The formula by which the historical Other is
in this way aligned with the unconscious is, as Jameson's title suggests, an
attractive one; it has the ring of promise about it, and implies an atonement with the past, if only in the form of a suspended opposition.[23] It is
worth pointing out, however, that by such assertions is usually meant not
that history is the unconscious, but that it resembles the unconscious:
it is at once real (it has happened) and unavailable in itself. The unconscious, whatever Jameson may say about its irreducible Otherness,
appears in his discourse as his most fond familiar, a mechanism for the
dialectical revelation of history's Real narrative structure: "It is in detect-
ing the traces of that uninterrupted narrative" – the great, Marxist story
of which we are all a part – "in restoring to the surface of the text the
repressed and buried reality of this fundamental history, that the doctrine
of a political unconscious finds its function and its necessity" (Jameson,
Political Unconscious, 20). The power of Marxist historiography lies in its

ability to resurrect the past and allow it to speak as what it most truly and in itself is: the "political unconscious."[24]

Jameson's text might be said to have, in this sense, its own "latent meaning" – not its own political unconscious, but what could more justifiably be called its own political *pre*-conscious. Although he spins his yarns in the constellation figured by the terms narrative, history, desire, and the unconscious, the central term at issue in his text is that of critical authority. His project is at every point one that engages literary history as an institutional province, and that joins battle in the methodological "class struggle" of the literary marketplace. Precisely because Jameson specifies historicism as the site of a rational redemption held perpetually in abeyance (whether by the structure of the dialectic or the hand of God matters little); precisely because he posits history as criticism's land of promise, the affective achievement of his argument is a reinscription of the authoritative, knowing (staying and passing) subject of history. The point is not that Jameson himself may occupy the position of such a knowing subject in his own narrative, or that he may posit a personal and professional triumph as his own conscious or unconscious goal in producing it. The point is rather that the appearance of the subject of knowledge in its paradoxical disposition of interment is a structurally necessary aspect (both a condition and a result) of Jameson's rational discourse. Presuming in advance history's "absolute horizon" as a discourse of knowledge, Jameson's project inevitably finds its own "absolute horizon" in this paradoxical constitution of the knowing subject.

All of this suggests that concern over history's denial is misplaced. On their own, accusations of willful amnesia neither demonstrate the importance of remembering history nor reveal better paradigms for historical engagement. At the heart of late twentieth-century criticism's return to history, and of the continuing discussion it has spawned, is rather the status of critical authority itself. It is this issue that defines the terms of a debate in which history only ever appears as an objective field, a known-unknown/knowable-unknowable terrain figured and refigured by knowing and ignorant critical subjects. Conceived in these terms, the effort to answer the "question" of history follows a trajectory as predictable as it is endless: What (in truth) happened? How do we know? How do we represent what we know? Is History a science or an art? How do we do justice to history, when our vision is skewed – when, as Hans Kellner puts it, we continually get the story "crooked"?[25] Despite its positioning as a bone of perpetual contention, history exerts its crucial force in this debate not as an apprehended object, but as the systemic form of subjective authority.

Indeed, it is, one suspects, a kind of nostalgia for this authority that motivates criticism's current "return" to history. Arguing over history's objective status, its use and abuse by various "historicisms," conveniently displaces the matter of critical authority to a field and a rhetoric in which values are seemingly transparent. Yet the denial of history allegedly perpetrated by one critical methodology is hardly remedied simply by history's affirmation in another. It is never enough, in itself, to supplant ignorance with knowledge, because ignorance has as powerful claims on the authority of the subject as knowledge does. The question of historical representation is unresolvable because historical representation itself is irreducibly commemorative; veering off toward the issues of "accuracy" and "adequacy," the writing of history never fails nonetheless to accomplish its principal goal: the memorialization of that death to which it is witness. The authority of the critical perspective – and not the knowledge of history – is once again confirmed in this sense as the principal result of historicism.

At the same time, the political effects of both the denial and the affirmation of history, or of history's importance as a field or discipline, cannot be discounted; it is the political dimension of historical engagement that precedes the appearance of historical events themselves for knowledge or ignorance. As Gerz's *2,146 Stones* suggests, the denial of the historical existence of the Holocaust is a political salvo before it is a "pure" statement of historical belief. Such a denial is disturbing because it suggests the loss of historical truth, and because it affirms a political appropriation of that truth that has real effects for the present, including the loss of history. Such a denial is, of course, construed by its proponents as a certain "knowledge" of history, but it is ultimately a political use of history, rather than history "itself," that is at stake. Indeed, the fact that denial appears in this context as affirmation is crucial. In terms of historical knowledge, the non-existence of certain historical events themselves is less important than the political will which posits those events as non-existent.

Similarly, the affirmation of the Holocaust as event or series of events is linked to the political priority of certain beliefs, such as that knowledge of such events will ensure that they will not be repeated, or that knowledge in itself offers a kind of justice to the victims of history. James Young's assessment of the Holocaust memorial's capacity to fetishize the past reveals, as we have seen, the ways in which such knowledge tends to isolate the knower from the very past that is his or her object. In the context of Holocaust memory, the mere mention of any number of current or recent historical situations (such as that of the former Yugoslavia in the 1990s – to cite, once again, an obvious example) demonstrates that historical affirmation has its own powerful component of denial.

Both positions are predicated not on the status of history as event, but on the political efficacy of the belief that history is knowable; that the subject is a stable locus of knowledge. In these terms, denial and affirmation serve the same function: both reserve the political effects of critical authority under the "natural" or "ontological" form of history, the "event." To underscore this kinship between history's denial and its affirmation, or between knowledge and ignorance, is not to insist on a facile relativism as history's final "truth." On the contrary, it is to insist on both relativism and positivism as the political effects of a gaze which posits the objective truth of history precisely in order to measure therein the stability and authority of its own position. Gazing toward the past, critical authority is invested in apprehending its object as a territory of promise, any remote corner of which is at any given time only partially charted, and which remains therefore perpetually available to further exploration. History, in this sense, is the ultimate prop for critical stasis, an inexhaustible source in which the gaze continually rediscovers its own coherence as knowledge. The debate over history and its status in current literary discourse matters, then, precisely because it is a political debate; what is at stake is not history, but the political effects of critical authority.

The attempt to establish an alternative methodology of critical engagement by "returning" to history seems, in this context, vexed at best. In light of Dante's Lethean encounter, it would seem to be precisely the historical dimension of inquiry that situates the critical subject so comfortably within its space of authority. Precisely because history is that which places the subject in a *knowing* relation with its Other, the effort not to deny history by always historicizing inevitably returns the subject of historical knowledge to the mountain-top space of Moses' far-sighted death. What Dante's example shows is that "seeing" historically is always, irreducibly, a writing of history, and that this writing is "lethal" to the extent that it situates or immobilizes a subject as "historical." In one sense, this is not new; written history has always maintained the trope of a certain death within it, insofar as it presumes to represent that which is past.[26] Historical writing is always funereal, always commemorative, restoring that which is absent to the plane of knowledge. Dante demonstrates that this burial of the past through its historical representation

masks the burial of the writing subject itself: "passing beyond" Lethe
with his eyes, the pilgrim accesses historical images or narratives, but in
so doing, is constrained to "present" himself in an aspect of unrelieved
paralysis (a kind of death), "staying" with his feet on the near bank. Historical writing's principal residuum is not the story of the past, but the
subject who knows.

Indeed, Jameson's own "transhistorical imperative" suggests an expression not of narrative's status as the "absolute horizon" of history, but
of the historical subject's own grounding in paradox. "Always historicize"
has an odd, almost oxymoronic quality that betrays, in a positive sense,
the contradiction internal to the concept of the "historical" as such. The
historicizing operation places the knowing subject in the way of history
as process, a dynamic plane of diachronic change to which dialectical
narrative is admirably adapted as its symbolic medium. But at the same
time, its very character as the discrete act of a rational subject, "the historicizing operation," specifies the irreducibility of its own locality and
stasis, its setting forth from a position of non-movement. The "always"
in Jameson's slogan is meant, of course, to suggest that the dialectic is not
only a structural but a moral imperative. Practitioners of literary criticism
not only "must" but "should" always (repeatedly, continually) confront
history dialectically, leapfrogging through progressively defined subjective and objective positions. Yet this "always" also signals historicism's
constitution as the field of paradox; it refers not only to a dialectical succession of historical positions (subjective and objective), but also to the
inconceivable coincidence of such positions with the process that connects them. "Always historicize" expresses the paradox through which
the historical subject is constituted in a non-relation with its historical
Other.

ALWAYS EROTICIZE!

Despite its more radical implications, the psychoanalytic "discovery" of
the unconscious has served well the traditional linking of history and
narrative. A convenient metaphor through which to comprehend history as Other, the unconscious is frequently designated as a repository or
holding cell for everything that knowledge excludes or "denies" in constituting itself as knowledge. What is "repressed" or "forgotten" (little, if
any, distinction is generally made between the two) remains nonetheless
there, promised, susceptible of a possible and, one imagines, inevitable
return. In these terms, the unconscious is not the Other of knowledge,

but a kind of promissory note inscribed within the very structure of rationality itself, the final guarantee that all may be known. What is lost to historiography is thereby reclaimed and accounted for, if only in its status as lost or forgotten. Historical knowledge can thus lay claim to mastery over history as a totality, numbering among its holdings precisely those elements of which it is not yet master. This "not yet" is crucial; it is audible in every engagement of the past by the present, and betrays the structure of promise in which historiography always beholds its Other.

Jameson's appropriation of Althusser seems the more disingenuous in this light. In 1964 Althusser composed his polemical essay, "Freud and Lacan," aiming to convince detractors that psychoanalysis was not simply a reactionary ideology.[27] Borrowing the vocabulary of empiricism, and celebrating psychoanalysis as "the science of a new object: the unconscious" (Althusser, "Freud and Lacan," 198), he argued that that object needed to be situated and defined in its specificity (Althusser, "Freud and Lacan," 192). Yet even in publishing these words he warned that they would lead to misunderstanding. In a letter to the essay's English translator, he wrote that certain of its theses needed to be corrected or expanded, and that Freud's term "the unconscious" itself should be "rechristened" as soon as possible. Indeed, even within the essay's appeal to the scientific model it is possible to discern its author's effort to deliver a more nuanced view of the psychoanalytic "object":

What is the *object* of psycho-analysis? It is *what* analytical technique deals with in the analytical practice of the cure, i.e. not the cure itself, not that supposedly dual system which is tailor-made for any phenomenology or morality – but the "*effects*," prolonged into the surviving adult, of the extraordinary adventure which from birth to the liquidation of the Oedipal phase transforms a small animal conceived by a man and a woman into a small human child.

One of the "effects" of the humanization of the small biological creature that results from human parturition: there in its place is the object of psychoanalysis, an object which has a simple name: "*the unconscious.*" (Althusser, *Lenin and Philosophy*, 204–05)

This simple name thus returns to designate the psychoanalytic object with all the persistence – and purchasing power – of a bad penny.[28] Yet it is clear that in broaching the question of "effects," Althusser is attempting to discuss something to which that name – by very reason of its being a name – is not entirely adequate. The importance of the unconscious for psychoanalysis is that it marks the fact that a certain passage to humanity has been accomplished by an organism. This passage to humanity is disposed for consciousness as an accession to history, an emergence of the subject as a being in relation to its own past: in becoming "human," the organism accedes to a subjectivity in which effects are "prolonged" and the history of its own passage persists.[29] It is these persisting effects of human subjectivity that are the principal object of psychoanalysis.

What Althusser specifies as the unconscious, in this sense, is not a stable object of science but the outward sign of the subject's accession to history.[30] The object of psychoanalysis is not, then, the unconscious as existing object, but the unconscious as historical effect. This is a crucial distinction, and one that becomes clearer when we recall that within the therapeutic scene, while the "talking cure" is taking its course, what is being talked about (discovered, constructed, recorded, encountered) is never anything but history. In speaking the histories of childhood, of dreams, of family systems, and so on, the subject reveals its own relation to the "extraordinary adventure" in which it came to be recognized as human. At the same time, the speaking subject encounters this historical relation at every step only through the vicissitudes of translation, fantasy, myth, projection, and so on – in short through the use of both affirmation and denial as instruments of apprehension. It is a persistent and pervasive cultural misunderstanding that psychoanalysis is, on the therapeutic level, about recovering the truth of a patient's past. In fact, the discovery of history in this sense is an important but, strictly speaking, provisional aspect of the patient's speech. The promise of a truth finally and absolutely known is what the analysand posits within the idea of "cure," and it is this promised accession to truth that fuels his or her discourse of history. Psychoanalysis never made such a promise, aware that it could not be made without reducing everything to the experience of the tragic hero. Instead, it remarks the function of a lure at the core of such knowing: the truth is not the cure, but only ever that which is promised, and which therefore remains unattainable even if it is always within sight.

Crucially, the subject's speech constitutes at every point a discourse of history that is not, however, exclusively a discourse of knowledge. While history provides the very structure of the analysand's search for truth in the Other – the prospect of a cure routed through an examination of the past – the speech that gives form to that search nonetheless betrays a continual encounter with history on another plane. The analysand's affirmations and denials – his frequent "Eureka!"s; her repeated "I don't know"s – mask a continuous and unbroken "I want" that is itself the very form of the subject's historical consistency. If psychoanalysis is the science of a new object in this sense, that object is not the unconscious, but rather history itself. After all, as many observers of the Freudian "discovery" have pointed out, the unconscious was known and even named long before Freud began listening to the speech of hysterics.[31] What is new in psychoanalysis is rather the apprehension of the historical disposition from and through which the subject of the unconscious speaks. The "new science" of psychoanalysis is founded in the discovery that history is a discourse not only of knowledge but also of desire.

To say that history is a discourse of desire is to acknowledge that the paradox which grounds the historicity of the subject (staying/passing) is not only a structure of promise, but also one of compromise. On the one hand, disposed as an exclusively rational being, the subject experiences the historical relation as an assurance of eventual atonement with its Other: the historical past, the unconscious, God, and so on. What is in fact an irreducible and insoluble disjunction is made whole by reducing history to its ideal totality as narrative. The principal product of this resolution – the subject constituted exclusively as knower – is the subject not of history, but rather of historical narrative. The chief manifestation of history as a discourse of desire, on the other hand, is not the knowing subject, but the symptom – the "effect," in Althusser's formulation, of the subject's having become human. The symptom is that which orients subjectivity inexorably toward its historical as opposed to its narrational integrity. It is the structure of inconsistency (staying/passing) in which the subject subsists. The absence of any promised atonement – either a reconciliation (absolute knowledge) or an end (death) – within this symptomatic structure is what identifies it as a structure of desire. The symptom manifests the subject's relation to history in a form inhospitable to knowledge, which is to say, as a non-relation. To redefine our terms, the symptom is the mark of the subject's erotic relation to being; the name of this erotic relation is history.

This appearance of the symptom at the crux of the subject's erotic relation to history suggests a reformulation of Jameson's methodological imperative by psychoanalysis: always eroticize! Such an injunction demands, in the literary context, that the historicizing operation not be undertaken merely as a submission to the dialectic; a belief in the narrative reality of history must be firmly in place before one can embark on either of Jameson's initial alternatives, the "contextualizing" or "theorizing" of one's readings that bring one inevitably to the same historicized (Marxist) "truth." To "eroticize" as a historicizing operation suggests that one cede to the inexorable and paradoxical function of desire a certain process in one's readings of texts, and that one do so precisely with reference to textuality's historical dimension.

The elaboration of such a process of reading (an "erotics of memory") and its concrete implications for modern Irish historical imagination will consume the balance of this book. It is through acts of symptomatic reading that the move from a lethal practice of historical knowing to an erotics of memory must take place. The following chapter offers a practical illustration of precisely this sort of reading, centering on Italian director Roberto Rossellini's neo-realist, cinematic repetition of a canonical Irish text, Joyce's "The Dead." In presenting a model for the critical reading of the past in general, this chapter will function as a necessary rhetorical and analytical bridge to the case studies in Irish historical imagination that follow in Part II below. Rossellini's *Viaggio in Italia* remembers "The Dead," re-presenting it as a prior, originary text now occurring for the first time in its re-covered form, a cinematic reading. In that sense, the film offers an example of a reading practice that acknowledges its textual other in an erotics of memory.

Before turning our attention to the theory of symptomatic reading, however, it is necessary to add a few comments about what it means, practically speaking, to approach memory as a discourse of desire. In the first place, if Jameson's "always historicize" is an essentially oxymoronic construction, then "always eroticize" must be acknowledged to be an essentially redundant one. It was perhaps Freud's most often-repeated (and misunderstood) dictum that all experience is sexual experience. By the term "sexual," of course, Freud meant not to isolate the biological or reproductive functions of the human organism, but to suggest desire's circulation within all aspects of experience, including that symbolic plane in which such experience is apprehended by consciousness. To "always eroticize" is redundant, since one's experience in every dimension, including the readings of texts, is in some sense expressive of this function of desire. Yet so far from undermining the force of our new injunction, this redundancy reveals its most compelling strength as the chief tool of a psychoanalytic historicism.

It is precisely repetition that was Freud's most trusted tool in eliciting the Other histories of his patients:

In analysing the dreams of my patients I sometimes put this assertion to the following test, which has never failed me. If the first account given me by a patient of a dream is too hard to follow I ask him to repeat it. In doing so he rarely uses the same words. But the parts of the dream which he describes in different terms are by that fact revealed to me as the weak spot in the dream's disguise . . . That is the point at which the interpretation of the dream can be started. My request to the patient to repeat his account of the dream has warned him that I was proposing to take special pains in solving it; under pressure of the resistance, therefore, he hastily covers the weak spots in the dream's disguise by replacing any expressions that threaten to betray its meaning by other less revealing ones. In this way he draws my attention to the expression which he has dropped out. (Freud, *The Interpretation of Dreams*, 553–54)

Repetition orients the dreamer away from the dream's narrative consistency (and therefore from his or her own consistency as a subject), toward what Freud called the "navel" (Freud, *The Interpretation of Dreams*, 564). The omphalos of the dream is the inexplicable, illegible point at which it might be said to express its dreamer's erotic relation to being, its subject's non-relation to history. Thus it is repetition – and not the single-thread linearity of narrative logic; not the once-and-for-all proclamations of Truth – that is psychoanalytic historicism's chief and most revered tool. As Auden wrote of Freud:

> He wasn't clever at all: he merely told
> The unhappy Present to recite the Past
> > Like a poetry lesson till sooner
> > Or later it faltered at the line where
> Long ago the accusations had begun,
> And suddenly knew by whom it had been judged,
> > How rich life had been and how silly,
> > And was life-forgiven and more humble.
> Able to approach the Future as a friend
> Without a wardrobe of excuses, without
> > A set mask of rectitude or an
> > Embarrassing over-familiar gesture.[32]

Repetition – the reciting of the past like a poetry lesson – as a mode of engagement with an Other (whether figured as the Past, the Unconscious, the Analyst, or anything else), is strictly antithetical to knowledge. By this I do not mean that having known certain things and then forgotten them, one can never know them again; this sort of knowledge-repetition, of course, happens all the time. The point is rather that knowing itself is structured for rationality as a discrete act of connection, and in this sense, it cannot be repeated. Moses, for example, does not gaze out from the top of Mount Pisgah again and again; that he does not, however, is not simply because to do so would be, in the context of his heroic narrative, redundant. In fact, Moses' act of seeing coincides with the act of burial that expresses his identity as a particular figure, the subject of a narrative history. What the intolerance for repetition in narrative demonstrates, then, is that it is precisely this effective burial that can never be repeated within a narrative of history. It is in repetition that the original sin against history lies: those who do not know history, we are told, are destined to repeat it. Repetition is not only boring, embarrassing, irresponsible; in the context of history, one should *know* better.

Psychoanalysis nonetheless insists on the theoretical and clinical validity of precisely the opposite lesson: those who do not repeat history are destined to know it. To understand this reversal as more than a rhetorical gesture it is necessary to read the phrase, "knowing history," not with the eyes of the critic, but with the ears of the analyst: knowing history, in that case, is also no-ing history; affirmation and denial are equal forces in the production of historical "knowledge." The point is that psychoanalysis apprehends historical knowledge (the lure of the truth) as that which is literally lethal to the subject; it is symptomatic, and as such, situates the subject in a disposition of boundedness (death or staying). The promise of knowledge is, of course, what supports the quest for history, but this promise is ultimately a detour that allows the historical subject to maintain a certain inertia, the comfort of interment that is the chief attribute of the authority of the subject.

Psychoanalysis begins by noting the paradoxical coincidence between a certain burial of the subject itself – figured as a radical immobility, the symptomatic consistency of the subject in history – and that subject's disposition as knowing.[33] This burial is what the subject's historical speech – and its silences as well – at every moment reveals. History, for the analysand, is spread out within the plane of rationality; pursuing its promise exclusively in that plane, the subject emerges in the lethal posture of the subject who knows. In its perpetual pursuit of the writing of its own history, the subject produces itself, literally, through an act of *en-graving*, in the aftermath of which it stands as memorial. The knowing subject itself is nothing other than this commemorative marker. As Althusser writes, "[T]hat is the test all adult men have passed: they are the *never forgetful* witnesses, and very often the victims, of this victory, bearing in their most hidden, i.e. in their most clamorous parts, the wounds, weaknesses and stiffnesses that result from this struggle for human life or death" (Althusser, *Lenin and Philosophy*, 205). This memorial status of the subject belies the traditional narrative logic according to which burial only occurs at the "end" of the story. "Humanity," Althusser adds a few lines later, "only inscribes its official deaths on its war memorials: those who were able to die on time, i.e. late." Psychoanalysis, however, never anything but an encounter with history, engages the subject's memorialization in its apprehension of the symptom.

In these terms, the symptom must be defined not only as an illness in the subject, a foreign body to be excised or isolated for the sake of the subject's health; it is also the subject itself constituted on the rational plane as a paradoxical living memorial. The symptom is the organized, living self, the marker placed over the space of interment and burial; it does not, for all that, constitute another region of promise, a space to be filled in the moment of cure. The subject's investment in the symptom is precisely the same as its investment in the particular past which, in its persistent resistance to change, supports its memorialized self. The gesture toward knowledge of the past is one calculated to maintain the status of the memorialized subject; knowing history reduces the system of present–past to a narrational relation, and thus refuses the repetition which is history's crucial mechanism. Reciting the past like a poetry lesson, on the other hand, allows us to weigh desire in the balance of our knowing and no-ing. Repetition reveals our investment in the narrative status of historical truth as well as history's objective status as Other. When we tell and retell the past, it is not history that shows through so much as our symptomatic fascination with its meanings, its rhythms, its style – all of the formal attributes that belie our memorialized, Pisgah vision. Reciting it in this way means repeating it over and over again, until the faulty lines show, the liminal boundaries at which our lethal histories are inscribed.

CHAPTER 3

A reservation under the name of Joyce: Rossellini's Viaggio in Italia *and the symptom*

Muta: Petrificationibus! O horild haraflare! Who his dickhuns now
rearrexes from undernearth the memorialorum?
Juva: Beleave filmly, beleave!

James Joyce
Finnegans Wake

"Je ne suis pas dans ma meilleure forme aujourd'hui, pour toutes sortes
de raisons" [I am not in my best form today, for all sorts of reasons].[1]
Such was the qualifying disclaimer with which Jacques Lacan began
one of his final theoretical investigations, a year-long seminar devoted as
much to literary as to psychoanalytic topics titled "Joyce le symptôme."
From a certain point of view, it is unreasonable to doubt the straightforward honesty of Lacan's disclosure. His health was at this time beginning the precipitous decline which would be halted only by his death, six
years later, at the age of eighty. Yet from another perspective, the statement's prominence in a crucial theoretical text devoted to the function
and formation of symptoms seems deliberately suggestive: the state of
Lacan's health aside, the comment is interesting since it refers obliquely
to Lacan's topic, the symptom that is itself precisely the evidence that
one is not in one's "best form." Moreover, what makes the statement's
appearance in the much-revised published version of the seminar particularly compelling is that it is the analyst, and not the analysand, who
is speaking.

Academic criticism typically requires that those who would interpret
literary texts do so with a degree of objectivity and mastery, closeting their
symptomatic inadequacies to as great an extent as possible. Lacan's bad
form is thus hardly consonant with what might be characterized as a
traditional scholarly approach to Joyce. Recognizing that Lacan himself
was not given to public confessions of intellectual limitation, it is worth
taking his comment seriously as a gesture toward symptomatic reading,
a critical discourse that issues from the position marked by the speaker's

66

own symptom. In principle, at least, such a practice empties out the critical pose of expertise, the falseness of reading as the process of becoming master of the master, and announces every reader's bad form, or symptom, as the condition of reading itself. Such a notion of symptomatic reading does not, however, simply license a new perspectivist relativism according to which every reader's bad form is as "good" as that of the next. It would be misleading – as well as naive at this point – to invoke the symptom as a kind of interpretive tool, a determinative strategy aimed at the definitive understanding of texts. For Lacan, the symptom is an enigmatic signifier; despite consisting as a kind of textual quantity within inter-subjective structures of communication, the symptom is not legible in itself. It is in this sense that reading "in bad form" – the apparent pejorative connotations of the metaphor notwithstanding – is not the same as reading "badly."

As we have seen, the authority of the subject who knows within practices of reading is fundamentally supported by the "Mosaic law" of a historical perspective that insists on the discrete autonomy of subjects and objects within an economy of hermeneutic exchange. Literary practice presumes that the engagement with texts is underwritten by the discrete coherence of a "historical relation." Put somewhat differently, the problem of reading in general can be construed as the effort to discern a meaningful text that is legitimately legible, a present, read text that is commensurate with and adequate to the past, written text in its disposition as ideal, originary object. In this sense, the act of reading engages what is a fundamentally historical task, the re-presentation of a radically unpresentable past within a discourse of knowledge – in other words, a textualization of history. *Finnegans Wake*, as we will see in Chapter 6 below, subverts this hermeneutic of re-presentation by submitting the historical object to its recovery/recovering within an "erotics of memory," a discourse that underscores the body of the past's illegibility as much as its legibility.

By emphasizing the structural role of the symptom in his own reading of *Finnegans Wake*, Lacan identified the theoretical structure that embodies precisely this coincidence of the legible and the illegible at the level of discourse. In reading Joyce, Lacan was not proposing to "psychologize" the author's texts – that is, to analyze the author's symptoms based on whatever evidence of them might appear in his writing. On the contrary, he registered a demand that literary practice grant to the illegibility of Joyce's text its proper affectivity, that reading begin to take into account the symptom's status as a signifier of the Real. In doing so he implied the viability of a textual practice no longer governed by the subject-supposed-to-know, a literary economy in which between the subject of reading and the object of reading there is no textual relation.

On 16 June 1975, "Bloomsday," the Fifth International James Joyce Symposium opened in Paris with a major address by an aging Jacques Lacan. The first salvo in what was to become an extended engagement with Joyce's texts in his seminar that year, Lacan's remarks initiated a complex elaboration of the symptom and, ultimately, the reconfiguration of his entire structural theory of the subject. In the course of his career Lacan had often used the interpretation of literary texts to effect changes in his own theoretical edifice.[2] The central gesture of this late turn to Joyce, however, was not an act of interpretation, but one of nomination: in his address at the Sorbonne that day, Lacan renamed Joyce "Joyce le symptôme."[3]

Noting a certain incongruity in his having been asked to address professional Joyceans on the subject of Joyce's writing, Lacan took pains to differentiate his own discourse from what he called the institutional hum of the academic Joyce-machine. Scholarly masters of Joyce reminded him, he said, of those four master historians so prominent in *Finnegans Wake*, the authors of the *Annals of Ireland*, and he was, after all, "une autre espèce d'analyste" (Lacan, "Joyce le symptôme," 23). Such puns aside, Lacan's act of naming does reveal a crucial disjunction between the subject of reading as it is apprehended by literary analysis and that apprehended by psychoanalysis. A name's traditional function, of course, lies in designating its subject's consistency within the symbolic order of language and signification; it is through the name that the subject comes to be rendered not only legitimate, but legible, a subject of knowledge. The symptom, on the other hand, names the subject in its peculiar relation to the unrepresentable, its determination by unconscious desire. The subject which Lacan reserves under the name "Joyce le symptôme" is thus a subject neither of literary history (the author, Joyce) nor of textual signification (the meaning of Joyce's texts), but rather one that, precisely in its designation as a subject, exceeds all economies of knowing.

In naming Joyce Lacan sought, paradoxically, to situate the emergence of the subject of reading precisely at reading's theoretical limit. For Lacan, the symptom is not simply that objective evidence of illness which the analysand drags like a bum leg or a sore thumb into the analyst's office; at stake in its apprehension is neither the localization of pain by a magisterial subject-supposed-to-know, nor the restoration of a healthy ego, "cured" by interpretative or excisive means. At its most basic, the Lacanian symptom is a kind of enigmatic name, a signifier which appears as a structural principle of illegibility resident within the very texture of signification. Loosely describable as the Real of language, the symptom marks the point at which unconscious meaning gains a kind of consistency on the plane of the Symbolic – in the form of bodily quirks, vocal tics, and so forth – without, however, making that unconscious meaning to which it refers immediately available to a practice of reading or decipherment. It is thus the point at which reading necessarily stops, the mark of (unconscious) desire's inscrutable play within symbolic systems of representation.[4] Lacan's act of naming thus designates the appearance of a literary, or textual, subject beyond the plane of legibility and knowledge. Noting the homophony between Joyce's name in its French pronunciation, and the French slang, *jouasse* (a vulgarism for "pleasure"), Lacan specified this subject as a subject of desire. Invoking the symptom as name, Lacan sought to mark the appearance, precisely within the Symbolic order of texts and language, of a particular Real (unspeakable, unrepresentable) erotic configuration, the subject of desire named "Joyce."

By bringing into focus the specific matter of the textual subject's illegibility in this way, Lacan's act of naming directly subverts the historical hermeneutic of recovery within normative processes of reading. To the extent that it centers on the issue of meaning, reading enacts a re-covery of the text as originary object, in effect restoring it to its ideal fullness as a signifying structure. Interpretation is the mechanism by which that "original" object which the text ideally contains (and which is in some sense the text itself), is not only understood, but recovered in the present. By redefining reading as a process of naming, Lacan suggests that the pivot on which such acts of re-presentation turn is the authorial status of the signifier. It is the name of the author, its legibility as name, that orients every act of reading (even those that explicitly critique the notion of authorship) exclusively toward what is legible in the text, toward a text that can be re-presented and restored to comprehension in the present. Put more simply, reading always enacts a reproduction of the text itself exclusively as legible object, and it is that legibility that reading regards as specifically licensed by the authorial signifier. Reading is not, in this sense, an act of engagement with a discrete and objectively distant text, but one that forges a textual relation on the historical plane, a connection between an unread originary text and its legitimate progeny, the legible text.

Initially, Lacan's naming of Joyce appears to support and affirm this fundamental hegemony of a historical dynamic of recovery within the practice of reading, and in fact, to reinscribe it within the paternal function of the name. The convergence of name and law in Lacan's famous homophony, *le nom / non du père*, after all, seems to suggest that Lacan is confirming, rather than subverting, the signifier's patrimonial function in Joyce's texts. For Lacan, it is indeed the case that the name is the fundamental index of the subject's constitution under Symbolic law; radically alienated on the plane of the Real, the "split" subject emerges as a coherent, integrated being only within the Symbolic order, acceding to identity through the agency of the signifier. Subjectivity is grounded as such, then, in the existence of a specifically paternal structure, a Symbolic familial relation in which identity is bestowed as a sort of patrimony.

In this connection, Lacan's *nom du père* appears to offer a striking confirmation of the truth, in the sphere of literary analysis, of Stephen Dedalus's suggestion in *Ulysses* that "paternity may be a legal fiction" (Joyce, *Ulysses*, 9.837 ff.). Stephen's notion of generational descent as "a mystical estate, an apostolic succession, from only begetter to only begotten," is realized literally in the relation between a text and its reading – a relation which, like that of father and son, stakes its claim to legitimacy on resemblance, but is in fact authorized through the "mystical," non-genetic bestowal of the paternal signifier. Just as the paternal signifier guarantees biological legitimacy as a legal fiction in the social realm, so the name of the author, "Joyce," licenses the legibility of its interpretative descendant as a Joycean text. In Lacan's formulation, the legal fiction of paternity produces, via the paternal signifier, the symbolic fixing, or "fixion," of the subject itself; through the mechanism of the name, the subject is constituted literally as a patrimonial effect, a fixion of the law.[5]

On the other hand, Lacan's use of the symptom, rather than the name, to designate Joyce as a subject of reading seems to effect a very different fixion of the textual subject. Freud had explained the symptom as a compromise formation, the result of a psychic conflict between repressed ideas and the forces of repression themselves. Thus, he postulated that the difficulty of the psychoanalytic "cure" resulted from the fact that the symptom was supported from both sides; it emerged as the effect of a consensual reconciliation between competing forces (for example, those of "defense-against" and "wish-for").[6] Deciphering the symptom, or uncovering the point at which such antagonistic forces serve as supports for one another, meant for Freud discovering the patient's relation to pre-historic scenes of guilt and loss, expressed in familiar, symbolic myths.[7] Lacan articulated the symptom's fundamental compromise structure in slightly different terms, stressing its status as a marriage of the Symbolic and the Real at the level of the subject. While it appears on the surface of the textual subject as a signifier, an identifying "name," the symptom points to that subject's determination in the Real, the inarticulable register of unconscious desire. The symptom cannot, in that sense, be read as anything other than an eruption of Real desire within the Symbolic coherence of the subject. The symptom marks the subject as a textual compromise formation, an unstable marriage of the legible and the illegible within the space of reading.

Lacan's conception of the symptom as a compromise between the Real and the Symbolic is clarified by a remarkable passage from the seminar titled "Sexuality in the Defiles of the Signifier." Here Lacan acknowledged that a second, alternative function exists alongside the name's patrimonial, authorizing function (its status as *le nom du père*), and even suggested the primacy of this second function in the constitution of the subject: "It is at the level of matrimonial alliance," Lacan wrote, "as opposed to natural generation, to biological lineal descent – at the level therefore of the signifier – that the fundamental exchanges take place."[8] In other words, the fixion of the subject "at the level of the signifier" conforms to a matrimonial rather than a patrimonial structure. The Symbolic unity of the subject, then, indexed by a name ("Joyce"), masks its formation in a tenuous compromise between the Real and the Symbolic, a fundamental disunity of which the symptom is the outward sign.

These two functions of the name reveal an inherent ambiguity of the signifier's disposition, a double agency that is ultimately respected by Lacan's formulation of symbolic law. Lacan's *nom du père* governs a subject that is constituted in a vertical plane of symbolic patrimony, a trajectory that echoes that of genetic (historical) descent. In its matrimonial function, however, the name disavows any relation of mimesis, genetic or otherwise, and thus implicitly belies its own designation of the subject as a historically generated identity. Under this second aspect of the signifier's agency, the subject of reading is constituted matrimonially, that is, in a horizontal relation of non-mimetic connection and disconnection. The designation of the matrimonial subject as an "identity," therefore, does not signal its inherent, natural unity, but rather precisely the illusion of its mimetic convergence. The matrimonial name reveals the subject as an identity constituted in difference as such. At one pole of symbolic law, then, the name marks the paternal bestowal of subjectivity in a vertical trajectory of generational descent, producing a Symbolic, "whole" subject. At the other, the name marks the subject's coupling on a lateral or horizontal plane of connectivity, the suturing of a Real division which produces a conjugal subject. In its double function, the name bears concrete witness to the fact that the legible subject re-covered and re-presented by reading is constituted on the basis not only of generation but also of connectivity and division, not only of procreation but also of conjugation and disjunction.[9] The subject of reading is, in other words, a symptomatic subject.

Lacan's re-naming of Joyce thus introduces a fundamental disjunction between the subject of reading as it is apprehended by literary analysis and that apprehended by psychoanalysis. While the literary scholars in Lacan's audience in Paris had gathered literally in Joyce's authorial name, psychoanalysts, Lacan suggested, apprehend the subject of their reading under the symptom. Prior to any notion of cure or treatment, the symptom is what constitutes the subject of reading as such for the discourse of psychoanalysis. In naming Joyce "Joyce le symptôme," Lacan explicitly refused the exclusive fixion of the subject by a patrimonial signifier, instead expanding the subject of his reading to include precisely that matrimonial subject of difference, the symptom.

The immediate and profound consequence of Lacan's act of naming, then, is a fundamental shift in what it means to read. Proceeding under the authorial name as symptom rather than as signifier, reading engages textual meaning as a locus of difference, division, and instability, rather than one of recovery. Interpretation continues to re-cover textual meaning, but it is never the "fixed" or "interred" likeness of an ideal (unrecoupable) originary object. Indeed, symptomatic reading in this sense dispenses with resemblance altogether as a criterion for legitimacy, opting instead to "recite the past like a poetry lesson," as Auden put it, bringing forth difference as the consequent effect of repetition.

RAISING "THE DEAD"

The cinematic adaptation of classic literary texts ought to provide confirmation of reading's eternal and successful resistance to precisely the sort of symptomatic engagement I have been describing. By definition, adaptational reading proceeds as a profoundly conservative exercise in mimetic fidelity, a displacement of textual representation, in a more or less linear fashion, onto a primarily visual medium. A specialized form of textual engagement in this sense, adaptation nonetheless reveals the crucial function that mimesis plays in reading in general. As we have seen, every act of reading conforms to a historical dynamic of re-covery: the legibility of the text is legitimated as the re-presentation of textual meaning under the authorial signifier. To return to our earlier formulation, every act of reading enacts the "lethal history" of its textual object, re-covering that object in its disposition as a fixed, "dead," interred body for knowledge. What the example of adaptation suggests is that the legitimacy of this interred body – the legibility of the text – is only confirmed by its disposition as a *likeness* to that original, lost, authorized textual object.

A remarkable, albeit inadvertent, acknowledgment of the authorial name's function in the forging of legitimate textual relations appears in Clive Hart's *Joyce, Huston and the Making of "The Dead."* Hart served as the Joyce estate's principal advisor to John and Tony Huston in the making of their film adaptation of Joyce's short story. Commenting directly on his role in the production, Hart wrote that his goal had been to "ensure that this film prove worthy of Joyce in general and that it should not, in particular, so misrepresent the tone and spirit of the story that *Joyce's name* could not be associated with it."[10] Such a comment explicitly confirms the valuation of authenticity that drives the filmic adaptation of literature as an act of reading. Ensuring that the film "prove worthy of Joyce" means, to most readers, insisting on its fidelity to the authority of Joyce's classic text as well as to the cultural history inscribed within it – precisely the terms that in fact dominated critical reception of the film.[11]

Yet at the same time Hart's comment explicitly subordinates this mimetic imperative to a more urgent goal, the appropriation of Joyce's name itself. Reserved under the name of the textual author, Huston's mimetic reading gains its proper, patrimonial identity as the legitimate descendant and heir of *Joyce's* "The Dead"; named thus, the film's faithful resemblance to its literary forebear appears not merely imitative but genetic. The name ensures that what the viewer will encounter is not merely Huston's film, but Joyce's original story, re-covered and restored to its textual fullness in the present. Quite literally, the success of Huston's filmic reading depends upon his viewers' accepting it as the legible version of Joyce's text, a version whose legibility is specifically authorized by Joyce's patrimonial signifier.

Curiously, though, Hart's designation of Joyce's name as an instrument of association between text and film also implies that Lacan's alternative legal "fixion" of the textual subject is also at work within adaptational reading's mimetic attempt to raise "The Dead." In precise terms, what the dominance of the historical hermeneutic of recovery means is that a binding reflexivity governs the act of reading: what the original text and its legible progeny share, on the most fundamental level, is a common source of authorship. The fact that this shared authorship is nominal rather than actual suggests that adaptation's product is not only a patrimonial subject – its legibility and legitimacy assured according to the laws of genetic, lineal descent – but also, in the most literal sense, a matrimonial couple: two texts joined at the precise point of their mutual association with a name. The duplicity of Symbolic law suggests in these terms that the forging of a cinematic relation of likeness between two texts also reveals, inevitably, their symptomatic non-relation.

An extraordinary example of this convergence of cinematic and symptomatic acts of reading exists in Roberto Rossellini's 1953 film, *Viaggio in Italia*, a work that offers a powerful counterpoint to Huston's mimetic reading of "The Dead" and an explicit rejection of the dominance of the patrimonial signifier that typically governs reading's historical hermeneutic of recovery. Universally panned on its release by critics and viewers alike, the film has enjoyed a certain limited fame among readers of Joyce as the "other" cinematic version of "The Dead."[12] While Rossellini's film displays none of Huston's compulsion to repeat a Joycean "parent" text, the fact that it reads Joyce's story, both cinematically and symptomatically, is undeniable.

A neo-realist domestic drama of post-war civilization and marital discontent, *Viaggio in Italia* tells the story of an English couple's sojourn in Italy. As played by Ingrid Bergman and George Sanders, the film's protagonists are petulant and edgy, quarrelling and squabbling their way through Naples as they try to sell off a piece of local property which they have inherited from a deceased Uncle Homer. As the film progresses, their marriage dissolves in jealousy, intolerance, and boredom, and then is patched up in a complex, epiphanic ending which, despite the characters' professions of renewed love for one another, leaves considerable doubt as to its status as a reconciliation.

The only overt indication of the film's connection with "The Dead" appears in a brief scene in which Bergman's character recalls a deceased former lover, Charles Lewington, who was stationed in Italy during World War II. This young, consumptive poet died, we are told, after passing a stormy night outside the window of his beloved, desperately and vainly trying to woo her on the eve of her marriage to another man. The story echoes the details of Gretta Conroy's memory of Michael Furey, even to the sound of pebbles thrown against a window, and Gabriel's jealousy is likewise repeated as Sanders's character angrily accuses his wife of having come to Italy merely to pursue a "love pilgrimage." Beyond this scene, the film's references to Joyce's writing, and to "The Dead" in particular, are more subtle, though frequent. A reference to Joyce's fondness for classical paradigms, for instance, seems implicit in the absent but powerful influence of the film's "Uncle Homer." In a more specific allusion to "The Dead," Sanders's character insists at one point, in a paraphrase of Gabriel Conroy, that he is "sick of this country, sick of it!"[13]

For most viewers, of course, a few such scattered allusions do not constitute an adaptation – and indeed, ignoring as it does the usual boundaries of mimetic correspondence, *Viaggio in Italia* can hardly be considered a version of "The Dead," even of the most free-wheeling sort. Refusing to claim its authority and legitimacy as the repetition of a text designated as both historically and hierarchically primary, Rossellini's film betrays none of Huston's self-conscious effort to reproduce, in broad, Hollywood brush-strokes, the "tone and spirit" – much less the plot – of Joyce's story.[14]

More importantly, *Viaggio in Italia* reverses the crucial authorizing function which Joyce's name performs with respect to Huston's filmic reading of "The Dead." While in Rossellini's case the name of Joyce occupies the site of a certain grafting between film and text, it does so not as the master signifier of literary and historical authority, but as a kind of familiar, though enigmatic, bodily tic – a textual symptom. This name connects film and text on a plane of difference, rather than sameness: the symbolic universe of Rossellini's film constitutes a space in which Joyce's name is entered, not unlike a signature, as the material enigma which structures the film's sense. This point is brought home, so to speak, when, midway through the film's second sequence, the protagonists arrive at their exilic home-away-from-home, a hotel in Naples. Speaking the couple's surname for the first time, Sanders's character identifies their rooms for the concierge – and for the viewer – as those which have been occupied in advance by their name: "I have," he says, "a reservation under the name of Joyce."

The one-time husband of Zsa Zsa Gabor is perhaps an unlikely source from which to expect lucid explanations of Lacan. Nonetheless, this phrase, "a reservation under the name of Joyce," pronounced in 1953 by George Sanders on a film set in Naples, is an admirably precise summation of Lacan's theory of the symptom. For Lacan, as we have seen, identifying the symptom is an act of nomination rather than of interpretation; his attention to the textual symptom does not reveal a mysterious exegetical procedure, but the name which he gives to Joyce and to the insistence of his signifier within his texts, "Joyce le symptôme."[15] A material, textual signifier, the symptom is not, for Lacan, a decodable attribute of Joyce's personality, but the name which marks the formation of the subject as a being who is spoken. As such, the symptom comes into focus as that material illegibility that is set aside, or reserved, in every reading of a text. Within the space of its reservation, the symptom is that in the text which speaks; it is the name, "Joyce le symptôme," which speaks its subject.[16]

In precisely these terms, the name of Joyce takes up a form of residence in *Viaggio in Italia* prior to the arrival of Joyce's text, "The Dead," as its structuring referent. Rather than producing a recognizable visualization of an ideal, prior text, Rossellini's film maintains within it the space of the symptom's insistence: "a reservation under the name of Joyce." In this space the authorial signature remains enigmatic and therefore non-authoritative, a symptom, the function of which is not reducible to a strategy of mimesis, but instead marks the signifier's material insistence at the joining of two texts.

WHAT DOES JOHNNY WANT?

In 1951, Rossellini began planning a film version of Colette's novel, *Duo*, a moral fable about marital alienation. Following the sudden critical acclaim of *Roma, Città Aperta* (1946), expectations had been extremely high for Rossellini's films, and his first efforts with Ingrid Bergman, *Stromboli* (1949) and *Europa '51* (1951), had failed miserably. As a result, the director scrambled to secure recognized Hollywood talent for his next project, eventually signing George Sanders to play opposite Bergman in the *Duo* adaptation. By the time Sanders arrived in Rome to begin filming, however, Rossellini had learned that the film rights to the novel had been previously sold, and that he could not therefore undertake the project. In order not to lose Sanders, the director immediately began writing his own screenplay, pursuing the general subject matter and theme that had originally attracted him to *Duo*.[17] Sanders later wrote of his frustration and mounting disgust at being repeatedly asked to perform, virtually without rehearsal, lines that had been hurriedly scribbled on pieces of scrap paper immediately prior to the day's shooting.[18] In fact, this sort of improvisation was not simply necessitated by the loss of *Duo*; Rossellini employed this technique often enough by choice, as a means of achieving the unrehearsed and unmannered spontaneity which his neo-realist aesthetic demanded.

It is worth noting that, in one sense, this aesthetic finds a ready analog in the "moral fables" of *Dubliners*. Like Joyce's short stories, Rossellini's films tend to subordinate dramatic gesture to a quotidian blandness, a "nothing happens" sort of mundanity which nonetheless maintains a powerful sense of pathos and emotional effect. On the other hand, the circumstances under which "The Dead" may have emerged as a specific replacement text for Colette's novel are unclear. In subsequent interviews and writings on the film, Rossellini never mentioned having been influenced by Joyce, or even having read him. On the contrary, the film's studied indifference to Joyce's text suggests that any such influence was, if anything, very slight. From "The Dead," Rossellini appears to have lifted a short scene, his protagonists' surname, and a few scattered, insignificant details to fill out and complicate his own, original plotline. In a positive sense, this paucity of direct allusion forces the viewer to forego predictable judgments of the film's effectiveness as a mimetic equivalent of "The Dead," without discounting its real connections to Joyce's text. Such connections are forcefully evident, particularly in the film's complex awareness of what is at stake politically in the cultural construction of love. "The Dead," like Colette's *Duo*, reveals a kind of resident alienation at the heart of the social propriety of marriage, and it is in these terms that *Viaggio in Italia* chiefly asserts its symptomatic connections with Joyce's text, its reservation of specific material signifiers under the name of Joyce.

Following the opening titles and credits, which are accompanied by a lilting voice singing a Neapolitan love song, the film's first shot places the viewer in the driver's seat of an automobile speeding down an Italian country road. The landscape lurches about in its frame in a manner suggesting that the viewer is in the car itself. The first of many banal conversations between the vehicle's occupants, Alexander and Katherine Joyce, begins: "Where are we?" "Oh, I don't know exactly." The dialogue serves to establish several random narrational details: Katherine and Alex have been married for eight years and are generally ill at ease with one another; Uncle Homer was "not a normal person"; Italy is a place eternally threatened by the unchecked passions and laziness of its citizens, as well as by malaria.

As the film continues, however, such dialogue – in which viewers might expect to find a chief source of basic narrative development – takes a back seat, as it were, to the ponderously material presence of the car itself. The automobile dominates the film, literally filling the screen to frame the Joyces' marital power struggles (Alex's "Do you mind if I drive?"), their interactions with Italy and Italians (Katherine's sightseeing; Alex's dalliance with a prostitute), and the film's culminating romantic and religious epiphany, in which the Joyces finally get out of the car and embrace. As the predominant site in which the progressive deterioration of the Joyces' marriage takes place, the automobile becomes a kind of "third subject" marking Alex's and Katherine's association as a couple. In this respect the car replaces marriage's traditional third subject and ruling cultural metaphor, the bed, inviting viewers and protagonists alike to contemplate issues of child-bearing, sexual betrayal, and political dominance through its dirty windshield.

Clearly, the image of the car can be read in these terms as a kind of metaphor for the Joyces' failing marriage. An island of shared experience, it isolates them at once from their surroundings and from each other, while at the same time propelling them, both literally and figuratively, toward the narrative's climactic choice between divorce and reunion. In this vein, the automobile's symbolic function supports André Bazin's contention that within Rossellini's neorealist aesthetic, objects frequently serve as dynamic reflections of the characters' own consciousness.[19] Similarly, Peter Brunette has written of the car's ubiquity in the film as symbolizing its occupants' xenophobia, their alienation and inability to really live life passionately as those outside in the Italian landscape do (Brunette, *Rossellini*, 165ff.).

Such readings, while viable and interesting, limit the function of the image to its symbolic decodability. Regarded from a slightly different angle, however, the automobile manages to bypass this decoding of its symbolic value, asserting its own status as a material signifier, the visual materialization of a verbal pun: *drive*. A word in image's clothing, the car accomplishes a textual effect in visual terms. Without compromising its legibility as a symbol, it maintains a material insistence within the cinematic text as a signifier, a written word. It is in these terms that the automobile functions in *Viaggio in Italia* as a symptomatic, rather than a symbolic, quantity. While the car may symbolize the progress of the Joyces' marriage, its circulation through the film as the signifier "drive" presses the viewer to apprehend its appearance there as the symptom of the inter-subjective path of desire itself. The crucial point is that the narrative goal of symbolic communion is not simply displaced onto this word-made-flesh. Through the insistence of its verbal or textual materiality in the film, the drive indexes – but does not represent or symbolize – the dialectic of desire which is played out in the film's marital metaphor.

As it happens, the text of Joyce's story also foregrounds a certain "drive" as the material signifier of Gretta and Gabriel Conroy's unity as a matrimonial subject. The drive in this case is that of Johnny the horse, whose story Gabriel Conroy relates in the Misses Morkan's entrance hall as the guests are preparing to leave. As Gabriel tells it, one fine day, Johnny, a mill-horse by trade, is granted a reprieve from his accustomed daily grind at the mill in order to satisfy his owner's sudden desire "to drive out with the quality" in the park:

– And everything went on beautifully until Johnny came in sight of King Billy's statue: and whether he fell in love with the horse King Billy sits on or whether he thought he was back again in the mill, anyhow he began to walk round the statue.

Gabriel paced in a circle round the hall in his galoshes amid the laughter of the others.
– Round and round he went, said Gabriel, and the old gentleman, who was a very pompous old gentleman, was highly indignant. *Go on, sir! What do you mean, sir? Johnny! Johnny! Most extraordinary conduct! Can't understand the horse!* (Joyce, "The Dead," 207–08)

The story of Johnny's drive does mark a point of symbolic correspondence, or "legibility," between *Viaggio in Italia* and "The Dead"; in a certain sense, the car's symptomatic presence in the film seems to repeat, with important differences, Johnny's symptomatic drive of helpless repetition. In another sense, however, this symbolic correspondence merely serves to emphasize the film's reservation of the symptomatic drive under the name of Joyce. *Viaggio*'s car is not, after all, a version of Johnny's drive but a point on the plane of the Symbolic at which the differences of the two texts can be symptomatically joined. This symptomatic joining is precisely mirrored, or rather, expanded, in the depiction of the matrimonial subject that is at the center of both Rossellini's film and Joyce's text.

In psychoanalytic theory, the notion of the drive denotes desire's aim, its orientation and movement along a particular path, rather than its specific goal or object.[20] The term is thus differentiated from words like "need" and "want," which express the necessity of a subject's reaching the object-cause of its desire, and instead refers to a dynamic of pursuit and deferral, in which desire itself is preserved and maintained precisely because its goal is not attained. The drive defines the subject's orientation *around* the object-cause of its desire, its consistency in a movement – or to use Lacan's term, *pulsion* – which perpetuates the drive itself. The question that Gabriel's story implicitly poses, "What does Johnny want?" is thus explicitly answered by Johnny's circular movement itself: what Johnny "wants" is not desire's goal, but desire's aim: the maintenance – rather than satisfaction – of desire itself. Whether the object of his circulation is chosen for reasons of love or habit, his pursuit is an iteration of the drive that works precisely because it defers any possible achievement of its end.

Likewise, the verbal pun implied by the automobile's perpetual circulation in *Viaggio in Italia* underscores the importance of that circulation itself. The image's symbolic value as a vehicle is subordinated to its role in marking a path of pursuit that at once defines its orientation toward a goal and defers any eventual arrival. In a similar way, the Joyces' movement through museums, houses, and various tourist sites defines the subjective orientation of their desire, without bringing that desire to any sort of resolution or fruition. Tourism, in this sense, is not a thematic preoccupation of the film, but a symptom of its protagonists' own circuits of desire.

This symptom dose not appear as a point of mimetic repetition uniting text and film, but rather figures their marital convergence under the name of Joyce. The symptom structures the relation between film and text as an organizational, though not mimetic, whole: a matrimonial body to be read. Here the designation of the object of our reading as a "body" rather than a "text" is entirely apt. As elaborated in Lacanian theory, the concept of the drive is indeed instrumental in the designation of the body as a symbolically coherent object for reading. Traditionally, the drive designates the organization of the subject according to specific organic desires: oral, anal, and so on. In other words, the drive configures the bodily consistency of the subject around Symbolic centers or "ends" of meaning that can be deciphered and read by a process of literary analysis or psychoanalysis. Strictly speaking, the drive isolates such "erogenous zones" from their metabolic functions (eating involves organs other than the mouth), and instead indexes their functioning with respect to desire.[21]

Lacan, for his part, was unequivocal on this score: for him the drive does not effect an apportionment of the body according to the requirements of biological need. As Lacan repeatedly pointed out, the translation of Freud's *trieb* into English as "instinct" implies a biologism that is fundamentally alien to the concept as Freud elaborated it. The problem here is not simply a difference in nuance, but that in favoring biologism, "instinct" licenses an understanding of drives as stemming from an already existing, whole, biological subject. In fact, as Lacan's reading of Freud reveals, the case is the reverse: it is the subject that is literally organized by the drives.

What Lacan traces again and again in terms of the drive is the body's division and organization by the signifier. In Lacan's formulation, the unconscious signifier determines subjectivity in such a way that the body is literally caught in the net of signification, and thus divided on the plane of the Symbolic into particular erotic regions, or zones. These zones are not organs in an exclusively biological sense, but are ends of the body situated in terms of the subject's desiring relation to its own being. As Laplanche and Pontalis put it in *The Language of Pyscho-Analysis*:

Although the existence and predominance of definite bodily zones in human sexuality remains a fundamental datum of psycho-analytic experience, any account of this fact in merely anatomical and physiological terms is inadequate. What has to be given consideration too is that these zones, at the beginnings of psychosexual development, constitute the favoured paths of exchange with the surroundings, while at the same time soliciting the most attention, care – and consequently stimulation – from the mother. (Laplanche and Pontalis, *The Language of Psycho-Analysis* at "Erotogenic [or Erogenous] Zone")

The organization of the body, as this passage makes clear, does not imply that the body is the natural origin of desire, but rather that it is a kind of residual consequence of desire; the apportionment of bodily organs depends on the subject's determination in the Symbolic by the unconscious signifier. While Laplanche and Pontalis suggest that certain portions of the body are disposed to be cathected over others, this determination is by no means "natural" or certain: "It is precisely to the extent that adjoining, connected zones are excluded," according to Lacan, "that others take on their erogenous function and become specific sources for the drive" (Lacan, *Four Fundamental Concepts*, 172).

In these terms, *Viaggio in Italia*'s ubiquitous automobile, read as a material signifier rather than as a symbol, marks an "end" of the matrimonially defined textual body (the "textual relation") that is forged as a result of the film's erotic – as opposed to mimetic – relation to "The Dead." As an image of symptomatic circulation, the car reveals, without imitating, the insistence of the symptom as material signifier in Joyce's short story. The presence of the drive as material signifier, then, does not establish a mimetic correspondence between film and text, but has the effect, rather, of reorienting our own process of reading "The Dead" within *Viaggio in Italia* toward a structure of deferral and, ultimately, non-relation. No textual object, definitively represented as a likeness of Joyce's short story, is ever re-covered (interred) by our efforts to come to know this film in its relation to Joyce. Instead, the name "Joyce" itself, an enigmatic signifier, enables our own reading to maintain its path of circulation around that object-cause of its desire, the recognizable, paternal body of "The Dead" in our midst.

LE NOM DU MARI

An oddly comical passage from Ingrid Bergman's autobiography suggests that *Viaggio in Italia*'s automobile may represent a version of Rossellini's own symptomatic tourism. When Bergman left the United States to begin filming *Stromboli*, her husband, Petter Lindstrom, along with most of the movie-going public, suspected that her connection with Rossellini was probably more than professional. Resolving at the very least to plead his case, Lindstrom pursued his wife to Sicily, where a meeting was arranged between Bergman, himself, and the director. Bergman's description suggests that the meeting was, in a word, volcanic:

Roberto had told me a dozen times that if I left him he'd kill himself, and often he was waving a revolver about. Another thing was his fixation about death in his car: he always had a tree picked out into which he was going to crash it . . .
So that night in Messina, Roberto had all his plans worked out. He was certain that Petter was going to induce me to leave with him, or kidnap me, and he knew that there were only three entrances to the hotel. So he had stationed a friend at each of them, and then off he went circling the block in his car – round and round – ready to chase us if we came out. Petter and I were in the room and Roberto was circling around and around every thirty seconds – vroom – vroom – vroom – with me saying "Here he comes again . . . here he comes again!" He never stopped all night long, hour after hour, and I just sat at the window and stared out and listened to Petter talking until the dawn came up. It was a nightmare.[22]

The story of Ingrid Bergman's departure from Hollywood while at the height of her career, and of her subsequent vilification for having abandoned Lindstrom and her daughter Pia – not to mention her adoring public – is well known. In 1948 Bergman penned her now famous letter to Rossellini:

Dear Mr. Rossellini,

I saw your films *Open City* and *Paisan*, and enjoyed them very much. If you need a Swedish actress who speaks English very well, who has not forgotten her German, who is not very understandable in French, and who, in Italian knows only "ti amo" I am ready to come and make a film with you. Ingrid Bergman (Bergman, *My Story*, 4–5)

Slavoj Zizek has remarked upon the Lacanian circuitousness with which this letter arrived at its destination: Bergman sent the letter to Rossellini's studio, where it was first lost and then burnt in a fire; subsequent delivery was then delayed because the director was not on speaking terms with his studio's representatives, and finally, when the letter did arrive, it had to be translated into Italian by his secretary. That Rossellini ever heard the contents of the letter at all seems justification enough for Zizek's reference to "the miracle of Rossellini's encounter with Ingrid Bergman."[23]

But the greater cause for wonder, Zizek goes on to say, is that the arrival of this letter, along with that of Bergman herself, fills out the space of a reservation, maintained in advance within Rossellini's most famous film, the 1945 *Open City*, in which the two central villains are a lesbian and a Nazi named, respectively, "Ingrid" and "Bergmann." "What," asks Zizek, "were [Rossellini's] thoughts upon receiving a letter signed by a person whose name condensed two impersonations of evil from his film?"[24] The director answered Bergman's letter with an urgent telegram saying that it was "absolutely true that I dreamed to make a film with you." And, in fact, Zizek adds, this statement was absolutely true: several years before she met Rossellini, "Ingrid Bergman . . . entered his life as *symptom*" (Zizek, "Rossellini," 19–20; Zizek's emphasis).

Zizek makes brilliant use of this miraculous encounter to illustrate and explain the rather notorious Lacanian thesis that "Woman is a symptom of man," a statement in which it is possible to hear, like a kind of distant music, a peculiar echo of Gabriel's famous question in "The Dead": "What is a woman . . . a symbol of?" (Joyce, "The Dead," 210). Gabriel, who stands in the Misses Morkan's stairwell gazing up at his wife, while the celebrated tenor Bartell D'Arcy sings "The Lass of Aughrim," is at once answered and corrected by Lacan's phrase:

What is a woman . . . a symbol of?
Woman is a symptom of man.

Placing Gabriel's question and Lacan's answer in dialogue in this way reveals the crucial point of difference between symptom and symbol. While in his early teaching Lacan concurred with Freud's approach to the symptom, his late engagement with Joyce brought him to assert that Freud had falsely conflated these two terms.[25] From the point of view of Freudian theory, the terms of Gabriel's question are not appreciably different from those of Lacan's answer. Gabriel seeks the meaning of woman as a decipherable *symbol*, and Lacan's notion of woman as *symptom* supplies that meaning: woman's meaning is circumscribed in this case in her being deciphered with reference to man, not as an autonomous being, but as his symptom. On the other hand, as Zizek writes,

If...we conceive the symptom as Lacan did in his last writings and seminars, namely as a particular signifying formation which confers on the subject its very ontological consistency, enabling it to structure its basic, constitutive relationship towards enjoyment (*jouissance*), then the entire relationship is reversed, for if the symptom is dissolved, the subject itself disintegrates. In this sense, "Woman is a symptom of man" means that man himself exists only through woman qua his symptom: his very ontological consistency depends on, is "externalized" in, his symptom. In other words, man literally *ex-sists*: his entire being lies "out there," in woman. Woman, on the other hand, does *not* exist, she *insists*, which is why she does not come to be through man only. (Zizek, "Rossellini," 21)

Rephrasing Gabriel's question in Lacanian terms, "What is a woman...a symptom of?" thus underscores the male activity of cir-cumscription as one that affirms man's own consistency as an ex-sisting subject. With respect to this activity, woman appears as the material, enigmatic signifier around which man circulates.

This notion of woman as the symptom that, when dissolved, causes the disintegration of the subject, is realized in the person of one of *Viaggio in Italia*'s oddest characters. The film's protagonists – and its viewers – first meet this character, Marie, in a bar at the Joyces' Naples hotel. Everything about this meeting seems trivial, from the Joyces' slight awk-wardness at bumping into old acquaintances, to the chattering exchange of pleasantries, to the impatient ordering of drinks. As the film contin-ues, Marie herself proves a decidedly minor personage, an out-of-place French woman with little to say and a bad accent to say it with; as a presence in the narrative, she is barely there, a sideshow attraction who draws Alex's sexual interest rather inexplicably and, in any case, tem-porarily. What draws our attention to Marie – and what literally draws her into the film – is an odd circumstance that repeatedly asserts its presence while seeming to have no discernible symbolic function in the film: Marie has a broken leg. While this injury may elicit a passing sympathy for Marie on the part of other characters, such feelings are quickly dispelled by her friend, who insists with a smile that "She will be alright tomorrow." For the viewer, however, the leg is a subject of paradoxical fascination. Its presence does not seem to make any compelling sense, and yet it continues to show up as a factor in the film's narrative. So far from being, like Marie, "barely there," the broken leg is ubiquitous, even gigantic; it steals the show.

Freud once described the manifestation of unconscious meaning in conscious life as having precisely the same effect as the telling of an unfunny joke. Beside *Viaggio in Italia*'s many decipherable symbols, Marie's broken leg may simply be an imponderable throwaway, a point at which interpretation finds its own leg being pulled. Yet precisely for this reason the leg invites attention to its status as an enigmatic signifier, or symptom, a sign that Marie herself is "not in her best form today, for all sorts of reasons." While it symbolizes Marie's physical "bad form" as a character in the film, the cast also carries the name of a certain symptomatic "bad form" inscribed within the Joyces' relationship and in the relationship between film and text: "Marie" as the signifier of "marriage." In a literal sense, the broken leg enters the name "Marie" as the signifier of the Joyces' own symptomatic marital "bad form," as well as of Rossellini's textual relation with Joyce.

In these terms, Marie also embodies a remarkable illustration and clarification of Lacan's claim that "Woman is a symptom of man." Lacan's point is that man ex-sists through woman as his symptom; without her, he disintegrates as a subject. In the context of the film, Alex's romantic pursuit of Marie allows him literally to ex-sist. By turning away from Katherine, and orienting his own desire around Marie, Alex can take pleasure in his own symptom. Marie is the external materialization of Alex's own "bad form," and it is by maintaining his ex-sistence through her as his symptom that he can perpetuate his desire in a pleasurable drive of pursuit and deferral. Thus, it comes as no surprise when, after an evening out, during which Alex ignores his wife in order to flirt with Marie, Katherine comments that she has never seen her husband "in such good form."

Moreover, Marie's in-sistence as symptom figures the relation between Joyce's text and Rossellini's film explicitly in matrimonial terms. In his description of the symptom, Lacan sought to demonstrate the name's fundamental convergence, not with Symbolic law (biological or Oedipal), but with Real desire. If the signifier governs the determination of the subject as a principle of Symbolic law, the symptom marks the eruption of the Real within the very exercise of that law. The word "symptom" derives from the Greek, συμπιπτειν, meaning "to fall together." Identified by Lacan as the precise point at which the split subject coalesces, the symptom is thus the enigmatic signifier which integrates the subject and allows it to "fall together" in the symbolic.[26] In his Joyce seminar, Lacan spoke of the symptom as a thread that binds the subject in its specific relation to being on all three levels, Real, Symbolic, and Imaginary; in terms of the subject's constitution, then, it might be said that the symptom is what literally "ties the knot," naming the subject's integration on a lateral plane of conjugation rather than a vertical one of generation.[27]

While the patrimonial signifier, the *nom du père*, designates a preexisting subject as a recognizable likeness, a legitimate and legible subject of knowledge, the matrimonial name marks the subject's consistency precisely as a symptomatic (which is to say, erotic) being, that is, one in which difference persists. Apropos of both Lacan's and Rossellini's encounters with Joyce, then, one might propose a new name for the symptom itself, one that recognizes it as the point at which the textual subject "falls together" in a structural non-relation: the symptom is then the affective, literal embodiment of the *nom du mari*, the name of the husband that designates identity itself as the very mark of the subject's constitutive difference and which reveals the subject of reading as a symptomatic subject of desire.[28]

THESIS, ANTITHESIS ... PROSTHESIS!

As a matrimonial symptom, Marie's plaster cast signals the fact that the subject of desire is not formed organically by a dialectic of generation or synthesis. As an organ, a zone on the body of the matrimonial subject invested with desire, the symptom marks not wholeness but its absence; it is the sign that the identity called a subject is radically fissured in its very constitution. In these terms, the symptom has a prosthetic rather than a synthetic function: it marks the existence of an absence or fissure, even as it sutures that absence to create a symbolic "whole" identity.[29] In this regard, the symptom betrays the false promise of the dialectic itself. What is supposed to be produced in the progression of thesis and antithesis is, of course, a synthesis, the moment of connection, of understanding and successful relation. Instead, desire's dialectic produces the symptom, which, illegible in itself, marks the integration of the subject as a being that is complete and whole, engaged in a meaningful system of symbolic exchange.

In precisely these terms, Marie's cast literally holds her together; without it, her body would dissolve, just as, without her symptomatic in-sistence, Alex would disintegrate as a coherent, male subject of desire. The symptom is in a certain sense what completes subjectivity. It is only through the symptom that a coherent subject emerges on the plane of the Symbolic: Marie's leg makes her "legible." In Real terms, of course, the subject remains radically incomplete, alienated from itself, or, as Lacan put it, "split." The symptom is thus something like an artificial leg. An addition to subjectivity produced by desire's dialectic, it gives the appearance of wholeness by masking a Real gap: thesis, antithesis... *prosthesis.*

Viewed as a prosthetic symptom rather than as a synthetic symbol, Marie's plaster cast suddenly emerges as a compelling, and surprisingly mobile, recurring signifier of desire's circulation in Rossellini's film. On the Joyces' tour through Uncle Homer's house, for instance, the symptom appears, in a somewhat different form, as a ceramic *objet d'art* in a display cabinet. As the Joyces' guide, Tony Burton, says, this miniature is "vieux Paris," a comment that connotes the presence of Marie's signifier, as well as that of her plaster leg: "plaster of Paris." In a similar way, the disturbance that Katherine feels upon seeing the statues in local museums suggests that in some sense they carry for her the symptomatic signifier of the plaster cast in altered form. It is in the film's penultimate scene, the visit to the archaeological ruins at Pompeii, however, that Marie's broken leg plays its command performance as a symptom. It is here that the plaster cast re-emerges as the floating signifier of the couple's past, the symptom that marks a space reserved under the name of Joyce.

At the precise moment in the narrative at which the Joyces have decided to get a divorce, their host, Tony Burton, arrives to insist that they accompany him to the archaeological site at Pompeii, where, he says, an extraordinary event is about to occur. The archaeologists are about to make a discovery; the workmen know something is there, just below the surface, and are about to dig it up. The Joyces' privilege will lie in being present at the unveiling, in seeing exactly what the unknown "thing" is. When they arrive at the site, Tony begins his explanation: "It's on this spot that they found a hollow space. When the men find hollow ground, they make a number of holes, and through these pour plaster. The plaster fills out the hollow space left in the ground by the

1. "It looks like a leg!" *Viaggio in Italia* (1953)

body which has disintegrated."³⁰ As is evident, Tony's speech betrays at every turn the insistence of the symptom, as well as language's effort to re-cover its space and to locate there a meaningful array of symbols. The "body" is, as Tony says, "disintegrated," and the plaster will fill out its shape in such a way that it will be recognizable. What is so disturbing for the Joyces about all this is the fact that their first glimpse of this plaster shape, despite Tony's attempts to integrate it symbolically in advance, reveals the symptom as an incursion of the Real: "Look! You can begin to see something. It looks like a leg!"

As if aware that something is awry, that the emergence of yet another prosthetic leg has allowed the Real to strike too close to home, Tony works hard to deflect its effects. Immediately, he directs attention away from the leg to an arm, then to two more legs, all the while interpreting each partial object as it emerges. The fascination of the onlookers (including the viewers of the film) is evident, but Tony works hard to diffuse or channel the desiring gazes of all present into safe regions, to integrate what they see into a safe reality. Thus, as soon as he sees that there are three legs, he rejects the possibility that the diggers may have uncovered a couple, and insists that "it must be a group." But one of the Italian excavators, as if unaware that his digging-up must remain a process of re-covery, finally makes the crucial, compromising identification: "un uomo e una donna." Tony tries again: "Perhaps a husband and wife . . ."

But the camera, as if responding to the fascination of the Real, draws our attention immediately to a sexless crotch, and thereby to a question: How did the excavator know? Clearly, this determination of gender is a truth staged by science, which, after all is a discursive form of desire also. The information, "un uomo e una donna," comes to us as a reintegration of the illegible signifier, the blank space reserved on a plaster cast under the name of the symptom.

This emergence of the symptom from a space of hollow ground suggests a further important aspect of the film's climactic scene. The recovery of the bodies at Pompeii reveals the crucial role played by official discourse in the present's apprehension of the past, and at the same time suggests that discourse's inability to symbolize adequately a Real return of the dead (or, for that matter, of "The Dead"). Lacan's readings of *Hamlet* and *Antigone* suggest that for him, such a return resulted from one thing: inadequate symbolization at the time of death. Precisely because it takes place in the Real, death requires that it be integrated by the symbolic universe that governs life; death must be taken properly into account, or it will return to haunt the living. In this sense, the viewer's gaze that meets the newly recovered bodies also re-covers them symbolically. While the primary action of the archaeologists in the scene is one of dis-covering (or re-covering), their discovery also produces the crucial, symbolic second burial that the ancient Pompeiians, surprised by death, never received.

The Pompeii scene thus repeats with remarkable exactitude the common representation not only of burial, but of its accompanying rituals. As the grave diggers complete their work, the familiar cast of characters gathers around the grave: the Joyces are the necessary mourners and Tony is the presiding priest who blesses the finality of death and resymbolizes it through prayer. Beginning with the archaeologists' discovery of "a hollow space," Tony integrates their find for his listeners: "hollow ground" becomes hallowed ground, the sacred space in which symbolic miracles take place. The drilling of holes makes this ground holy, and the action of pouring plaster through these holes completes, by way of sexual metaphor, the symbolic integration of whatever lies beneath, waiting to be found. Most importantly, this scene makes clearly evident that which the graveside funeral is calculated to obscure: our own fascination with the body.

In other words, burial of the dead always requires the services of a priest-like subject, one who will literally re-cover the (symbolic) body. It is the priest who inters, and thus the circuits along which desire flows trace a path *inter-prètes*, between and among priestly subjects who strive through symbolization to integrate the answers of the Real where they emerge as symptoms. This reserved space in the ground, then, is the Lacanian Real. In an inter-subjective exchange of language, "wherever two or more are gathered in my name," this ground is made holy to allow us to see the object for what it is ("a body ... a group ... perhaps a married couple"). The white, plaster bodies are in "fine form" indeed – "exactly as they were when they died."

Given the power of this priestly presence, it is perhaps difficult to understand just what Alex and Katherine find so upsetting about the discovery of the bodies. Symbolically, the Pompeiian couple affirms everything the Joyces, at least on an abstract level, supposedly value: love, togetherness, and commitment even in death. The problem for the Joyces is that the bodies' emergence from the ground marks an eruption of the Real within their own controlled, symbolic universe. The discovery of the bodies, is, for them, a discovery of the Real body in their midst. This body is not in this regard available to the Joyces as an objective and separate symbol, but only as the object that completes and defines their own consistency as a marital subject: it is their symptom.

Viaggio in Italia is literally teeming with these symptomatic dead bodies. Until the discovery at Pompeii, however, all are kept in fine form and continually re-covered by a process of symbolic *inter-prète-ation*. Within the Joyces' symbolic systems of communication, the imperative that such bodies remain buried is figured as a series of jokes concerning their ignorance of various deaths. At one point Alex, for example, teases Katherine rather maliciously for not having realized until two years after the fact that Charles Lewington had died. Similarly, Uncle Homer's friends are immensely amused by the fact that he managed to keep his own death a secret from them until "long after he was buried." Moreover, they are confident that "our deaths will come as a surprise to him." In this context, the discovery of the bodies at Pompeii after hundreds of years takes on an added force. The very image of "commitment unto death," these bodies reveal the principal dead body in the Joyces' midst, that of their marriage, dead but unmourned for eight years.

In this light, the Joyces' marital reconciliation at the film's conclusion seems extraordinarily ill-conceived. Immediately following the debacle at Pompeii, Alex's and Katherine's gushing professions of mutual love seem a rather perverse non sequitur. Yet, like most of Rossellini's films, *Viaggio in Italia* holds out the false lure of an apparent narrative logic. From a certain point of view, the perversity of this ending is quite easily, and comfortably, resolved. In the image of the Pompeiian couple, married in

2. The cure of the symptom. *Viaggio in Italia* (1953)

death, the Joyces seem to see a clear analogy to their own situation. This terrible image of a marriage that is literally dead impels them toward one rendered healthy and alive by vows of renewed commitment and respect. Yet the meticulous structuring of the closing epiphany belies this logic of a return to romance. As it has throughout the film, the symptom takes center stage in this final scene, forging a new point of connection between the Joyces.

Returning from the archaeological site at Pompeii, Alex and Katherine enter a town in which a religious festival is in progress. Their car is immediately engulfed by a crowd of worshipers, and they are forced to stop. While they continue to discuss arrangements for the divorce, the two get out of the car to try to see what is going on:

ALEX: How can they believe in that? They're like a bunch of children!
KATHERINE: Children are happy. Alex, I don't want you to hate me. I don't want it to finish this way.
ALEX: Oh, Katherine! What are you driving at? What game are you trying to play? You've never understood me. You've never even tried. And now this nonsense. What is it you want?
KATHERINE: Nothing. I despise you.

(*Hommage à Roberto Rossellini*, 130–31)

It is this conversation that marks an unprecedented break in the Joyces' interaction. Spoken in exasperation, their words nonetheless reveal, for the first time, the truth of their situation: "What is it you're driving at?

What is it you want? Nothing." The goal of the drive is, and has been all along, precisely nothing – nothing, that is, apart from its continuation. Its aim is all, and once the drive is arrested, the center of gravity around which it orbits dissolves. What Alex and Katherine have lost is not exactly love; nor is it the will to make their marriage work. (It is apparent that on these terms they have not, at this point, even agreed to disagree.) Rather, they have rescinded the very thing which pulls them together, which defines their being as a couple, their symptom.

What happens next is not a random event, but neither does it cohere satisfactorily within the narrative logic of the film. In a compelling expression of the sudden absence of the symptom's gravitational pull, the Joyces attempt to re-enter their automobile, when Katherine, now literally without an anchor in the symbolic, is suddenly swept away by the crowd. As her hands and voice reach in terror back toward Alex and the familiar safety of the car and the drive – "Alex! Alex!" – the viewer catches a different voice issuing from the crowd itself: "Miracolo! Miracolo!" A miracle has occurred: an old man who was lame has apparently been restored to health. While it is impossible to view this miracle itself through the teeming crowd, the evidence that it has in fact taken place emerges in the background, where two crutches are held aloft in triumph: the symptom has been cured.

Despite an undeniable allusion here to the film's earlier broken legs, there is no question of Marie being the lucky recipient of this miraculous divine intervention. When she last appeared several scenes ago, she had abandoned her own crutches and was well on the way to full recovery. The point is that the cure of another leg comes back as an answer of the Real to the Joyces' abandonment of their symptom. The terror in Katherine's face leaves no doubt that the effects of such a miracle are far from pleasant. The loss of the symptom, far more than the loss of a marriage, marks the entrance of the subject into the vertiginous, disintegrated space of the Real. In its dissolution, the symptom does not leave behind a cured, whole, and fully integrated subject; on the contrary, the split subject quite literally cannot survive its own cure. It is for this reason that Alex and Katherine so willingly and desperately reinscribe themselves – using every romantic cliché they can think of – within the familiar circuits of marital desire:

KATHERINE: Oh, I don't want to lose you!
ALEX: Katherine!
KATHERINE: Oh!
ALEX: Katherine, what's wrong with us? Why do we torture one another?

KATHERINE: When you say things that hurt me...I...I try to hurt you back,
   don't you see? But I can't, I can't any longer, because I...because I love
   you.
ALEX: Perhaps we get hurt too easily.
KATHERINE: Tell me that you love me.
ALEX: Well if I do, will you promise not to take advantage of me?
KATHERINE: Yes. But tell me. I want to hear you say it.
ALEX: All right. I love you.

FINIS

(*Hommage à Roberto Rossellini*, 131–32)

Rossellini's film thus returns, finally, to the fact of a marriage. Yet in doing so, it reveals the marital scene as a symbolic masking of the Real symptom at the center of inter-subjective circuits of desire. It is in these terms that the textual relation between *Viaggio in Italia* and "The Dead" can be acknowledged as a marital connection, the joining of two texts at the name. Reading Joyce, Rossellini manages to subvert the usual demands of mimetic correspondence, while revealing adaptation's dependence on a myth of identification. The symptom does not, in simple terms, replace the symbol at the center of Rossellini's textual connection. On the contrary, what the symptom's gravitational pull on its orbiting subjects most compellingly demonstrates is the fact that, to paraphrase Lacan, there is no textual relation. In Rossellini's film, this absence of a textual relation resides at the very center of an act of repetitive though non-mimetic reading, an act that in counter-memorial fashion continually re-covers the body of "The Dead" in its midst.

In reading "The Dead," Rossellini's film exposes the dynamic of historical recovery at work in every act of critical interpretation: reading aims not only at the discovery of a discrete objective meaning, but at the presentation of a past text, one that is "originary" and yet has never before "occurred" in the present. As a cinematic counter-memorial, *Viaggio in Italia* provides a powerful model for charting the relationship between modernism, with its pledge to "make it new," and the obligation of every culture to return to the past, repeating and rehearsing its own insistent histories. In particular, because it pursues its "erotics of memory" in relation to a classic work of Irish literature, Rossellini's film opens up extraordinarily rich possibilities for apprehending the spectacles of history as they occur within Ireland's cultural and political struggle to establish its "own" modernity.

As we turn our attention to a series of case studies in modern Irish historical imagination, it is worth noting that in the miracle of Rossellini's

cinematic encounter with "The Dead," it is already possible to discern a radically different, symptomatic disposition of the Irishness of
Joyce's text. Approached through Rossellini's symptomatic discourse,
"The Dead" never emerges in its "own" terms – the conventionally
"authentic" terms of Irish culture, Irish writing, or Irish history. Instead, Irishness is constituted in Rossellini's reading through the play
of a signifier, the protagonists' name, "Joyce," operating as that discourse's symptom. As if acknowledging that the words "Ireland" and
"Irish" also textualize realities that are deeply symptomatic, Rossellini
refuses to present "The Dead" as a specifically Irish text. Instead, he
enables Irishness to occur in the film "ex-centrically." Joyce, it is worth
remembering, conceived "The Dead" while living in Rome.[31] In a fitting
response, Rossellini quite literally takes Joyce's Ireland on a voyage to
Italy. Gleefully foregrounding its own exoticism and Otherness, the Italy
beloved of Rossellini acknowledges the Ireland of an exiled Joyce, along
with the buried Irishness of its homesick British protagonists, as its own
symptomatic form of ex-sistence.

Viaggio in Italia thus offers a powerful new model for cultural and
historical criticism's encounters with Ireland, and for its re-covery of
the Irish Other in an erotics of memory. If the stability of Irishness – an
Irish "state" – has been the acknowledged or implicit goal of much of
Irish history, Rossellini's "memory-work" pushes us to ask what sort of
"Irishness" and what sort of "Ireland" is or has been the compensatory
result of a culture and politics so powerfully centered on memory and on
its lethal historical function. It is to this investigation of modern Ireland's
crisis of historical imagination that we now turn.

The spectacles of history

CHAPTER 4

The birth of a nation: Irish nationalism and the technology of memory, 1891–1921

> The modern literature of Ireland, and indeed all that stir of thought which prepared for the Anglo-Irish war, began when Parnell fell from power in 1891. A disillusioned and embittered Ireland turned from parliamentary politics and the race began, as I think, to be troubled by that event's long gestation.
>
> W. B. Yeats
> *Address to the Swedish Academy upon accepting the Nobel Prize*

On September 18, 1916, three weeks shy of the twenty-fifth anniversary of the death of Charles Stewart Parnell, the "Uncrowned King" himself appeared to an audience assembled at Dublin's Gaiety Theatre. The occasion was the Irish debut of D. W. Griffith's *The Birth of a Nation*, a film already notorious at that time for the technical brilliance and unvarnished racism of its director. In the days immediately following Parnell's death in 1891, a rumor had circulated that his coffin buried in Glasnevin Cemetery was filled with stones. The idea that the great leader might not really be dead had led to Elvis-style sightings all over Ireland and as far away as Germany, where Parnell's sometime political ally John Dillon claimed to have seen the great leader attending a performance of the Wagner opera, *Götterdammerung* [The Twilight of the Gods] (Lyons, *Charles Stewart Parnell*, 603). In a country as rife with unresolved histories as Ireland, the appearance of ghosts is probably to be expected, and even, perhaps, taken for granted. What is slightly shocking about the Gaiety apparition is that it was *not* that of a ghost. Parnell appeared on that evening not as a spectral member of the audience, but as a cinematic spectacle onscreen, a sort of memory-effect, disrupting the narrative that contained it, and occasioned entirely by the new technology of the cinema.

The sequence in which this figure of the past appeared to the Dublin audience occurs near the beginning of the second half of Griffith's three-hour silent film. A series of titles designed not only to reorient viewers within the narrative, but also to guide their valuation of its characters and events, prepares the audience for Griffith's treatment of the period of Reconstruction after the American Civil War. The title that concludes the sequence employs the phrase, "the uncrowned king" (Parnell's customary epithet among Irish nationalists) to introduce the character of Austin Stoneman, a congressional leader and the unqualified villain of Griffith's cinematic narrative, as he is poised to seize power in the wake of Lincoln's assassination:

> *Fade in.*
> TITLE: *The Birth of a Nation*
> *Second part – Reconstruction.*
> The agony which the South endured that a nation might be born.
> The blight of war does not end when hostilities cease.
> *Fade out.*
> TITLE: This is an historical presentation of the Civil War and Reconstruction Period, and is not meant to reflect on any race or people of today.
> TITLE: Excerpts from Woodrow Wilson's "History of the American People": "Adventurers swarmed out of the North, as much enemies of the one race as of the other, to cozen, beguile, and use the negroes ... In the villages the negroes were the office holders, men who knew none of the uses of authority, except its insolences."
> TITLE: "The policy of the congressional leaders wrought ... a veritable overthrow of civilization in the South ... in their determination to '*put the white South under the heel of the black South.*'"
>   WOODROW WILSON
> TITLE "The white men were roused by a mere instinct of self-preservation ... until at last there had sprung into existence a great Ku Klux Klan, a veritable empire of the South, to protect the Southern country."
>   WOODROW WILSON
> TITLE: The Uncrowned King.
> The Executive Mansion of the Nation has shifted from the White House to this strange house on the Capitol Hill.
>
>   (Griffith, *The Birth of a Nation*)

This textual presentation of "The Uncrowned King" is followed by an image of Stoneman seated in his study and surrounded by fawning colleagues and politicians, all seeking the ear of the man who has newly emerged as the most powerful political figure in the land.

With the exception of *Citizen Kane, The Birth of a Nation* is probably the most written-about and commented-on American film in history. But as with *Kane*, scholars and critics have tended to emphasize the importance of Griffith's film as a cultural artifact, the essential identity

3. "The uncrowned king." *The Birth of a Nation* (1915)

of which is not subordinated by its performance and reception in specific
contexts. Conventional interpretive rules would thus suggest that the
Irish audience saw Griffith's film as nothing more than an evening's
entertainment, and that it might have moved from it to, say, a production
of Boucicault's *Arrah-na-Pogue*, which was also playing in Dublin that
week, as easily as it might have gone from luncheon to tea.

In suggesting, as I am here, that Ralph Lewis in the character of the
Honorable Austin Stoneman recalls Parnell for the Irish audience, I do
not mean for a moment to imply that through some kind of nostalgia-
induced cultural or technological myopia, naïve Irish viewers mistook
Stoneman for their own fallen leader. Of course, the Irish audience knew
that the film it was watching was an American one, that it told the story
of the American Civil War, and that it was not concerned with any
aspect of Irish politics let alone with any specific portrayal of Parnell.
For them, as for us, the "Uncrowned King" of Griffith's title refers,
within the narrative, to Austin Stoneman's assumption of authority in
the wake of Lincoln's assassination; clearly, Griffith uses this epithet to in-
fer Stoneman's narcissism and lust for monarchic power in a supposedly
democratic society. Viewing *The Birth of a Nation* as a document purport-
ing to relate an episode in American history – treating it, in other words,
as a discrete cultural object to be read – the meaning of this sequence
within the film's larger narrative purpose is absolutely clear. On the other

hand, considering the film in terms of its performance in the Irish context underscores its considerable ambiguity for particular viewers.

To begin with, Griffith's title, with its uncanny resonance for Irish political hopes, signals the film's potential for inviting a unique sort of interest from its contemporary Dublin audience. As an advance advertisement in the *Irish Times* of Tuesday, 12 September put it: "SEE what your American SISTERS and BROTHERS did when THEIR country was plunged in War. The Part the WOMEN played and the evolution of their Country after the WAR ENDED . . . **HIGHLY IMPORTANT**."[1] In a more specific way, the appearance of the phrase "The Uncrowned King" in this context would certainly have opened a sort of breach in Griffith's historical presentation for viewers, a lapse in its celebrated narrative continuity in which the words would also have resonated as Parnell's epithet, bestowed on him during a speaking tour in Toronto by his greatest supporter and eventual betrayer, Tim Healy.[2] Indeed, while it is conventional to speak of discrete "films" rather than "performances of films," to do so in this case seems to me slightly ludicrous. Less than six months after the Easter Rising, and particularly in the wake of its leaders' martyrdom, Griffith's melodrama of a nation's "birth," through a North / South war pitting brother against brother in racial conflict, would certainly have resonated in Ireland with a power – and an ambivalence – it did not evoke elsewhere.

In a startling way, the Dublin premier of *The Birth of a Nation* reiterates a historiographical convention linking the Easter Rising and its aftermath to the death of Parnell. In his speech accepting the Nobel Prize for literature in 1925, Yeats spelled out the logic of this connection. Parnell's great political achievement, the bringing together of disparate political factions – the violent agrarian movements of John Dillon and Michael Davitt, Parliamentarians, the Church – dissolved with his political demise and death. At that point the possibility of the nation's taking a parliamentary route to Home Rule collapsed and Home Rule itself acquired the aura of a national fantasy. In this reading of history, the Easter Rising emerges, along with the War of Independence in the second decade of the twentieth century and the Civil War in the early twenties, as a cultural and political symptom of Parnell's loss. Without the Uncrowned King of Ireland's ability to bring Parliamentarians, rural guerrilla fighters, and the Church to common ground, the turn to a peculiarly romantic – and brutal – brand of violence was inevitable.[3]

What is striking about Yeats's comment is his suggestion that, for Ireland, the period following Parnell's demise is one characterized by a crisis of historical imagination, a breach in Ireland's ability to imagine

itself and, especially, its history. In his reference to "modern Irish literature," Yeats implicitly and retrospectively acknowledges the passing of his
own movement, and its vision of history. The Irish literary and cultural
renaissance of the late nineteenth century had served to embody Yeats's
early belief in the authenticity and viability of "romantic Ireland"; it was
Yeats, after all, who had invested in the construction of a new Ireland
based on the revival of its past. Yeats had hoped that through his writing
and the Abbey stage the mythic figures of Ireland's past would become
palpable cultural presences in the early years of the twentieth century,
heralding the arrival of Ireland's modernity as a recovery of its animating
Celtic essence. In 1925, on the other hand, Yeats could acknowledge his
own belief's precariousness in the political and cultural vacuum left by
Parnell. Even as he attempted to resurrect Cathleen ni Houlihan and
Cuchulain as figures of Irish modernity, a new imagination of history was
being shaped in Ireland's modern literature, a warts-and-all conception
that Yeats had earlier associated with Joyce and the "Cork realists."[4]

In a crucial, although occluded way, Yeats's reading of the Anglo-
Irish War's rootedness in Parnell's death attempts to solve this crisis of
historical imagination even as it concedes its power as a symptom of
Ireland's modernity. In Yeats's reading, Parnell died for a cause which,
had he lived, might have been realized. Like Robert Emmet, Wolfe
Tone, and countless others before and after him, Parnell seems to gain
his importance not in articulating Irish nationalism's political goals, but
in realizing the seemingly inevitable necessity of Irish self-sacrifice. In
that sense, Yeats's comments reserve a prominent place for Parnell in
Ireland's historical narrative as that least modern of figures, the Irish
political martyr. Yeats's words do not so much register the profoundly
disorienting effect Parnell's loss actually had on Irish politics, as explain
that loss through recourse to a familiar historical narrative of Irishness.
Once Parnell is understood as a martyr to a lost cause, the national
trauma that his death *was* is strangely soothed, or at least contained, by
the narrative explanation of what it *means*. In this way, Parnell becomes
another touchstone for Ireland's lethal histories.

The importance of the cinema's birth precisely at a moment of modern Irish culture's crisis of historical imagination lies in its ambivalence
toward this process of historical telling by which the traumas of Ireland's
past might be converted into meaningful, familiar stories. As a narrative medium, to be sure, the early cinema was powerfully complicit in
subordinating the events of the past to their preferred meanings within
Irish history's dominant narrative teleologies. On the other hand, as a

documentary medium that for the first time seemed to hold out the technological possibility of capturing events as they "really happened" – the
possibility of showing rather than telling the past – the cinema introduced a radically alternative historiographical process into Irish culture.
In the cinema, the past could be narrated, but it apparently could also
simply occur; it could be represented, but it seemed that it could also
be, simply and disturbingly, present. The Dublin screening of *The Birth
of a Nation* in September 1916 seems, in that radical sense, to reintroduce
Parnell's loss as event. In the moment of viewing, the announcement that
"The Uncrowned King" will appear in the film's next shot has nothing
to do with Irish history's narrative coherence, but with its sudden and
momentary eruption as spectacle.

Parnell's posthumous onscreen "appearance" suggests the urgency,
in the Irish context, of the relationship between modernity and reproducibility queried by Benjamin in "The Work of Art in the Age of
Mechanical Reproduction." For Benjamin, the crucial question with
respect to photography, and after it the cinema, is not whether the images mechanically reproduced by these technologies can be called works
of art, but whether and how these technologies change art as such, and
with it our very mode of perception.[5] My argument here is that during
this period the cinema, a profoundly foreign cultural discourse, was not
only a mechanism for representing Ireland's past, but also for presenting
it. In that sense, it was a significant and largely overlooked factor in the
transformation of modern Irish historical imagination.

Indeed, as an instance of that most modern of qualities, mechanical reproducibility, the spectacle of Parnell's sudden presence in *The
Birth of a Nation* underscores the curious historical convergence between
the moment of his death and the prehistory of the cinema. In April
1891, about six months prior to Parnell's passing, an American inventor
named Thomas Alva Edison had submitted patent applications for two
new machines designed respectively to capture and reproduce "genuine
segments of life in motion."[6] Edison's inventions, the Kinetograph and
the Kinetoscope, led directly to the Lumiere brothers' smaller and more
portable cinematographe, a machine that would shortly make documentary screenings of the "real lives" of public and political figures a normal
event in music halls all over the world. The appearance, twenty-five years
later, of an "Uncrowned King" in *The Birth of a Nation* suggests Parnell's
curious – and thoroughly modern – distinction among Irish political
martyrs: the last great Irish leader for whom the possibility of appearing
in a motion picture did not exist, he was also the first whose posthumous

legacy would be formed entirely in an age in which the cinema would quickly emerge as a dominant and transformative technology of Irish memory.

The birth of the cinema as we know it – surely one of modernity's great beginnings though not one conventionally associated with Ireland – occurred on December 28, 1895, when the brothers Auguste and Louis Lumiere first screened their films for a public audience at the Salon Indien in the basement of the Grand Café in Paris (Ceram, *Archaeology of the Cinema*, 150). The Lumiere films were "actualities," so called because they presented short real-life subjects; at under a minute or so in length, they seemed to capture small slices of actual, everyday experience. As many film scholars have noted, historical accounts of these screenings have exaggerated both their "reality effect" and the naiveté of early audiences. The most familiar, and sensational, example centers on *Arrival of a Train at La Ciotat Station* (1897) in which a train rushes from the distant background toward the audience. According to many reports, early audiences were so convinced of the reality of the moving image before them that they reacted as though the train were about to run them over. The evidence for such accounts has not been forthcoming, leading many cinema historians and film critics to comment that the story says much more about how we would like to view early film audiences than it does about those audiences themselves.[7] Contemporary film viewers reserve a measure of sophistication for themselves by assuming that the pleasure early audiences took in the new medium lay in their own naiveté.

The first Irish screenings of the Lumiere films took place in April 1896 at Dan Lowrey's Star of Erin Theatre of Varieties in Dublin, and by early the next year they had become a primary draw for music-hall audiences. A contemporary review of *Arrival of a Train* in the *Freeman's Journal* provides an indication of the sophistication with which the film was received, and thus a practical counter to the sensational, but apocryphal, legend of its reality effect. Acknowledging the film's "startling" impact, the writer nonetheless does so precisely by emphasizing its constructed quality:

[O]ne is almost apt to forget that the representation is artificial. When the train comes to a standstill the passengers are seen hurrying out of the carriages, bearing their luggage, the greetings between themselves and their friends are all represented perfectly true to life and the scene is an exact reproduction of the life and the bustle and tumult to be witnessed at the great Railway depots of the world.[8]

The insistence here that "one is *almost* apt to forget that the representation is artificial," along with the use of words like "represented," "reproduction," and even "scene," clearly betrays the actual source of the reviewer's pleasure in these early films. It is not the pleasure of narrative film in its dominant form as contemporary viewers know it today, that of being caught up in a fictional world that seems real. It is, rather, the pleasure of the spectacle of actuality presented as artificial.

The power of the medium for early audiences thus lay not in the play of situation- and character-based tension and resolution that characterizes narrative discourse, but in the obvious attraction and novelty of the cinema's capacity to display a photographic image that appeared to move. Within five or six years of the first screenings, however, film had already become a predominantly narrative medium. While still presenting short subjects, the cinema now brought to life fictional stories or documentary images that implied narrative elements of suspense or conflict ultimately resolved by the last frame: chase sequences became common, for example, as did films of firemen rushing to extinguish staged fires. This incipient narrativity is apparent as well in the earliest Irish documentaries, *Life on the Great Southern and Western Railway* (Louis de Clerq, 1904), *London to Killarney* (Arthur Melbourne-Cooper, 1907), and *Whaling, Afloat and Ashore* (Robert Paul, 1908). In the last, for example, the British inventor and cinema pioneer Robert Paul used a camera he developed only months after the Lumieres' cinematographe to shoot a ten-minute sequence of Irish and Norwegian whalemen plying their trade. Filmed primarily from a boat, the sequence of shots and titles implies a loose story structure, moving from the "First sight of a whale" to images of a harpooneer shooting the whale and reloading, the whale being towed alongside the boat, the removing of blubber and whalebone, and finally the "Norwegian and Irish Whalers at play," a sequence of shots in which the men dance with one another on the docks and stage sack races, leg-wrestling matches, and contests of physical strength.

The cinema's emergence as a medium for telling stories, coupled with its apparent ability to capture and exhibit "real life" subjects, meant that in Ireland, as elsewhere, history quickly became one of its dominant genres. The first director of Irish historical subjects was Sidney Olcott, a Canadian working for the American Kalem Film Company. Olcott made a number of narrative films based in whole or in part on Irish historical topics such as 1798 and the Land War. With titles like *Rory O'More* (1911) – about a political activist on the run from the British – *For Ireland's Sake* (1912), and *Ireland the Oppressed* (1913), Olcott left no doubt as to his sympathies for the concerns of Irish nationalism. The historical veneer of his films frequently gives way to unabashed political allegories of Irishness; Olcott's primary purpose in that sense is not to show the events of the past but to clothe them in narratives that will divulge their political significance without complexity or ambiguity.

In *The Lad from Old Ireland* (1910; 12 minutes), for instance, a young Irishman emigrates to the United States to find work. On receiving word of his mother's death, he returns to the old country, stepping off the boat to find a landlord's agent in the act of evicting his family. Having made good in America, the "lad," Terry O'Connor, pays off the agent, dispatches him and restores the family farm. *Rory O'More* (1911; 10 minutes) offers a similarly generalized view of Irish politics and history localized in a representative cast of characters: Rory is an Irish patriot attempting to elude British soldiers after his sweetheart, Kathleen, warns him that a price has been placed on his head. The nobility of the Irish race is in clear evidence as Rory, captured while swimming across a river, dives back in to save a drowning British soldier. Sentenced to hang in spite of this service to his enemy, Rory is led to the scaffold. As he approaches the gallows, his local priest, Fr. O'Brien, demonstrates the nationalist mettle of the Irish clergy by untying the prisoner, only to be shot for a martyr as Rory escapes. In the film's final sequence, Rory reads a note, passed to him by Fr. O'Brien before his death, that reads: "Go to Crager's Point, Kathleen and your mother will be there with a boat from the waiting ship. Godspeed you to America. Father O'Brien." Olcott's longer feature, *For Ireland's Sake* (1912; 25 minutes), follows a narrative structure virtually identical to that of *Rory O'More*, but makes more overt use of the land as national symbol. The opening "Explanatory Title" indicates that "This entire production was produced in County Kerry, Ireland, amid the beautiful Killarney District. The Gap of Dunloe, the Black Valley, Muchross Abbey, Sweet Innisfallen and the lakes are shown among many other pretty spots famed in song and story."

The quality of romantic propaganda Olcott brought to his Irish subjects is clearly motivated by his perceived market, which consisted not only of Irish nationalist audiences but more importantly (from a financial perspective) their American counterparts. Even *Bold Emmet, Ireland's Martyr* (1915; 30 minutes), while it treated the actual historical event of Emmet's trial, couched it in a sentimental narrative about a representative United Irishman ("Con Daly," played by Olcott himself) and a "true daughter of Erin" ("Norah Doyle," played by Valentine Grant), replete with allegorical views of domestic life: Con out fishing in a curragh; Norah's mother making "rush lights" (reeds dipped in wax); Irish women, young and old, together by the fireside; two cute puppies.

Another director, Walter MacNamara, while producing for the same market, placed slightly greater emphasis on the attempt to represent actual historical events. In *Ireland a Nation* (1914; 31 minutes), MacNamara offered an astonishingly ambitious treatment of Irish history from the 1798 rebellion to 1914, featuring among other historical scenes, a recreation of Robert Emmet's famous speech from the dock. While Emmet's story seems to provide more than adequate material for a historical narrative, MacNamara's film continues after Emmet's execution to include historical treatments of Daniel O'Connell, emigration, Home Rule meetings, and actual newsreel footage of contemporary public figures such as De Valera and Arthur Griffith, as well as of demonstrations in support of Terence MacSwiney, the Lord Mayor of Cork who died in a hunger strike.[9]

The film opens on Napoleon, seated in his room beside a great globe, as Emmet arrives to deliver his appeal on behalf of Ireland: "To Napoleon Bonaparte: – We, the United Irishmen of Ireland, do hereby implore you to send us aid to break the yoke of our eternal enemy England. The time is ripe for you to invade our shores, because England's difficulty is Ireland's opportunity. United Irishmen." Napoleon's willingness to "send ships, guns – and men to aid Ireland" is thwarted by that stock figure of Irish historical allegory, "the most infamous of things – the informer." Stooped and lascivious-looking, the informer gives barely human form to the consummate evil that dogs Ireland's quest for self-determination throughout its history.

The sequence of titles in which MacNamara records Emmet's speech at trial is remarkable, from a historical perspective, both for its comprehensiveness and its sense of history as high drama. Following the style common to narrative films of this period, the interior shots of the trial have a theatrical, staged look. A stationary camera reveals Emmet, passionately declaring that he has:

Nothing to say that can alter your predetermination. [And] Much to say why my Reputation should be rescued from false ACCUSATION and CALUMNY.

Charged with being an Emissary of France and to sell the INDEPENDENCE OF MY COUNTRY – and for what! – I wish to place her INDEPENDENCE beyond the reach of any POWER on EARTH.

Am I to be APPALLED and ALSIFIED [sic] by a mere remnant of mortality here – BY YOU?

Were it possible to collect all the INNOCENT BLOOD that you have SPILLED in your UNHALLOWED MINISTRY in one great RESERVOIR, your lordship MIGHT SWIM IN IT.

Let no man defame MY MEMORY by believing that I could have engaged in any CAUSE but that of my COUNTRY´s LIBERTY and INDEPENDENCE.

I tried to achieve for my COUNTRY, what WASHINGTON achieved for AMERICA.

Fade in to Washington reviewing troops.

Until my country takes her place amongst the nations of the earth, then and not till then, let my epitaph be written. (MacNamara, *Ireland a Nation*)

Clearly, the prominence of works such as those of Olcott and MacNamara suggests that in Ireland the early cinema was at once a medium for the telling of historical narratives and a political tool helpful in making sense of them for a nationalist politics. Answering a dominant perception that, in the absence of an indigenous industry (the first Irish studio, Ardmore Studios, did not open until 1958), the phrase "Irish film" is something of an oxymoron, scholars such as Luke Gibbons and Kevin Rockett have responded by showing that film was a crucial presence in twentieth-century Irish politics from the start. Gibbons in particular has advanced a useful and powerful critique of cinematic representations and misrepresentations of the Irish by early British and American film industries long before the appearance of such exemplary classics as *The Quiet Man* and *Darby O'Gill and the Little People*.[10] Such a critique does not, for Gibbons, presume the possibility of a more "correct" or "truly Irish" image on film. Rather, it offers a starting point for a cinema that would reveal the contradictions within Irish cultural representation as such.

On the historical side, Rockett has supplied fascinating evidence of the links between cinema and republican political movements. In *Cinema and Ireland*, for instance, Rockett reports that John MacDonagh's production work on *Willy Reilly and His Colleen Bawn* was halted when some of the cast were arrested and imprisoned as members of the IRA. When MacDonagh made a short film featuring Michael Collins, Arthur Griffith, and others for the Republican Loan Bond campaign, Irish Volunteers showed up to force theaters to show the film at gunpoint. Another instance involves Olcott's *Bold Emmet, Ireland's Martyr*. During the shooting of the film, Olcott had allowed the Irish Volunteers to use the film's prop-guns for a parade. When the film was screened in Dublin's Rotunda, its run was cut short when it was found to be interfering with England's attempts to recruit Irish soldiers for service in World War I (Rockett, *Cinema and Ireland*, 23–24).

This historical/cultural critique of early Irish cinema has been crucial in developing a critical sense of the role early film technology and its reception played in the transformation of Irish historical imagination. Its limitation lies in the fact that it sees film's historiographical importance exclusively in terms of its emerging dominance as a narrative medium. Through this lens, film appears as a non-factor in Irish culture until it begins to represent that culture and its past through stories. Interestingly, this historical selectivity is the direct result of a primary concern with a cinema that could be construed as specifically Irish. The need to locate and define the cinema's role in shaping or reshaping "Irishness" in the early twentieth century has tended to limit scholarly attention to those instances in which film is clearly operating in Irish culture as a medium for cultural and political representation. If the phrase "Irish cinema" refers to a set of historically discrete documents depicting Irish subjects (historical events and figures, locations, themes, and so on), then Irish cinema properly begins no earlier than 1908 or 1909. In this historical frame, the documentary work of non-Irish film-makers such as de Clerq, Melbourne-Cooper, and Paul can be designated as isolated precursors to Irish cinema's proper foundational events, the opening of Ireland's first cinema, the Volta Theatre, by James Joyce in 1909 and Olcott's series of Irish narrative pictures beginning in 1910–11.

Yet film was a cultural presence in Ireland, no less than in other countries, from 1896 on. That the vast majority of films screened in Ireland during the first decade of the century were foreign-produced seems an odd basis on which to ignore them as a significant part of Irish popular culture. The Lumieres printed numerous films of boxing matches, parades, images of President McKinley strolling in his garden, and so on, for international distribution, and these played in Irish music halls and as novelty attractions in variety shows. Moreover, recognizably Irish locations and subjects were not unknown: the Lumieres themselves traveled to Ireland in 1897, making a series of local Irish "actualities" in Belfast and Dublin.[11] Furthermore, while there was no indigenous film industry within Ireland itself, it is not entirely the case that no films were being produced by locals during this period. In the 1890s, Horgan's shoe and photography shop in Youghal became the site of magic lantern slide shows produced and organized by the proprietor's two sons. The

Horgan brothers took their own pictures and made slides for exhibition, or bought slides of world scenes. Around the middle of the decade, they purchased a movie camera and began to shoot and exhibit films of people coming out of church, a paddle steamer, a fire brigade, and so on. This sort of activity by local amateurs was relatively common from 1896 on.

What distinguishes the pre-1908 cinema from the work of Olcott, MacNamara, and others are differences not of content, location, and subject matter so much as of cinematic discourse itself. The films to which the earliest audiences, in Ireland as elsewhere, were exposed were not narrative films, but short real-life subjects, the central discursive purpose of which was not to involve the audience in the plot twists of an unfolding narrative but, more simply, to exhibit an image. While film's capacity to tell the past enabled it to function, within Irish culture, as a powerful mechanism for the exploration and description of Irish political identity, it was in its capacity to show that it issued a profound and far-reaching challenge to the strategies of cultural memory. As a medium of spectacle, the cinema opened a counter-memorial space, a space in which the complexities of individual and collective memory-work in the present could occur.

In part, what I want to suggest here is simply the significance for studies of Irish and other national cinemas of a now standard revision of film history undertaken by scholars such as Tom Gunning, Miriam Hansen, Lynne Kirby, and others in the late 1980s and early 1990s.[12] Noting the tendency to view the pre-narrative cinema as primitive and its audiences as naïve, this scholarship sought to explore early film not as a stage in a continuous development of film art and technology, but as a rupture, a cultural form distinguishable from later (narrative) film by its own fundamentally different set of priorities and claims. This historical approach opposed the dominant "continuity model" of film history which, according to Gunning, relied on three assumptions: first, that early film is a primitive form in which cinema's real potential is latent but not manifest; second, that cinema does not begin to develop until its essence as a distinct art form is realized (in other words, that early film just mimics theater); and third, that cinema did not really develop until it became a narrative form.[13]

Arguing that the turn to narrative cinema was not a discovery of cinema's "natural" form, but a calculated redefinition of the medium based in significant part on particular directors' and production companies' strategic adaptation to market forces, Gunning introduced the now familiar term "cinema of attractions" in the mid-80s to characterize the early cinema.[14] Early actualities did not record events neutrally, but presented them through a cinematic gesture of capturing for view. As compared to the narrative cinema, then, the cinema of attractions addresses its audience in a fundamentally different way: "[T]he cinema of attractions directly solicits spectator attention, inciting visual curiosity, and supplying pleasure through an exciting spectacle – a unique event, whether fictional or documentary, that is of interest in itself" (Gunning, "Cinema of Attractions," 58). Narrative cinema, by contrast, seeks its audience's investment of interest in a developing story, an experience that produces pleasure and satisfaction as functions of narrative tension, intensified and modulated until the achievement of a resolution that strikes the audience as both logical and earned. "Rather than early approximations of the later practices of the style of classical film narration," Gunning suggests, "aspects of early cinema are best understood if a purpose other than storytelling is factored in. Cinema as an attraction is that other purpose" (Gunning, "Now You See It, Now You Don't," 73).

A crucial component of Gunning's writing on early cinema is his insistence that the terms "narrative" and "attraction" do not present a simple case of binary opposition. Implicit narratives are present in film from the start, as, for instance, in the case of the Lumieres' "Arrival of a Train" (1897), which suggests the teleology of a "journey" and "arrival" as its implied narrative context. Another early Lumiere film, *Le Repas de bébé* [Baby's Lunch] (1895), featured a family group (actually August Lumiere with his wife and child) sharing an outdoor meal together in the garden of the family home. Although nothing much happens in the minute-long film, the potential clearly exists for the viewer to form narrative expectations, such as that the baby will spill his soup, and so on.[15] At the same time, and perhaps more importantly for the present discussion, the cinema of attractions, and the moments of spectacle on which it relies, are never fully eclipsed by the narrative cinema. The fascination for a cinema that presents a series of views, "[a]lthough different from the fascination in story telling exploited by the cinema from the time of Griffith . . . is not necessarily opposed to it. In fact the cinema of attractions does not disappear with the dominance of narrative, but rather goes underground, both into certain avantgarde practices and as a component of narrative films . . . " (Gunning, "The Cinema of Attractions," 57).

Gunning's insistence on the "underground" presence of a discourse of attractions within narrative cinema helps to make sense of one of the most startling – and as far as I know, completely ignored – aspects of the narrative films of Olcott, MacNamara, and other pioneers of Irish film, namely, their prominent use of cinematic special effects. One of the most striking examples occurs in Olcott's first Irish feature, *The Lad from Old Ireland* (1910). During the sequence depicting Terry O'Connor's return to Ireland from America, Terry turns from the boat rail, dreaming of the Irish girl he will soon see again. Suddenly, she appears beside him. He moves to kiss her, and just as suddenly she is gone. As a moment in the narrative, this hallucination is clearly designed to convey Terry's deep sense of dislocation from his beloved and from his homeland. But its effect is, on the contrary, to displace the viewers' attention away from the narrative's continuity and, momentarily, toward the medium of film itself. Involved in a story of cultural displacement (the story of Irishness), the audience is suddenly reminded that it is watching a film: "Look," Terry's hallucination seems to say, "at what this medium can do!" At such a moment, the narrative pulse of Olcott's film seems to scatter as the audience experiences the cinema of attractions and its distinctly different, indeed slightly jarring, form of pleasure.

Another example is found in MacNamara's *Ireland a Nation* (1914), in which a priest, on the run from the British for illegally saying mass, is pictured coming along a path in a wood. Suddenly his black frock and collar turn magically into street clothes, as if to suggest that he is protected from his enemies by some miraculous or magical power, the source of which remains obscure. Again, the viewers' attention is jarred out of its narrative channel and trained on the cinematic medium itself. A similar effect is produced by different means in a shot near the opening of *For Ireland's Sake* (Olcott, 1912), in which a blacksmith is seen making a sword in a forge. Here, each frame of the black and white image is hand-tinted with red, suggesting the heat of the flames but once again – ironically – reminding the viewer of the artificiality of the image itself. Such examples serve to remind us that even as early Irish viewers entered into the narrative histories the cinema presented, they, like the *Freeman's Journal* reviewer watching the earliest actualities before them, likely felt "*almost* apt to forget that the representation is artificial."

The importance, in the Irish context, of this attention to the historical specificities of cinema's origins is that it reveals the hidden dependence of the debate about racial or cultural identity in film – the represen-tation of "Irishness" – on a presumption of narrative representation as cinema's exclusive mode of discourse. Gunning suggests that cinema became "narrativized" between 1907 and 1913, precisely the period in which "Irish film" has been judged to have begun. During this period, feature films began to present a self-enclosed diegetic universe, into which the spectator looks as an outsider, or hidden voyeur; the narrative film does not "acknowledge" the spectator. Paradoxically, it is this distance from the story onscreen that enables viewers' identification with it, or rather, their ability to see it as analogous to the narrative of their own history and identity. As we have seen in the case of Gerz's *2,146 Stones*, the historical narratives viewers choose to accept can reveal their own powerful investments in keeping the past safely distant and objectified. The narrative films of Olcott and others perform this memorial function for their intended Irish and Irish-American audiences, remembering a past that is contained by its familiar meanings – a past that, most importantly, never threatens to become present. It is narrativity in this sense that gives an absurdly vague and abstract term like "Irishness" its form and sense in the first place; more than any particular collection of characteristics, it is the primacy of narrative, therefore, that makes it possible to designate a film as recognizably "Irish" or "not Irish."

By contrast, when the early cinema is acknowledged as having "a purpose other than story-telling," based on a grammar of visual effects or attractions, it appears powerfully transnational in its discourse. It is more difficult to locate national (much less nationalist) qualities in the earliest films because they define cinema as a medium not of stories but of effects: magic, spectacle, attractions. The difference is not one of content or theme, but mode of address. Put simply, attractions foreground the role of the spectator differently. As Gunning points out, the attraction directly addresses the spectator as an exhibition, and can even be aggressive, as in the case of *Arrival of a Train*. The crucial point in the present context is not only this openness of acknowledgment, but the fact that cinematic tricks acknowledge the Irish viewer in exactly the same way as they do the French or American viewer; there is nothing that essentially distinguishes the Irish reception of the Lumieres' *Arrival of a Train* from its French reception. In that sense, a cinema's putative "Irishness" – indeed, the notion of "national cinema" in general – can no longer be understood as a complex function exclusively of that cinema's thematic content, the national or racial identity of its directors, actors, and producers, the location of its production, and so on, but also of the extent to which it gives a discourse of telling, as opposed to one of showing, primacy of place.

Griffith's *The Birth of a Nation*, or rather its presentation in Dublin at a particular historical moment, offers the potential for a different sort of reading of "Irish cinema." The work most frequently acknowledged as the first, best, and most influential example of narrativity in film, *Birth* suddenly appears in the Irish context as a work of local spectacle. While acknowledging that its narrative contains elements loosely analogous to the Irish political situation, we are precluded from reading and estimating its impact on nationalism by any of the traditional measures precisely because the film is in its content and production so obviously not Irish. Indeed, the curious proposition to which all of this leads is that it may be precisely the film's foreignness, along with the historically non-Irish origins of cinematic technology in general, that enables Irish memory to speak within it; Griffith's film offers an ex-centric presentation of authentic Irish history. If narrative film refuses as a rule to acknowledge its spectator, *Birth's* Irish debut challenges us to acknowledge and read those places where, in spite of narrativity, the comfortable separation of viewer and history nevertheless breaks down, where the past suddenly occurs, and demands that the viewer undertake the complex and ambivalent task of memory-work.

BLOO . . . ME? NO.

The Birth of a Nation tells the story of the American Civil War by focalizing it through a melodramatic romance plot involving two families on opposite sides of the conflict, the Camerons of the Old South and the Stonemans of the abolitionist North. Austin Stoneman, whose image is here reserved under the title of "The Uncrowned King," is the head of the northern family, the most powerful member of the US Congress, and the film's unequivocal villain. Griffith represents Stoneman as a power-hungry autocrat, rising to power during Reconstruction and, in the wake of Lincoln's assassination, imposing harsh penalties on the rebel South. Stoneman's policies include the institution of black State Parliaments in the South, the installation of blacks and mulattos in positions of public trust and the more or less direct sanctioning of rape by black freedmen of Southern white women. In the end it remains to the Ku Klux Klan, the heroes of Griffith's film, to ride to the rescue of the Old South, restoring decency and the "proper" disposition of the races.

Griffith's film was and is seen as a viciously racist document of American culture, worthy of suppression. From the first screenings in California in 1915 and later that year in New York and Boston, the film was attended by protests and boycotts organized by the newly formed NAACP (National Association for the Advancement of Colored People) and other concerned groups; the film has also been blamed for a resurgence of the

Ku Klux Klan in the 1930s.[16] At the same time, *Birth* was and is seen by critics and students of film history as a work of technical genius. Griffith's use of close-up photography to enhance the emotional impact of particular scenes, the mobile camera-work necessary for the famous "Ride of the Klansmen" sequence, and double-exposure effects are among the innovations he perfected in the service of his narrative. Unprecedented was Griffith's capturing of full-scale battle scenes in extreme long shot, a technique that allowed audiences to feel for the first time as though they were witnessing real historical charges, retreats, cannon-fire, and so on.

Despite the film's rather questionable telling of history, Griffith insisted on its historical objectivity and truthfulness, adding titles after the film's first screenings to answer charges of racism. Prefatory to the film's opening sequence, for example, a title reads: "If in this work we have conveyed to the mind the ravages of war to the end that *war may be held in abhorrence*, this effort will not have been in vain" (*The Birth of a Nation*). For all his idealism, however, Griffith appears to have been either astonishingly naïve or brilliantly calculating in his use of the cinematic medium: in order to secure his audience's trust, he invokes the familiar model of literary historiography, quoting print sources and even including footnotes in many of his titles. Literary sources also define the structure of Griffith's narrative, which ultimately subordinates the central political conflict to a romantic one. When at the narrative's conclusion, the daughter of the North marries the son of the South, Elsie Stoneman's and Ben Cameron's romantic union implies political resolution as well, and the healing of the nation takes place under the benevolent eye of Jesus Christ, seen in an extraordinary double exposure, separating the saved from the damned in one of the film's final shots.

In other words, Griffith's greatest achievement in *The Birth of a Nation* was that he brought the cinema's capacity for spectacle – the sense that one was witnessing an event, an "actuality" – under the rein of an outdated, but comfortably familiar literary form of historical narrative. Griffith's models in the making of his narrative film are not the pioneers of film spectacle, such as Méliès or even the Lumieres, but the giants of literary narrative. One of the opening titles contains Griffith's oddly literary "Plea for the Art of the Motion Picture":

We do not fear censorship, for we have no wish to offend with improprieties or obscenities, but we do demand, as a right, the liberty to show the dark side of wrong, that we may illuminate the bright side of virtue – the same liberty that is conceded to the art of the written word – the art to which we owe the Bible and the works of Shakespeare. (Griffith, *The Birth of a Nation*)

4. "The honorable member for Ulster." *The Birth of a Nation* (1915)

Claims such as these have figured prominently in the film's critical indict-
ment as a profoundly immoral document of racist ideology. What they
also reveal is Griffith's masterful use of narrative discourse to reconfigure
cinema as an ideological medium.

At the time of its Irish debut, *The Birth of a Nation*'s reputation was
already a year-and-a-half old. Except through recourse to metaphor
or analogy, its ideological claims would certainly have been perceived
as having nothing specifically to do with Irish experience. If the film
produced a local political impact on the Irish audience, then, it is not
because it narrated Irish historical experience, but because it created a
discursive space in which local Irish references – and memories – could
appear in the guise of spectacle. The film's thematics of national birth
coupled with its implementation of a literary historiographical model
are what initially open this discursive space. Indeed, in the midst of
such themes and strategies, Griffith's "Uncrowned King" title is not
the only reference that might have appeared oddly familiar to the Irish
audience. Shortly after Parnell's "appearance," for example, Griffith
offers a "historical facsimile" of "The negro party in control in the State
House of representatives" in 1871. One of the black representatives, while
seated at his place, furtively removes a bottle of liquor from beneath his
desk and takes a drink. The title that precedes this image identifies him
as "the honorable member for Ulster."

In most cases of early film screenings, confirmable records of audience response are few or nonexistent, and it is therefore difficult in this instance to know precisely how to interpret the impact such titles might have had on the Irish audience. Contemporary notices of *The Birth of a Nation* focus on the film itself, its technical brilliance, its racism or its sheer scale: "18,000 people, 5,000 horses, cost £100,000," ran an ad in the *Freeman's Journal*, for Tuesday 19 September, 1916. A review published following the film's opening day screenings ran as follows:

Mr. D. W. Griffith's production, "The Birth of a Nation," was screened at the Gaiety Theatre yesterday at 2:30 o'clock and in the afternoon at 8 o'clock. At both performances the theatre was crowded. The exhibition of the film, which is in two acts, extends over a period of fully three hours.

"The Birth of a Nation" deals with the American Civil War, that bitter feud between the North and South which culminated in the disfranchisement of the white race in the South at the instigation of Abraham Lincoln's successor in the field of American politics, the Radical Leader, Austin Stoneman. The enthusiasm of the audience becomes gradually roused as the Northern and Southern Armies mobilise . . . The film, during its progress, was marked by repeated outbursts of enthusiasm from the audience, who followed the different phases of the story with an unflagging interest, which is the greatest indication of the success of the production. (*Freeman's Journal*, Tues. Sept. 19, 1916)

This notice is typical in that it recognizes that the film inspired "outbursts of enthusiasm," while offering no indication of their motivation. It is impossible to tell whether such responses connote a critical awareness of the film's political content, satisfaction with its technical execution, or sheer exuberance at being able to "follow the different phases of the story."

An invaluable resource in this case exists, therefore, in the diaries of Joseph Holloway, held at the National Library in Dublin. Because they are so singular, Holloway's comments about the film should probably be taken with caution. Still, they provide valuable indicators for an aspect of this film's performance excluded from contemporary reviews in local papers. The "publisher's note" to his diaries provides the following introduction to Holloway:

Series One provides the theatrical diaries of Joseph Holloway who must be regarded as one of the most fanatical theatre-goers of all time. In the period 1895 to 1944 he attended almost every major performance at the Abbey Theatre, the Gate Theatre, the amateur theatres of Dublin, the commercial theatres, and plays performed by touring companies . . . His experiences were recorded in daily diary form. His own comments were supplemented with clippings from papers. In all there are 221 volumes containing perhaps 25,000,000 words.

Part Two covers the years 1912–1917, a period overshadowed both by the Great War and by the Irish Uprising of 1916. Holloway continued his theatre-going in these years, recounting performances of many major plays by European figures such as Ibsen alongside the native Irish drama. However, it is perhaps the press-cuttings and Holloway's comments on his own personal experience of war – which make these diaries a unique picture of Dublin theatrical life.[17]

It turns out that Holloway also attended film screenings, although not quite so obsessively, and his comments on Griffith's *Birth of a Nation* are certainly illuminating. The entry for September 20, 1916 begins as follows:

20 Wednesday. I saw the stupendous film historical drama in 2 acts – *The Birth of a Nation*, founded on Norman Dixon's story, *The Clansman*, at the Gaiety matinee & to say that I was thrilled by most of it is to state but downright fact. It is a story of the war between North and South & its after-affect [sic] until the negroes were again put in their proper place. (Holloway, *Diaries*, 654)

Holloway leaves little doubt here as to his own reading of the film's narrative, and refers later in the same entry (p. 655) to having witnessed "long queues" outside the Queens Theatre, " – children and women mostly – attracted by the unsavory title of *The White Slave Traffic*! How is it women are always curious to see what they shouldn't?" (Holloway, *Diaries*, 655).

But Holloway's most interesting comment does not concern his own views on race or unsavory entertainments. Here is his entry for September 23, 1916:

23 Saturday . . . – Miss Conroy said a friend who was at *The Birth of a Nation* the other evening at the Gaiety said that there was great conflict [at] one incident in which Lincoln refuses to deal harshly with the Southern Leaders, and says "he'll treat them as if nothing occurred at all!" – In a shout coming from one of the audience, "Where is Sir John Maxwell to hear that?" followed by great approval and the contrary, till she got quite frightened of there being a row. (The [illegible] assistant, who was present at opening show first night said one in gallery called out aft[er] seeing the above incident – "For our second Cromwell!"). (Holloway, *Diaries*, 682)

The sequence in question, near the end of the film's first part, just prior to the appearance of "The Uncrowned King," depicts Stoneman meeting with President Lincoln and pressing him to implement a policy of harsh retribution toward the recalcitrant South: "Their leaders must be hanged and their states treated as conquered provinces," the title depicts

5. "I shall deal with them as though they had never been away."
The Birth of a Nation (1915)

Stoneman as saying. As the congressional leader shakes his fist passionately in the air, Lincoln rises and quietly demurs: "I shall deal with them as though they had never been away."

Any doubt that Griffith's film was perceived as politically relevant to the Irish situation by some members of the Irish audience is removed, it seems to me, by Holloway's recording of these two separate incidents. Both register a negative identification of Lincoln with Sir John Maxwell, the British Military Governor responsible for punitive measures taken after the suppression of the Rising. Martial law under Maxwell brought large-scale arrests and deportation of rebels to British prison camps, the indiscriminate murder of civilian residents in North King Street, and, perhaps most notoriously, the murder of pacifist Francis Sheehy-Skeffington after he witnessed a British officer shoot and kill an unarmed boy.[18] The second comment, naming Maxwell as "our second Cromwell" gives some indication of the bitterness of Irish feeling toward him and the British policy he represented.

If the fact that there were incidents of this sort indicates *Birth*'s political relevance to the Irish situation, the nature of the outbursts themselves reveals quite clearly how it was relevant. In both cases, audience members reiterate Holloway's own apparent identification with the film's white Southerners. Such identification is understandable as a matter of historical analogy – as, in other words, evidence of the audience's identification with the narrative – since Ireland's political position with respect to England at the time might be said superficially to resemble that of the American South to the North, or rather to the Union as a whole. In this view, Patrick Pearse's reading of the Proclamation on the steps of the General Post Office had essentially attempted to establish Ireland as a breakaway republic. More importantly, Irish identification with the film's beleaguered Southern whites reflects local opposition to the push for a unified, autonomous Ireland as the central goal of parliamentary change. It is certainly not difficult to imagine that to nationalist supporters of the Irish Republican Brotherhood or the Irish Volunteers, Griffith's heroic depictions of sheeted Klansmen riding to the rescue of the Old South might stir sympathetic memories of the Whiteboys and other Irish secret guerrilla societies. Furthermore, it is worth mentioning that identifying with the film's "protagonists" reserves the virtues of "whiteness" for Irish viewers, possibly in opposition to the British Victorian tradition of identifying the Irish as black.[19]

The film's Irish audience thus participates in Griffith's narrative through a complex dynamic of identification, rather than through a mimetic structure of cultural representation, such as would operate in a recognizably "Irish film" like Olcott's *For Ireland's Sake* or *Rory O'More*. It is the fact that the viewers' involvement is so dynamic that allows them to follow the story of American history unfolding before them, a story that is separate and distant, and at the same time to identify with a narrative of Irishness that is in some way being referenced in the film. This complex of identification thus preserves both the film's integrity as a narrative of historical truth and the audience's separation from it; indeed, its coherence demands that audience members actively ignore the spectacle of Irish identity as it suddenly occurs in the other major "Irish" signifiers presented in the film: "The Uncrowned King" is an abolitionist, and the "Member for Ulster" is black.

This play between elements that are recognizably Irish and those that are not, a play between a certain willed ignorance and knowledge of one's own history, is the point to which I want to draw attention. Griffith's film clearly contains elements that its Irish viewers would have experienced as momentary visual curiosities, that for them would have satisfied Gunning's description of the attraction as "a unique event, whether fictional or documentary, that is of interest in itself." In a cinema of attractions, according to Gunning, "[t]he spectator does not get lost in a fictional world and its drama, but remains aware of the act of looking, the excitement of curiosity and its fulfillment" (Gunning, "An Aesthetic of Astonishment," 121). Just so, the appearance of "The Uncrowned King" momentarily reminds the Irish audience of its own act of looking, and places it in anticipation of the imminent revelation of a spectacle of Irish history. The title opens a fleeting moment in which Griffith's film, contrary to every expectation or intention, directly addresses and acknowledges its Irish spectators and offers them an exhibition of the Irish past.

The poignancy such an address might have contained for viewers is considerable, especially in light of a historical perception (of which viewers could not have been unaware) that Ireland had not only suffered Parnell's loss but had caused it as well. In the bitter, final lines of his essay, "The Shade of Parnell," Joyce gave some indication of the implications a return from the dead by Parnell might have held for Irish witnesses:

> The ghost of the "uncrowned king" will weigh on the hearts of those who remember him ... but it will not be a vindictive ghost. The melancholy which invaded his mind was perhaps the profound conviction that, in his hour of need, one of the disciples who dipped his hand in the same bowl with him would betray him. That he fought to the very end with this desolate certainty in mind is his greatest claim to nobility.
>
> In his final desperate appeal to his countrymen, he begged them not to throw him as a sop to the English wolves howling around them. It redounds to their honour that they did not fail this appeal. They did not throw him to the English wolves; they tore him to pieces themselves.[20]

Of course, such moments, regardless of their spectacular effect in par-ticular circumstances, are intended by Griffith exclusively to support the *narrative* purposes of the film; there is no discernible intent on the director's part to "show" Irishness. Gunning does not discuss the possi-bility that an element of a film motivated by the narrative in one context might appear as an attraction, or spectacle in another, but this is appar-ently precisely what happens in the screening of Griffith's *The Birth of a Nation* in Dublin. Griffith's use of the title, "The Uncrowned King" sets up, in the Irish setting, an expectation of an attraction, a thing of local significance that will appear and then disappear. It is not a moment of narrative suspense, but a moment of visual expectation.

In the "Lestrygonians" episode of *Ulysses*, Joyce presents a similar case in which a spectator anticipates a showing, rather than a telling, of the self. As he reads the throwaway flyer handed him by a "sombre YMCA man," Leopold Bloom thinks to himself: "Bloo ... Me? No." The text of the throwaway (it actually reads, "Blood of the Lamb") sets up Bloom's expectation of a visual appearance, an exhibition of

Bloom's own name (Joyce, *Ulysses*, 8.8–9). When the signifier "Bloom" fails to materialize, there is no narrative resolution implied, but only the disappointment of a visual expectation. In the case of Griffith's title, a similar expectation is created based on the profoundly local point of view of the Irish audience. Suddenly Griffith's film ceases to be an exclusively narrative construction and openly acknowledges the audience in the manner of a cinema of attractions. As in Bloom's case, the expectation is that a kind of Irish self, or at least its signifier, will materialize: "The Uncrowned King . . . Parnell? No."

While the narrative of *Birth* involves its audience in a play of iden-tification, the attraction attracts differently. Its mode is surprise rather than suspense, and whereas all narrative implies temporal progression and change, the temporality of attractions is not progressive, but exhibi-tionist. It is motivated by a present/absent dynamic, a "here it is!" and "now it's gone!" mode of spectatorial pleasure. As Gunning puts it, "The temporality of the attraction itself, then, is limited to the pure present tense of its appearance . . . The act of display on which the cinema of attractions is founded presents itself as a *temporal irruption* [sic] rather than a temporal development." What is paramount is "the sudden ap-pearance and then the disappearance of the view itself" (Gunning, "Now You See It, Now You Don't," 75–77). The title thus sets up the expecta-tion of Parnell's appearance as specter/spectacle, an expectation that is quickly disappointed by the dominance of the title's narrative logic: it is Austin Stoneman we see, and not Parnell. In the Irish context, the result is not the pleasure of narrative suspense, but a momentary eruption of the past within the present, an eruption that is quickly contained and swallowed by the ruling narrative, a narrative that is not "Irish."

THE CINEMA OF APPREHENSIONS

The promise of Parnell's momentary, epiphanic showing forth – of his occurrence to the audience as historical actuality – and his subsequent concealment as Griffith's film resumes its narrative mode of address, indicates in microcosm the role narrative film has played, and indeed continues to play, in Irish culture. It is in its narrative moment that film becomes representational, a revealing of events through staged narratives that seem real. As spectacle, film does not represent but present. Early film's profoundly transformative potential lies in its capacity to make possible the presence of the past, a capacity it realizes not in the telling of historical narratives, but in the showing of the spectacles of history. It is this historiographical function that suggests a slight reformulation of Gunning's conception of the early cinema: a cinema of apprehensions. The cinema's radical historiographical discourse is one that offers, in lieu of a narrative explanation, the revelation of the past's disturbing presence.

"Irish film" is a term forever linked to the adequacies and inadequacies of cultural representation; what announces itself as the spectacle of Irishness or Irish history always turns out, inevitably, to be someone else's story about Irishness. The crucial point to register here is the extent to which Griffith's historical fantasy reveals the overwhelming power of narrative cinema as a memorial medium, a mechanism for the construction and dissemination of Ireland's lethal histories. In its ascendency as a narrative medium during this period, cinematic technology despite its novelty loses its radical potential as a progressive instrument of cultural memory in the Irish context and becomes a conservative one. Sending its originary grammar of attractions increasingly underground, it returns Irish historical imagination to the lethal heroic model of nineteenth-century literary narratives, a model which is, as we have seen, based on the primacy of a knowing, rather than a desiring, subject.

In "The Work of Art in the Age of Mechanical Reproduction," Benjamin comments wryly on the tendency of early film critics to speak about the medium in terms more appropriate to painting or literature. The cinema's radical transformation of art, and indeed, of seeing, writes Benjamin, "did not keep Abel Gance from adducing hieroglyphs for purposes of comparison, nor Severin-Mars from speaking of the film as one might speak of paintings by Fra Angelico" (Benjamin, *Illuminations*, 227). As the work of Olcott, MacNamara, and others demonstrates, in Ireland this regressive discourse *about* cinema took the form of a regressive discourse *of* cinema. In spite of film's capacity for spectacle, it quickly became the medium for nineteenth-century literary-historical narratives; its cultural power rested primarily with its resurrection of popular melodramatic narrative forms that were current during the Irish literary and cultural renaissance.

Because the birth of film coincided, in Ireland, with a crisis of historical imagination, this regression to non-cinematic imperatives for narrative continuity and resolution had profoundly negative – and lasting – effects. While the Irish Civil War of the early twenties was not rooted in the impact of Griffith's cinematic example, that example provided a powerful model for the narrative shape Ireland's own birth as a nation might take.

In his speech featured in Walter MacNamara's film, *Ireland a Nation* (1914), and referenced earlier, Robert Emmet had proclaimed that he tried to achieve for Ireland what Washington did for America. Here was Griffith, offering another American experience as a paradigm for Ireland's own political independence.

On a more concrete level of cultural production, the impact of narrative cinema on Irish historical imagination can be measured in the kinds of films *Birth* inspired. Chief among these was Fred O'Donovan's large-scale film adaptation of Charles Kickham's popular nineteenth-century novel, *Knocknagow*. An announcement of an advance private screening of the film in *The Irish Limelight* in February, 1918 suggests that in the film, set during the Famine in 1848, the people of Irish history "come out of the past to live and have their being in the present."[21] Like *The Birth of a Nation*, *Knocknagow* uses strong characters and personal conflicts to articulate and resolve the larger political and land issues it addresses; in particular, it depicts an imaginary Irish public in which Catholics and nationalists are united in opposition to Britain. That the film's nostalgic vision of Irish hardship was intended to fan political passions is evident in the scheduling of its public premiere on April 22, 1918, the two-year anniversary of Easter Monday. The full text of the *Irish Limelight* announcement gives some indication of the scale of the production, if not of its creators' hopes for its impact:

"Knocknagow," the Film Co. of Ireland's super-production, will be shown to the trade at the Sackville Street Picture House on February 6th. Having seen the film, we confidently predict that it will prove to be the greatest attraction ever offered to Ireland's cinema-loving public. Produced amongst the very hills and valleys where Kickham laid the scenes of his immortal story, it visualises the genius of its famous author in a manner that cannot fail to appeal to all classes and creeds. Here the characters, costumed with historical accuracy, come out of the past to live and have their being in the present.

Photographically perfect, this homely yet wonderfully powerful Irish story grips our attention at the outset and holds it while it flows naturally throughout the eight long reels necessary for its portrayal upon the screen. To attempt anything in the nature of a descriptive write-up would be futile, for the story was conceived of genius, and it has been sympathetically handled with an ability that cannot fail to gladden the hearts of all who are interested in the future of Irish motion photography. (*Irish Limelight*, February 1918)

Kevin Rockett has argued that *Knocknagow*'s epic sweep was modeled directly and consciously on Griffith's *Birth*, a position that seems difficult to maintain after viewing the film: although impressive for its time,

Knocknagow reveals no specific evidence of the influence of *Birth*'s narrative scope or its technical brilliance. What is clear, however, is that the
film inherits its historiographical strategy, a return to the Irish past by
literary means, directly from Griffith, and for that reason provoked direct
comparison to its predecessor. Rockett reports that *The Evening Telegraph*
of 13 December 1919 proclaimed that in Boston, the picture "took more
money than the much 'boosted' [*The*] *Birth of a Nation*" (Rockett, *Cinema
and Ireland*, 23).

Another film influenced by Griffith's narrative model was *Willy Reilly
and His Colleen Bawn*, which also received its premiere on an anniversary
of the Rising (the fourth). Shot on location at St. Enda's – the school
founded by Patrick Pearse and an important symbol of nationalism –
Willy Reilly, like *Birth*, solves political and religious conflicts at the national
and historical level by reducing them to a romantic family plot at the end
of which a Catholic and a Protestant marry. Interestingly, the film was
directed by John MacDonagh, who had written the script that became
Griffith's earlier film, *The Fugitive*, and whose brother Thomas was among
those executed for his role in the 1916 Rising.

Such evidence of Griffith's influence lends support to the notion that
Irish nationalists realized early the narrative cinema's potential as political propaganda. While the phrase "Irish cinema" may seem contradictory when set against the better-known film traditions of countries like
Italy, France, Germany, and the United States, what is clear is that the
forging of modern Ireland's national identity and its cinematic tradition
go hand in hand. The concurrence of these historical developments, the
one political, the other technological, spawned a cinema preoccupied
with issues of nationalism, political division, religious faith, mythological
tradition, and the codes of personal and social identity. Implicit in much
of the critical writing about this tradition is the awareness that in its
narrative moment, the cinema has been, despite its identification with
new cultural expression and progressivism, a profoundly conservative
force in Irish culture. As a representational medium, film has served to
perpetuate images and meanings of Irishness that, while comfortable,
are at best simplistic and at worst culturally compromising.

But if the cinema betrays its true power as a historical medium in
becoming a medium of narratives modeled on literary sources, its more
radical counter-influence can also be measured, ironically enough, in
literary texts that register the influence of film's earlier aesthetic of spectacle. Three such texts, all of them narratives of Easter 1916, register
the Rising's importance as a prominent locus of modern Ireland's crisis

of historical imagination. As different as these treatments are, all reveal narrative as a discursive mode the power of which lies in its capacity to admit the apprehension of history as something contrary to narrative: the spectacle of history. The event of the Rising is not controlled and clarified by these narratives; rather it haunts them.

James Stephens' *The Insurrection in Dublin* is a day-by-day, journalistic account of the Rising as it happened. Stephens records his own confusion, and that of fellow citizens, as he wanders about the city, following up rumors, gathering information and misinformation from neighbors and sizing up the rebels in St. Stephen's Green. The terms that define Stephens' account of the Rising are confusion, disbelief, and impatience with the rebels. Sean O'Casey's account in *The Plow and the Stars* produces a similar effect through dramatic treatment of character. O'Casey's Dubliners are not uniformly starry-eyed nationalists preaching Sinn Fein's "Ourselves Alone," or "Ireland for the Irish." Their number includes working-class drunks, theoretical Marxists, and bourgeois dreamers seeking a better life. The nationalists are exposed as cowards and glorified boy-scouts; the bravest of the characters is a transplanted Protestant from the North. Like Stephens, O'Casey leaves one with an overall impression of the Rising's complex and ambivalent impact on a confused citizenry variously invested and disinvested in its leaders' goals. Finally, Joyce offers a remarkable treatment in *Finnegans Wake* in which an account of the Easter Rising emerges through a tissue of references to horse races and particularly the Grand National, the outcome of which we learn: "Peredos last in the Grand Natural. Velivision victor" (Joyce, *FW*, 610.34–35). What might be a profoundly idealistic and romantic – if ironic – treatment of the *Irish* race and its grand, national vision, turns out to be Joyce's deeply historical consideration of the Rising as a concrete and spectacular event. Joyce's focus on horse races to the exclusion of rebel sallies and retreats registers the concrete historical fact that Easter Monday, the day the Rising began, was a bank holiday. The historical event of the Rising would have been experienced, then, by many Dubliners just as Joyce records it, simply because much of Dublin was, quite literally, off to the races at the time.

What these very different accounts uniformly demonstrate is the capacity of conventional historical treatments to shroud historical events themselves in a narrative structure intent on revealing causes, effects, and meanings. In a sense, conventional historiography indicates that the Easter Rising does not become a historical event until it is so narrativized. As Conor Cruise O'Brien puts it: "All observers report that Dubliners,

and Irish people generally, were at first almost unanimous in condemn-
ing the revolt; they also report that, after the executions, feeling very
rapidly changed into one of veneration for the fallen leaders, and respect
and support for their surviving comrades."[22] Once the metaphor implicit in an Easter *rising* had been realized, the narrative of the event and
its significance as Irish history was clear – so clear that ten years later an
audience at the Abbey Theatre could riot at Sean O'Casey's alternative
view as blasphemous.

What is striking in the accounts by Stephens, O'Casey, and Joyce is
their entirely different treatment of narrative as a historical medium.
None of these writers dispenses wholly with narrative, but neither does
narrative serve to cover and obscure the complexity of the historical
event they treat. In these texts, the narratives that are made about the
Easter Rising continue to struggle with and against the spectacle of
the Rising, since its historical actuality is never fully apprehensible in
language, narrative, or any discursive form.[23] This creates, or rather
allows, what I would call a persistent apprehension in the apprehension
of history, a sense that the narratives of the past are continually haunted
by the events themselves, that the events threaten to erupt, to recur
as spectacle, or otherwise to disrupt the narrative resolution they have
received. Film's profound impact as a historical medium lies precisely
here. It is the possibility that a discursive or cultural medium can reveal
the event as "actuality" that draws the fascination of the audience. In the
midst of Ireland's formative cultural and political imaginings – "all that
stir of thought," as Yeats put it – the cinema proposes a narrative space
in which the profound Otherness of the historical spectacle can breach
the heavy shroud of narrative sense.

CHAPTER 5

Fighting the waves: Yeats, Cuchulain, and the lethal histories of "romantic Ireland"

> History is necessity until it takes fire in someone's imagination and becomes myth or passion.
>
> W. B. Yeats
> *Autobiographies*

Among modern Irish writers, William Butler Yeats is certainly among the least likely to be considered as having been influenced by the cinema. At one extreme, the poet's cosmopolitanism aligns him with the traditional elitism of literary "high" culture, rather than with the public immediacy and pervasiveness of popular mass media. At the other, his fascination with rural Irish life officially locates his perception of cultural authenticity in an ancient oral tradition rooted in the land itself rather than a modern visual one based on perceptions of Ireland. Yet it is worth noting that in his prose writings, Yeats detailed his own active participation in the nineteenth-century parlor culture that in fact constitutes the prehistory of the cinema's culture of spectacle. The popularity of seances and occult practices, institutionalized by groups such as Madame Blavatsky's Order of the Golden Dawn, revolved around the very discourse of attractions that the cinema would realize with a new technological force in 1895.[1] The projection of "familiars" on waving screens or on columns of smoke to effect apparent visitations by ghosts, for example, was common practice at such events. Yeats, whose genius with language appears to have been matched only by his credulousness, seems not to have fully understood the importance of such spectacles as games and illusions.

In the literary sphere, Yeats's concern with formal spectacle is evidenced by his fascination with drama, and in the lyric poetry, too, it is images that are most prominent, especially in the poet's handling of history. Early on, Yeats sought to express the vitality of "romantic Ireland" in terms not of stories, but of vivid images operating within stories: past figures whose actions could quite literally be made present through the medium of poetry. Such figures – Red Hanrahan, Cuchulain, the

Countess Cathleen, Cathleen ni Houlihan, and so on – are important
for Yeats not because they are representative heroes on whose stories he
felt Irish citizens should model their lives: in each of them, he sought to
locate and transmit what he called "character isolated by a deed," the
enduring vitality of the figure itself rather than its scripted or proscriptive
meaning. Yeats intuited poetry's power as a mechanism for expressing
the force such figures continuously maintain in the present, rather than
for laying them to rest in an explanatory discourse of the past. The poet's
handling of the Irish past thus never produced a narrative of Irishness so
much as a series of presentations, an exhibition of images that resembles
in its cultural impact the serial "attractions" that define the early cinema.

   The devolution of such images into "circus animals" in the trajectory
of Yeats's career, and the poet's sense of "desertion" at their hands, is
one of the developments that make Yeats's writing so vitally important
for an understanding of the memorial function in Irish culture. In a
corpus overwhelmingly dominated by the lyric, a form in which narrative potentialities are severely confined while visuality is on the contrary
enhanced, Yeats recovered Irish history as a succession of "players on a
painted stage." The poet's middle and late writing acknowledges that the
romantic figures through which he hoped to make the vitality of the past
present were ultimately read as commemorative images; transformed in
the crucible of Irish nationalist politics, they came to form the iconography of what Patrick Keane has called "the lethal political mythology of
modern Ireland."[2]

   In this iconography, the figure of the legendary hero Cuchulain, whose
"fight with the sea" and other feats are detailed in the Red Branch Cycle
of tales, is surely among the most compelling, and ambivalent, for Yeats.
As Lady Augusta Gregory's translation of the tale has it, Cuchulain's
lover and opponent in battle, Aoife, angry at having been abandoned
by the hero, sends their son Conlaoch to kill him. Neither Conlaoch nor
Cuchulain is aware of their familial relation and, in the ensuing duel,
Conlaoch is killed. Cuchulain, learning his son's identity just before he
expires, rages uncontrollably so that Conchubar the king becomes fearful
that he will vent his anger on his own comrades and thus slay them all.
Conchubar sends Cathbad the druid to cast a spell, or "gessa," upon the
hero, saying, "Go now . . . and bind him to go down to Baile's Strand,
and to give three days fighting against the waves of the sea, rather than
to kill us all." The enchantment causes him to go mad, and to turn his
rage against the waves of the sea, which ultimately engulf him.[3]

   Because it couples blind courage and pathetic futility at such a visceral
level, the image of Cuchulain fighting the sea has become a curiously

negative emblem of Irish political identity. As such, the image seems to confirm what Denis Donoghue and others have suggested, that failure is somehow Ireland's special privilege; that the country's political identity is that of a "lost cause known to be lost."[4] If such a characterization seems hardly desirable as a political representation, it is powerfully compelling as a literary one. Indeed, to more than a few observers the history of modern Ireland has seemed eminently literary, an allegory of failed liberation in the tragicomic mode: its series of bungled offensives, unplanned revolutions, misinterpreted symbolic martyrdoms, and internally divided political movements structure Irish freedom from British oppression as an almost literary ideal which in any case never entirely seems to materialize.

The role played by the figure of Cuchulain in this literary version of Irish history is indicative of the extent to which identities, national or personal, are essentially commemorative projections of historicized consciousness. A striking example of this commemoration is found in the memorial to the Easter 1916 revolutionaries which stands in what is arguably one of the most significant public buildings in the Irish Republic, the General Post Office in Dublin. The bronze statue by Oliver Sheppard depicts a dying Cuchulain, bound to a stone pillar, while the Morrigu, or Goddess of War, perches on his shoulder in the shape of a raven. The image reflects the story of Cuchulain's death on a battlefield: having been wounded six times, he bound himself to a pillar in order to die nobly on his feet.[5] In its commemorative capacity, the monument takes up its position in the Post Office as a synecdochic or metonymic indicator of the historical real. In its evaluative function, however, it recreates those events metaphorically in order to assert their efficacy in the expression of an ideal heroism, and, by implication, of an essential Irishness. The structuring of national identity in this instance thus takes place between a "never forget" imperative which aims to preserve the truth of the past, and a nostalgic, idealistic elevation of events which paradoxically places knowledge of them at a certain remove from the fact of their having happened. The image of Cuchulain thus fulfills the function of a conventional memorial, juxtaposing the methodological goals of historicism and idealism as counterparts in the formation of national identity.

Like the image of Cuchulain's fight with the sea in Yeats's early writing, the statue marks this complex intersection between history and myth in a commemoration of failure, an idealization of Ireland as the "lost cause known to be lost," and does so in the explicit terms of Christian devotion. Indeed, to say that the figure's features and posture are Christlike is to understate the obvious. In a Catholic country, the image of the sacrificial hero, bound and dying, is hardly ambiguous. If Oliver Sheppard translates Christ's cross into Cuchulain's stone pillar; if the crown of thorns becomes a less painful headband, the iconographic references are no less potent: even the enervated sag of the hero's limbs seems worthy of a Michelangelo *pietà*.

Yeats's interest in the creation of a modern Irish national identity through the revival of its myths and legends is, of course, well known, and many critics have read his passion for "Romantic Ireland" as a nostalgic idealism of which the sentimentalism represented by the Cuchulain statue in the General Post Office is the inevitable result. Donoghue particularly credits Yeats with the forging of this link between the remembrance of the past and the value of Ireland's continued identification with failure. In his essay, "Romantic Ireland," Donoghue appropriates Yeats's announcement in "September, 1913" that "Romantic Ireland's dead and gone," in order to disparage a modern philistinism and to argue for the establishment of a true and authentic (and implicitly Yeatsian) Irish identity in the commemoration of the past. He suggests that whether or not "Romantic Ireland" is dead and gone, its value as cultural currency is something modern Ireland cannot afford to do without, that the phrase "We Irish" relies for its continued vitality and significance on its connections with the past, with myth, and with belief.

Donoghue proposes "thinking of modern Irish history as a drama at once romantic and revolutionary" (Donoghue, *We Irish*, 22), a practice which tends to retain the image of "Romantic Ireland" as the determining force of Irish identity; memory is always memory of an ideal. As Donoghue puts it, "Romantic Ireland is a set of values espoused, promoted, bought and sold in the market-place" (Donoghue, *We Irish*, 33), a commodity too valuable – or at least too ubiquitous – to ignore. The implication is that if it is removed from circulation, the cultural economy will simply collapse; there will be no currency in which to reckon the value of Irishness. Even as its reality is belied by the political divisions and social hierarchies of current history, "Romantic Ireland," Donoghue concludes, must remain a measurable force within Irish experience, "sequestered . . . so that it may be preserved for a quieter time, a future more hospitable to justice" (Donoghue, *We Irish*, 33). The price of such preservation is that life and allegory become blurred in the creation of an idealism that drives the force of history.[6]

Despite its critical appropriation, the death of "Romantic Ireland" suggests, for Yeats, not so much the loss of an ideal as precisely this transformation of the heroic image into a debased currency of prayer and pence – a compensatory structure of memorialization. Yeats's response was to return to the Cuchulain image rather than abandon it, and it is this tendency to return, repeatedly, to a thematics the poet himself questioned as outmoded that is so prone to misunderstanding. The futile inadequacy of Cuchulain's defiance of the sea may, for many, seem a particularly eloquent symbolic expression of the condition of Irish political identity. Yet the clichéd sentimentalism and negativity implicit in this reading of the Cuchulain image is at sharp variance with Yeats's own employment of it. Yeats's Cuchulain is not reducible to the value of noble failure; nor does his "bitter tide" consume itself in the trivial banality of a "sea of troubles." Even as his image expresses the idealization of failure, it reveals the terms in which that idealization is brought to bear, and by which Irish identity is bound to a commemorative historicism.

In a figural dimension, the iconographic image of Cuchulain fighting the waves captures, within modern Irish historical consciousness, that odd coincidence of movement and paralysis embodied in Dante's encounter with Lethe and in Moses' Pisgah sight of Palestine. In his madness, the hero is at once active (indeed, heroically so) and tragically, lethally confined. An understanding of the Cuchulain figure's cultural ambivalence is crucial to a reconsideration of modern Irish memory because it expresses precisely memory's role in the compensatory, commemorative constitution of Irishness in the present. At the same time, this figuring of Ireland's historical relation to its past marks the starting point for an apprehension of "counter-memorial" alternatives, cultural discourses of memory in which desire emerges as the central term around which Irishness is configured.

EVERYBODY'S GONE

The tradition according to which Irish history unfolds as a tragic morality play has produced a thematics of Irishness as repetitive as it is emotionally unambiguous. Paternal inadequacy, maternal passivity, Celtic violence, rural authenticity, and natural beauty are among the conventional themes and images that bear, much as Yeats's "circus animals" do, a complex relationship with actual Irish history. One of the most familiar, not to say clichéd, of these images appears late in N. G. Bristow's brilliant and hilarious 1995 short film, *Everybody's Gone*. Against the bleak background of a Connemara beach, we see the father of Davey, the film's protagonist, vainly searching the icy surf for his son, presumably drowned. The tragic pathos of the sequence suggests a historical resonance for Bristow's title, linking the phrase "Everybody's Gone" not only to the Wild Geese of the seventeenth and eighteenth centuries and the famine-occasioned diaspora of the nineteenth, but also to the theme of lost Irish youth mythologized by Yeats in *Cathleen ni Houlihan* and ironized by Joyce in *A Portrait of the Artist as a Young Man*. Such pathos is countered, however, by the more immediate source of the film's title, revealed in a scene near the film's opening. Here Davey sits on a bluff above the beach near his home, gazing wistfully out over the pathetically small waves of the cold, grey Atlantic, and listening on a small portable tape player as the Beach Boys sing, "Everybody's Gone Surfin'." Undaunted by his obvious limitations of national identity and wave-size, Davey sets out to realize his American dream: cutting off the door to his father's tool shed, he fashions a surfboard of fabulous, and indeed mythic, sleekness, fixes it atop a giant spring and practices "hanging ten," hilariously, in the shed. Bristow's subversion of conventional Irish tragedy is complete when Davey, having set out to test his dream board against the reality of the icy Irish "surf," fails to return home. Just as Davey's father finds the broken remains of the surfboard, convincing himself (and viewers) of his son's tragic loss, Bristow cuts to a shot of Davey himself, very much alive, hitch-hiking on a country road. Over a hill in the near distance there appears a microbus full of American hippies, ready to drive young Davey off into the sunset to realize his dream in Connemara's perfect elsewhere, California.

Everybody's Gone serves to illustrate a contemporary Irish ambivalence regarding the past and its continued articulation through now conventional themes and figures, particularly that of Cuchulain's fight with the sea which it both reiterates and subverts. For the contemporary film audience, the shot that reveals Davey's "drowning" inevitably recalls the much more familiar closing sequence of Jim Sheridan's 1990 feature-length film, *The Field*, in which a deranged and hoary Bull MacCabe (Richard Harris) wades Cuchulain-like into the crashing waves, brandishing his shillelagh to avenge the death of yet another Irish son. *The Field* is a beautifully wrought and powerful film, but it is quite rigidly conventional in the emotional values and meanings it ascribes to Irish history. Through Sheridan's lens, Irish history seems less a tragedy unfolding before us, than a series of events required, through some divine or profane edict, to unfold according to Ireland's assigned tragic script. As in any script, human action is subordinate to the notion of role and outcomes are already defined; this landscape, this language, this population, this history will always and necessarily, it seems, produce in some form a

Cuchulain raging at the sea. The frequency with which the Cuchulain image and others like it surface and resurface in contemporary culture as markers of authentic Irishness seems to reinforce the conventional notion that tragedy is not a sad fact of Irish history, but rather its "ineluctable modality," its ruling formal structure.

Interestingly, *The Field* and *Everybody's Gone* follow identical narrative strategies, both returning, self-consciously, to the image of Cuchulain's fight with the sea precisely because it is part of the conventional thematics of Irish historical representation. What is clear, however, is that the investments made by each film in this strategy of repetition are profoundly different. To understand more clearly what is at stake in this difference, it is necessary to examine these films' memorial function, as distinct from their participation in a particular historiographical tradition centered on failure and loss. The issue chiefly in contention in these films' use of the Cuchulain figure is not the historical representation of the past but, in fact, the historical condition of the present. This condition, perhaps best described as a specific, local, and highly personal circumstance of historical loss, is implicit in the narrative structure of Cuchulain's fight with the sea.

Cuchulain's madness, according to the legend, is a response to his own belated arrival at the knowledge that the young man he has fought and killed is his son. At an allegorical level, this belatedness expresses the fact that the events of history are, in Ireland as elsewhere, experienced subjectively as lost events; the modality of pastness is, universally, that of an insistent absence. I say insistent because, so far from staying put, the absent past constantly threatens to overwhelm the present in its effects, much as the waves of the sea threaten to overwhelm Cuchulain. Conventionally, the memorial provides a kind of compensation for historical loss to a present hungry not only for historical sense, but more profoundly, for historical control. Indeed, the need for accuracy in historical representation actually bespeaks a human psychological and emotional need for control over realities that, in spite of their distance, continuously insist and persist in the present. Returning to the theoretical vocabulary of Chapter Three above, we might say that Cuchulain's memorial function enables the present to ex-sist through a past that continuously in-sists as its symptom.

A memorial is, then, by definition that which stalls present acts of memory altogether or, more precisely, renders them unnecessary. Indeed, in its particular strategy of repetition, *The Field* serves what I would call a conventionally "memorial" function in precisely this sense. Recognizing its "market," a present in need of historical control, Sheridan's film appropriates traditional images and themes it can treat as adequate to their meaning. Cuchulain here stands, quite literally, for the whole colossus of Irish historical failure. There is nothing to read here, nothing to analyze, and most importantly, nothing to remember. It may be that part of the film's structuring of memorial payoff can be traced to the intensity of felt emotion it provides, a sort of affective evidence that a whole range of Irish historical references – the famine, the coffin ships, the land war, and so on – have been adequately indexed. In the case of *The Field*, the emotional force of mythic tragedy displaces the otherwise unavoidable and devastating effects of Cuchulain's waves, and in that sense offers a compensatory structure in place of history's loss.[7]

Bristow's film, on the other hand, responds to the historical condition of belatedness quite differently. Following a structure of repetition identical to that of *The Field*, *Everybody's Gone* nonetheless returns to Cuchulain's fight with the sea in order to maximize that image's invitation to memory. The image of Davey, "surfing" in an authentic Irish toolshed followed by the comic shattering of the surfboard (a mythic dream of Irishness) by tiny waves, both distills and transforms the essence of Irish political failure. Davey both is and is not Cuchulain and, at the same time, he is and is not Cuchulain's defeated son Conlach. In complicating both the imagery and its conventional emotional content, *Everybody's Gone* invokes the thematics of failure not as a compensatory resolution but as a persistent question. Cuchulain is not here appropriated as an already inscribed memorial, but adopted as an image repeatedly begging (and begging for) inscription: repetition becomes re-petition. If in a generic sense the memorial is a cultural construction that uses imagery to obviate and devalue the work of memory in the present, Bristow's film constitutes a subversion of this function: it presents conventional images as opportunities to engage a past the meanings of which continue to unfold, and therefore to be relevant in the present.

In other words, *Everybody's Gone* works as a "counter-memorial" in precisely the sense that this term has emerged in connection with the German post-war memorial artists, Jochen and Esther Gerz. As against the compensatory structure of the memorial, the counter-memorial is in a general sense a cultural form of historical imagination that responds to the belatedness of the present by affirming the vitality of the past within present viewers' capacity to imagine it. Its emphasis is not on historical resolution so much as it is on a continually unfolding relationship to the past; its key characteristics are not accuracy and control, but connection and disconnection, figured in an ongoing dialogics of repetition and re-making. Not surprisingly, counter-memorialization does not confine history to a discourse of affirmative recovery, but includes forgetting and denial as practical, indeed unavoidable, functions of historical imagining. In this sense, there rests at the core of the counter-memorial a conviction of the past's vitality, and even subjectivity, rather than, exclusively, its dead, factual objectivity. History is not exclusively a past that can be variously told, but an unfolding, developing Other, constituted provisionally and dialogically in its encounters with a present that is both remembering and forgetful.

Inasmuch as the cultural prominence of Cuchulain's image can be traced directly to its treatment in Irish literature, it is tempting to identify these memorial and counter-memorial strategies respectively with Joyce and Yeats. It is easy – too easy, I would argue – to see Sheridan's memorialism as Yeatsian in its piety and nostalgia, appropriating as it does the hero's action as a way of embodying or illustrating a series of positive and negative qualities it then presents as identifiably Irish: courage, commitment to the land, cultural fundamentalism, provincial paranoia, and so on. *The Field*, after all, appears to adopt something very close to Yeats's strategy for cultural revival in the 1890s, and in particular his use of Cuchulain as "character isolated by a deed" to define a once and future compensatory Ireland of his dreams. In a parallel way, Bristow's parodic and subversive humor in *Everybody's Gone* easily fits a Joycean model of ironic repetition and comic inversion offered as a corrective to Yeats's romantic monumentalism.

In an essay in Jonathan Allison's collection, *Yeats's Political Identities*, Terence Brown has suggested that it is usual, even traditional in a sense, to locate in Joyce a corrective to everything that is monolithic, heroic, aristocratic, and nostalgic in Irish literature, which is to say, it is common to see Joyce as a positive alternative to Yeats and to Yeats's influence on the culture of his time.[8] The greater loss in the comparison is clearly suffered by Yeats, and it is therefore important to weigh carefully the critical impression of memorialism in his work against the work itself. Before turning to such an analysis, however, it is worth noting that this separation is also strictly inaccurate with respect to Joyce in that it portrays him as narrowly and exclusively reactive in his relationship to Yeats, a characterization that is belied by the complexity of Yeats's influence evidenced in Joyce's work itself.

It is true enough that the mythic figure Joyce chooses to feature in *Finnegans Wake* is not Cuchulain but Finn MacCumhail. Vicki Mahaffey has argued that this displacement constitutes a corrective to Yeats's own

attention to Cuchulain. In their book, *Celtic Heritage*, Brinley and Alwyn
Rees suggest that the Tales of the Red Branch Kings, the cycle of myths
in which Cuchulain is the dominant hero, emphasizes values of individual action and heroic feats of daring. By comparison, the Ossianic cycle,
which features Finn MacCumhail, focuses on the collective exploits and
camaraderie of the Fianna warriors.[9] In light of this difference in emphasis, it is not difficult to see that Joyce found in Finn a better model
for his own hero-as-collectivity, HCE ("Here Comes Everybody"). Indeed, in the Ricorso of *Finnegans Wake*, Joyce emphasizes the distance
between Finn and Cuchulain as models of Irishness by referencing the
"Ossianic" tales in a cluster of references to Ireland's geographic an-
tipode, "Osseania" (Joyce, *FW*, 593.5).

   Joyce's displacement of the Cuchulain image might be traced to his
own specific experience of belatedness with respect to Yeats. Upon first
meeting Yeats, Joyce reportedly asked the elder poet his age and, on
hearing the answer, replied that he was too late to be able to help him
(Ellmann, *James Joyce*, 101–3). Here and elsewhere Joyce's antipathy toward what he would later call Yeats's "cultic twalette" (Joyce, *FW*, 344.12)
is evident. At the same time, a useful and perhaps more precise way to
refigure his displacement from his countryman and literary precursor is
to think in terms of Joyce's own use of the prefix "counter" in *Dubliners*.
"Counterparts" figures a model of identity in which that which is opposite
or different expresses a repetition or version of the prior term: thus the
character of Alleyne, Farrington's boss, is a version of Farrington himself
in that the latter's cruelty to his son late in the story reflects Alleyne's
cruelty to him (Joyce, *Dubliners*, 86–98). Joyce's purpose here is both to
show the cyclical nature of social and cultural roles, which he saw as a
matter of choosing moral inaction (contrast Stephen Dedalus' departure
at the end of *A Portrait* to "forge in the smithy of my soul the uncreated
conscience of my race"), and to point to repetition with a difference as
a way out. It is in that sense that Cuchulain is present in *Finnegans Wake*
mostly as counterpart, an ex-centric re-petitioning of Irish heroic identity. Because they entail a more extreme level of identification through
difference, the stylistic markers of the counter-memorial strategy in Joyce
tend to be more overt, and more self-consciously subversive. Cuchulain
himself is directly present mostly to be undermined or displaced by less
heroic figures, such as Finn MacCumhail, HCE, and even ALP, who
becomes a kind of counter-Cuchulain when, as river, she is overcome
(and reborn) in a return to her "cold mad feary father" (Joyce, *FW*,
628.2), an overwhelming sea figured both as "tide" and "dad" ["tid"].

Joyce, then, returns to Cuchulain out of a recognition that repetition makes all the difference. What is less obvious is that the same can be said of Yeats in his poetic response to historical belatedness. In the lyric poetry, there are two main stylistic characteristics that reveal Yeats's repeated return to Cuchulain as serving a counter-memorial strategy: the smoothness, or deceptive simplicity, of his writing and the fact that while he writes primarily in lyric form, the poetry follows a cross-referential pattern that belies the simple containment strategy a lyric might otherwise represent. The breadth of connotation implied by, say, old age in "The Tower" must be read in the context of a broader selection of poems so that the boundaries of the "context" are, as a practical matter, dynamic (which is not to say that they are infinite). Yeats returns to Cuchulain as he returns to symbols and images (the Rose; the wind, scarecrows): by returning to the same figure again and again, Yeats preserves not its meaning but its interpretability, its dynamism and its vitality.

The image of Cuchulain fighting the waves was, to be sure, immoderately compelling to Yeats, who announced in his *Autobiographies* that a childhood desire to become a magician "competed for years with the dream of being killed upon the seashore" (Yeats, *Autobiographies*, 57). In the course of his career the poet turned repeatedly to the events of Cuchulain's life, producing a cycle of five plays, one prose drama, and some eight poems, many of which he revised continually over a period of fifty years between 1889 and his death in 1939. In this corpus, the episode of the hero's battle with the sea figures prominently.

Within certain strains of Yeats criticism, it is common to see this interest as obsessive, rather than, to use a word the poet would himself have preferred, passionate. That the two tendencies should coexist in one man is hardly remarkable, and there doesn't seem to be any compelling reason to treat them as mutually exclusive in Yeats. In any case, it is worth pointing out that the Cuchulain of *On Baile's Strand*, the play which opened the inaugural performance of Yeats's national theater (later the Abbey) in 1904, is not the Cuchulain of *The Death of Cuchulain*, the play Yeats was revising at the time of his death in 1939. The distance between these two figures, and that between passion and obsession as well, in my view, can be measured in Yeats's own transformation as a poet of historical imagination. The touchstones of this transformation are Yeats's Easter Rising poems, which in their ambivalence and "bewilderment," register a curious belatedness with respect to the poet's own construction of Cuchulain. Because those constructions are, as Yeats painfully learned, rooted "in the foul rag-and-bone shop of the heart," it is first necessary to return to their formation in the poet's imaginative vision; understanding the circus animals as constructions themselves is what makes their metamorphosis intelligible.

In the commemoration of the poetical hero, the literary value of Irish history emerges. As Yeats recalled Oscar Wilde once commenting over a shared Christmas dinner, the political validity of the term "We Irish," or of any representation of Irish national identity for that matter, is married to its poetical force within a descriptive narrative of tragicomic failure: "We Irish are too poetical to be poets," said Wilde. "We are a nation of brilliant failures" (Yeats, *Autobiographies*, 166–67). The remembered image of the hero marks the historicization of a mythic ideal, the birth of Irish history out of the spirit of literature.

Reading the Cuchulain image as an expression of the binding of identity recalls one of its primary sources, for Yeats, in the poetry of Shelley. As a young poet, Yeats modeled his own dramas and lyrics on those of Shelley, and took to referring to *Prometheus Unbound*, in particular, as his "sacred book" (Yeats, *Autobiographies*, 108).[10] Indeed, a passing comment in one of Yeats's essays on Shelley reveals an influence that apparently remained well beyond the writing of his early poetry: "When in middle life I looked back I found that he and not Blake, whom I had studied more and with more approval, had shaped my life."[11] George Bornstein goes so far as to assert that Yeats considered Cuchulain an Irish Prometheus, and indeed, there is much in Yeats's early representations of the hero to substantiate the claim.[12] The resemblance appears not so much in a depiction of Cuchulain as a political revolutionary, an agent of deliverance and liberation, as it does in a heroic resistance to idealization that can only be called Promethean. Yeats's depictions of Cuchulain emphasize the problematics of memory, historicism, and the representation of identity, rather than a drama of heroic success or failure. While the figure of Shelley's Prometheus has been regarded, from the poem's first publication, as an ideal image of political and social liberation, that is, as an icon precisely of heroic success, it is this battle with the idealizing forces of historicization that is foregrounded in Shelley's poem.[13] Shelley's *Prometheus Unbound*, then, aids an examination of Yeats's representation of the hero precisely in that it places that representation within a problematics of remembrance.

Even so, as has been pointed out by numerous readers, the success of Prometheus's battle against tyranny is a foregone conclusion. As an immortal, Prometheus has merely to wait long enough, and eventually the hour that brings Jupiter's demise will arrive. Moreover, the very title of Shelley's poem prefigures this inevitability of salvation in two ways. "Prometheus Unbound" in a literal sense insists on the freedom of the poem's hero as its initial condition; that is, rather than signalling the possibility of the hero's dramatic release, the title from the outset inscribes the events of the ensuing drama, the hero's action and the salvation of the world, within Prometheus's condition as already unbound. More indirectly, the presence of Prometheus's name in the title foreshadows the inevitable conclusion of the drama: stemming from the Greek word meaning "foresight," the name Prometheus marks the signal proof of the revolution's already having happened. Thus, in a remarkable flouting of what would seem an important dramatic law of epic poetry, it is the acknowledged inevitability of the hero's success – and not the false possibility of his failure – that Shelley's poem holds out to the reader. This name, Prometheus, which signifies both promise and conclusion, "the prophesy which begins and ends in thee," spends the poem's entire dramatic capital in the sounding of its first word.[14]

But whereas the inevitable triumph of Shelley's hero is legible in his very name, Ireland's narrative of deliverance maintains no such promise at its core. Instead, Irish history remains bound to a literary ideal of failure, a lethal history as literally confining as the watery perimeter of its islanded identity. For Yeats, the importance of Cuchulain lies in the fact that, as a figure, he embodies a poetical and heroic resistance to idealization. His image is neither iconic nor commemorative; it does not evaluate or petrify the past, but inscribes Irish history in terms of the image-less vitality of "myth" and "passion." To this end, Yeats's revision of Shelley's Prometheus goes well beyond the addition of what Bornstein calls the "more earthy" qualities of Cuchulain. To be sure, Cuchulain is more humanly passionate than Prometheus, more sexual and so on. But he is not, as Bornstein insists, an idealized form of human passion – at least not in the sense that he represents for Yeats the "type" of human perfection, a figure which the modern Irish would do well to emulate. Bornstein argues that Yeats's use of the Cuchulain figure is essentially allegorical, that the poet depicts a political, rather than poetical hero, whose passion is expended *for* the Irish. Such an image would hardly be an adequate corrective to the allegory of revolutionary justice in

Prometheus Unbound, which Yeats, in spite of his admiration for Shelley, called a "vague, propagandist emotion" (Bornstein, *Yeats and Shelley*, 127). If Shelley's Promethean justice produces mere allegories, so too does the simple adoption of learned heroic qualities create the mere allegorical value of the Easter 1916 martyrs.

In "A General Introduction for My Work," Yeats related the stony-hearted idealism of the 1916 patriots to the death of "Romantic Ireland," the "same country" in Ireland's past of which Cuchulain was representative. He wrote of being informed by newspaper reports, both Irish and English, "that my movement perished under the firing squads of 1916... If that statement is true, and it is only so in part, for romance was everywhere receding, it is because in the imagination of Pearse and his fellow soldiers the Sacrifice of the Mass had found the Red Branch in the tapestry; they went out to die calling upon Cuchulain" (Yeats, *Essays and Introductions*, 515). In other words, if heroic vitality "died" in 1916, it was because the rebels embraced a kind of Christification of their actions, an image of themselves as martyrs.[15]

This passage, along with many others both in the prose and in the poetry, betrays Yeats's consistent and deep-seated aversion to the officially sanctioned idealism that the GPO statue serves to embody. An antipathy toward monumentalism of all sorts – political, aesthetic, religious, historical – particularly in Yeats's later work, suggests a devotion to the mythic or legendary image that is altogether different from one which would commemorate or idealize it for political purposes.[16] Indeed, Yeats's approach to the revival of Irish myth opposes the process by which such images become the marmorialized effects of national memory, and by which the state locates its identity in the status of images.

More importantly, this passage, along with many others both in the prose and in the poetry, subtly registers the poet's awareness of personal responsibility in creating the Cuchulain image, a responsibility expressed more explicitly in later poems such as "Man and Echo" and "The Circus Animals' Desertion." Yeats believed that the Easter Rising gave birth to a "cult of sacrifice," the ideal of a tragic death, which Irish politicians were subsequently constrained to fulfill: "I am told that De Valera has said in private that within three years he will be torn in pieces... No sooner does a politician get into power than he begins to seek unpopularity. It is the cult of sacrifice planted in the nation by the executions of 1916."[17] Reading Yeats's work as an attempt to infuse modern Ireland with its proper and ideal heroic purpose may grant to his difficult poetry a certain efficiency of understanding and interpretation. But "Easter, 1916" is not simply an attempt to ennoble the given social order by eulogizing the failed effort of heroes. Yeats's celebration of the Rising veils a keen understanding of the price such heroes pay in becoming allegorical images, static and immobile stones "to trouble the living stream" (Yeats, "Easter, 1916," 44), as well as of the artist's own responsibility in recreating them as "lost causes known to be lost."[18]

In a letter to Lady Gregory dated May 11, 1916, Yeats wrote of his sorrow at the "many miscarriages of justice" in the wake of the rebellion, and refers to a letter which he had recently received from Maud Gonne: "Her main thought seems to be 'tragic dignity has returned to Ireland.' She had been told by two members of the Irish Party that 'Home Rule was betrayed.' She thinks now that the sacrifice has made it safe" (Jeffares, *A New Commentary*, 190–91). While it is not possible to ascertain whether or not this letter became a source for his poem, there can be no question about the difference between Yeats's and Maud Gonne's views of the Rising. The poet's enigmatic (even if now somewhat clichéd) phrase, "terrible beauty," stands in stark contrast to Gonne's "tragic dignity," the latter serving to rehabilitate the failure of the insurrection in much the same way that Sheppard's statue does.

For Gonne, it is the sacrifice of martyrs that invests the Irish cause with dignity – a lofty seriousness and nobility in failure, which, after all, is recoupable as a kind of tragic success. Yeats's phrase at once mirrors, or echoes, Gonne's, while betraying none of her moral certainty. Whether or not the martyrs' deaths succeeded in making sacred the event of the revolution; whether or not their actions proved worthy of their adopted symbols, those of the resurrection of Christ at Easter, to Yeats their deaths represent in a certain, irreducible sense, the non-recoupability of their lives. Their eloquently symbolic actions do indeed speak the unspeakable "terrible beauty"; but the phrase itself draws attention to the fact – as well as to the means by which their deaths are aesthetically rendered as sacrifice. "Terrible beauty" refers as much to the rebels' re-creation as symbolic ideals as it does to the irreversible fact of their deaths.

Thus, Yeats's poem questions the political effect of its own eulogy, even as it carries it out. It does not stop at demonstrating the revolutionaries' nobility, but insists on noting that that nobility is aesthetically rendered, that their transformation from dead men into heroes and martyrs is an act of image-making. The poet's "I," which begins the poem recalling chance, mundane meetings with the "vivid faces" of friends, speaks not only the regret of the living for moments lost in "polite meaningless words," but also the poet's awareness that now no words are meaningless:

"motley," a word that not only connotes the nonsense of clownish color combinations, but the casual indifference of the words typically used in such polite exchanges, becomes the hyper-inflected, symbolic "green" of the poem's conclusion.

Yeats's poem is a eulogy for dead heroes, but one that calls our attention to the unsentimental fact of their end – "not night but death" – and to the marmorialization which makes their death a sacrifice, a symbol, and a success. The poet does not shrink from criticizing the heroes, as when he writes, "Too long a sacrifice / Can make a stone of the heart. / O when may it suffice?"; or when he calls to mind Pearse's vow in the lines, "We know their dream; enough / To know they dreamed and are dead; / And what if excess of love / Bewildered them till they died?"[19] But neither does he shrink from recognizing his own complicity, as eulogist, in creating their memories: "I write it out in a verse – ." At the time of the writing of "Easter, 1916," Yeats had already written three of his Cuchulain plays and most of his poetry on the hero. Thus he was aware of his own role, as a poet of international stature, in creating the cult of Cuchulain to which Pearse and the other rebels pledged their Easter sacrifice.

Yeats remembers, and even honors the dead revolutionaries, without idealizing their claims and their symbols – without, in other words, capitulating to an ideal image of Ireland and of Irish freedom in remembering their actions. Yeats's memorial is thus less selective in its depiction than most: it points out that the revolutionaries' power lies precisely in their martyrdom, and therefore in their failure. They have become images, players on a painted stage, rather than living, fighting men and women. What is left in the wake of such a tragedy is nothing but the ability, as in "Easter, 1916," to name the dead; their passion is gone, and their poetic action is gone as well. Yeats's elegy for the dead martyrs reflects the reality that the revolution was not widely supported by the citizenry of Dublin, or of Ireland, and that it only became a victory of sorts when its martyrs became tragic symbols of the oppression of the Irish State.

What is crucial here is the fact that "Easter, 1916," while it is sometimes read as a celebratory eulogy to political martyrs, reveals Yeats's loss of clarity and direction with respect to Cuchulain's image and a growing sense of the costs of the poet's own program of mythic idealism. "Easter, 1916" is hardly a full-scale condemnation of heroic sacrifice; rather it expresses Yeats's ambivalence through observation ("Hearts with one purpose alone / Through summer and winter seem / Enchanted to a stone / To trouble the living stream.") and questioning ("Too long a sacrifice / Can make a stone of the heart. / O when may it suffice?" and "What if excess of love / Bewildered them till they died?").

Yeats's own bewilderment here is palpable enough to raise a serious question about his continued commitment to the image of Cuchulain. One explanation has been that Yeats's continued interest in Cuchulain as romantic hero is consistent with his political sympathies for Mussolini and fascism in the 1930s, that in other words he joins a personal reactivity and defensiveness to a larger political agenda. Such a reading disregards the fact that Yeats specifically distanced his last play, *The Death of Cuchulain*, from the national "mood" that had earlier allowed a romantic treatment of the Cuchulain legend by writers like Standish O'Grady, Lady Gregory, Synge, and himself. Attributing that mood to a willful escapism and denial following the event of Parnell's political defeat and death, Yeats wrote, "Repelled by what had seemed the *sole reality*, we had turned to romantic dreaming, to the nobility of tradition."[20] This impulse eventually gave way to the "Cork Realists," who, "instead of turning their backs upon the actual Ireland of their day ... attacked everything that had made it possible" (Yeats, *Variorum Plays*, 568).

Citing these passages, Philip Marcus has remarked that "By 1938, Yeats must have decided that the mood of the world, and consequently of Ireland, had changed enough so he could attempt to finish the task of bringing back 'the heroic ideal,' could write *The Death of Cuchulain*."[21] Yet as the opening of *The Death of Cuchulain* makes clear, its author – and, indeed, to a certain extent the play itself – are painfully aware of being "out of date." The scene is not that of "Romantic Ireland," nor even of an Ireland sympathetic to romantic representations of itself, but "a bare stage of any period." The figure who introduces the drama, an Old Man who bears an undeniable resemblance to Yeats himself, extols neither the high-minded virtue of its message nor the exemplary character of its hero. He has been asked to produce the play, he says, precisely "because I am out of fashion and out of date like the antiquated romantic stuff the thing is made of."[22] Thus, it is his own bitterness and rage, coupled with a hopeless sense that the audience is not only uninterested but emotionally ill-equipped to appreciate the play's passion, that contextualize this portrayal of Cuchulain's death. Insisting that the play's composition was occasioned by the inevitable return of Yeats's historical gyres, a revival of romance, in effect, thus only allows Marcus to impose an artificial continuity on Yeats's treatment of the Cuchulain tales, and to reinscribe the play's singular use of the hero's image within romantic values trumpeted not by Yeats, but by Standish O'Grady over a half-century before.

A singular aspect of the play's introductory monologue, and one of particular importance to the narrative that follows, involves the terms in which the Old Man expresses his almost paranoiac certainty of being misunderstood. It is the intellectually pretentious whom the Old Man most reviles, "people who are educating themselves out of the book Societies and the like, sciolists all, pickpockets and opinionated bitches. Why pickpockets? I will explain that, I will make it all quite clear" (Yeats, *The Death of Cuchulain*, 209–10). While the Old Man does not in fact return to the stage to explain his reference to "pickpockets," the term introduces a theme of betrayal which is central to the play and which emphasizes in its economic metaphor the debased valuation of heroism decried in earlier poems like "September, 1913." The image of the hero, the Old Man seems to say, functions here not as an abstract idealization, but as an occasion for intellectual thievery of a particularly ignominious sort.

Although this theme of betrayal is hinted at in Eithne Inguba's and Emer's attempts to influence the hero, the central referent of the Old Man's "pickpocket" charge is found in one of Yeats's major additions to the Cuchulain legend, the character of the Blind Beggar. It is the Blind Man, of course, who brings about the singularly unheroic death of Cuchulain. Even more than the ignominy of the death itself – the hero is all but spent from fighting by the time the Beggar arrives to cut his throat – the Blind Man's act comments on the worth of the heroic ideal as such. His "good sense" says that twelve pennies is the price of Cuchulain's head, but also that that is the price of his image as hero; in establishing the circumstances of his death, the pennies express the whole value of that death. In a sense, Yeats's use of a Judas figure in this context would seem to create, just as Sheppard's statue had done, a specifically Christ-like cult of sacrifice around the hero. Yet it is the audience that is implicated in an economics of betrayal by the Old Man's opening monologue and by the Blind Man's act of murder. It is the audience that has paid to witness this heroism, to see with its own eyes the reality of a romantic ideal.

Thus, to read within the death of "Romantic Ireland" Yeats's bitterness over an ideal lost or rejected is to reduce his entire endeavor to that of an antiquary who, having brought his arcane and inconsequential interests – the stories of Irish mythology – to publicity, is angered that they are not valued by all. Yeats was not interested in reviving the old myths for their own sake, however, but in order to locate within them imaginative masks for modern Ireland. To say that "Romantic Ireland" is dead and gone is not to say that the images are lost, but that they are being bought and sold *as* images, instead of as imaginative, passionate, and dynamic intensities or identities:

> What need you being come to sense,
> But fumble in a greasy till
> And add the halfpence to the pence
> And prayer to shivering prayer, until
> You have dried the marrow from the bone?
> For men were born to pray and save:
> Romantic Ireland's dead and gone,
> It's with O'Leary in the grave.
> (Yeats, "September, 1913," 1–8)

Yeats's play thus reveals a pronounced, if somewhat veiled, ambivalence both toward the unvarnished romanticism of the 1890s and toward the political uses to which such idealism has been put. In particular, as Marcus notes, the "sole reality" of Parnell's betrayal which had prompted the flight of the Irish imagination into romantic dreaming in the 1890s, re-appears in the series of questions in the play's final lyric, a lyric which disparages the apparent "sole reality" that the heroic ideal is available for virtually any price to those who pay:

> Are those things that men adore and loathe
> Their sole reality?
> What stood in the Post Office
> With Pearse and Connolly?
> What comes out of the mountain
> Where men first shed their blood?
> Who thought Cuchulain till it seemed
> He stood where they had stood?
> (Yeats, *The Death of Cuchulain*)

The explicit inclusion of the events of Easter Week, 1916 in a play about the death of Cuchulain further discredits the notion that Yeats's play represents a return to romantic idealism. On the contrary, the Rising grants historical perspective to the issue of image-making which Yeats is here exploring.

In this context, the Easter Rising becomes the historical equivalent of the play's dramatic image-making. Yeats referred to the revolutionaries as "the poets of 1916," and considered the Rising itself to have taken place upon a "painted stage." But what is at issue is the image of the hero that the Rising produced. That is, Yeats does not celebrate the effort of the insurgents here, but questions the value of the images that they produced, of themselves and of Cuchulain, and their political efficacy as martyrs. Indeed, the final stanza of the lyric focuses the Old Man's raging at the "pickpockets" directly on the memorial statue of Cuchulain itself, an image which marks the place in which passionate action has been sold for a romantic and propagandistic ideal of martyrdom:

> No body like his body
> Has modern woman borne,
> But an old man looking on life
> Imagines it in scorn.
> A statue's there to mark the place,
> By Oliver Sheppard done.
> So ends the tale that the harlot
> Sang to the beggar-man.
>
> (Yeats, *The Death of Cuchulain*, 218)

A letter to Sir William Rothenstein dated December 29, 1938, reveals that Yeats regarded the statue with antipathy: "some of the best known of the young men who got themselves killed in 1916 had the Irish legendary hero Cuchulain so much in their minds that the Government has celebrated the event with a bad statue" (Marcus, *Death of Cuchulain*, 15). The lack of sympathy communicated by the phrase, "got themselves killed," suggests that Yeats's dislike for the statue was not based merely on aesthetic preference, but also on a certain ambivalence toward the events of the Rising themselves, and toward the statue's translation of them into political idealization.[23]

Much of Yeats's later poetry can be read as a response to the official creation of an Irish political and cultural identity by appeal to a peculiarly Christ-like Cuchulain. The sacrificial values commemoratively sanctioned by the GPO statue have ultimately little to do with Yeats's effort to recreate modern Ireland through the revitalization of its myths. For Yeats, Cuchulain's heroic actions, and the retelling of them, do express an essential Irishness, but that expression is not necessarily exemplary in its forms. That is, the image of Cuchulain is not a propagandistic or idealistic representation of what the Irish could or should become. Rather, that image embodies a heroic passion, the "Irishness" of which is not wholly susceptible to a logic of cultural or political value.

Thus Yeats's final play, "The Death of Cuchulain," further clarifies his ambivalence toward the use of heroic images. Written in the final year of his life, and revised continually up until a few days before his death, the play not only stands at a historical remove from the rest of the Cuchulain cycle, but registers a shift from an early form of national historical imagining that had contextualized the writing of the earlier plays. Marcus's reading of a return to romance in Yeats's last play clearly supports the notion of Yeats's literary appropriation of Cuchulain for a fascist politics. While I think it entirely logical and therefore possible that at a human level Yeats's response to artistic bewilderment included a need for greater artistic control, I am hesitant (to say the least) to apply to that control a term that has gained its primary historical resonance after Yeats's death. What I can say is that in my own reading, Yeats's middle and later work evidences a continuing struggle with the costs of stabilizing, controlling images, as well as a growing acceptance of the rewards of that struggle itself. This struggle, which is artistic, personal, *and* political, is in my view traceable directly to the experience of historical and artistic loss that the 1916 Rising occasioned for Yeats. What 1916 gave him in a way he had not previously experienced was a tangible and belated sense of the memorial status Cuchulain's image had realized in his own work. While the middle and later poetry provides ample evidence of Yeats's reactivity and rage at this circumstance, it also reveals the depth of his commitment to maintaining a place within his writing for precisely the "counter-memorial" function that I have described above.

REPETITION MAKES ALL THE DIFFERENCE

In Yeats's poetry, the line is finely drawn indeed between mythic passion and political idealism. The distinction becomes clearer, however, when we note the importance of the concrete in the poet's mythic representations. In Cuchulain's fight with the sea, for instance, the isolation of character by deed has as much to do with the landscape that contextualizes the heroic act as it does with the alleged nobility of the hero. Yeats's symbols are never simply stand-ins for a transparent evaluation of events and characters, but nodal points at which the genuine complexity of those events emerges unsimplified. Yeats replaces the Promethean rock with its antithesis, a more complicated symbol of fixity that is no less powerful – and no less binding – for being indeterminate and in motion: the sea. Whereas Shelley presented Prometheus bound to the rock as an image of motiveless endurance, and therefore a corrective to the ideal image of Christ on the cross, Yeats's vision of the scene of binding finds Cuchulain in a tragic battle with the sea.

Clearly, the waves of the sea are a far more dynamic and unstable image than the rock of Prometheus, and in replacing that rock with the waves, Yeats seems to literalize the movement, both syntactical and actual, implied in the word "rock." Cuchulain is bound to the sea not with the heavy chains of metaphor, as is Prometheus, but rather in terms of a literal restriction, his restriction as hero, as ideal. That it is the sea he faces is important not least because Ireland is an island, and faces the sea on all sides. Thus a real complexity of waves, an actual depth of the sea, jostles with the image's status as symbol. As Yeats wrote in the introduction to his edition of Blake's poetry:

When Shakespeare compares the mind of the mad Lear to the "vexed sea," we are told at once something more laden with meaning than many pages of psychology ... The chief difference between the metaphors of poetry and the symbols of mysticism is that the latter are woven together into a complete system. The "vexed sea" would not be merely a detached comparison, but, with the fish it contains, would be related to the land and air, the winds and shadowing clouds, and all in their totality compared to the mind in its totality.[24]

This emphasis on the material basis of the symbol frees it from the allegorical idealisms to which it would otherwise be bound: "I try always to keep my philosophy within such classifications of thought as ... to include in my definition of water a little duckweed or a few fish. I have never met that poor naked creature, H_2O."[25]

If Cuchulain is somehow an exemplary Irish hero, it is not because his acts are appropriately sacrificial; Yeats's point, after all, is that they are incommensurable with the commemorative valuation of sacrifice. Rather, it is because those acts emerge from and are carried out in the context of the boundedness of Irish identity. Yeats's Cuchulain is, in the words of "The Tower," a hero who is "Bound neither to Cause nor to State," yet his battle expresses a boundedness which is both poetical and political. Nationalism, like historicism, is a question of topography as well as of philosophy: "Have not all races had their first unity from a mythology that marries them to rock and hill?" (Yeats, *Autobiographies*, 240). Cuchulain's fight with the sea is not an exemplary expression of what is rightly or wrongly or nobly done in the wake of the slaying of a son, but an expression of a nation's literal and geographic boundary, its binding to an islanded consciousness. "Married" to its rock and hill, Ireland's liberation, its becoming unbound, is, for Yeats, undivorceable from its geographical and historical binding.[26]

The materiality of the symbol was thus crucial for Yeats, and he mourned for the "reality lost to Shelley's *Prometheus Unbound* because he had not discovered in England or in Ireland his caucasus" (Yeats, *Essays and Introductions*, 350). The poet's insistence that the scene of Cuchulain's poetical passion be not simply an abstract "sea of generation" but a sea of duckweed and fish implies a similar materiality behind the hero himself.

History, as the final lyric of *The Death of Cuchulain* reveals, is a "tale that the harlot / Sang to the beggar man"; indeed, many of Yeats's Cuchulain figures are bound to the social and economic realities of Ireland, just as their heroic actions – "married to rock and hill" – are bound to its geographical ones. Of these figures, the Crazy Jane of Yeats's later poems is a familiar, and singular, example. "Crazy Jane on the Mountain," for instance, reverses the heroic ideal and recreates it within the bounds of poverty and madness, forces which, within the Crazy Jane poems, are equally constitutive of authentic "Irishness." Originally titled "Ireland After the Revolution," the poem depicts Jane turning from the Bishop, with whom she has become bored, to remark that she has discovered "something worse" in the confining ideals of a nation. The image of Jane on the mountain thus becomes a playful subversion of the central image of *Prometheus Unbound*; as Shelley's poem is an embodiment of the condition of being unbound, so Yeats's poem reveals, perhaps as a reversal of the allegorical Cathleen ni Houlihan, the figure of Crazy Jane as an image of post-revolutionary, unbound Ireland.

A profoundly different re-petitioning of the Cuchulain image appears, moreover, in the image of Margot Ruddock, an actress and poet in whom Yeats had a romantic interest and for whose volume *The Lemon Tree* (1937) Yeats wrote an introduction. Yeats wrote at least two poems for Ruddock, "Sweet Dancer" and "A Crazed Girl." Like Cuchulain, Ruddock had suffered from episodes of madness, and Yeats, without condescending to attribute a creative value to that madness, nonetheless implored readers not to try to understand or contain it:

> If strange men come from the house
> To lead her away, do not say
> That she is happy being crazy;
> Lead them gently astray;
> Let her finish her dance,
> Let her finish her dance.
> (Yeats, "Sweet Dancer," 8–13)

Here, as elsewhere, Yeats is aware that the dancer is only artificially separated from the dance, and that the meaning of passion is only available in an idealized form.

Moreover, Ruddock's madness expressed, just as Cuchulain's had, a boundedness that was not simply imagined but actual. In a letter to Olivia Shakespear dated May 22, 1936, Yeats wrote that Ruddock had come to see him "to find out if her verse was any good. I had known her for some years and had told her to stop writing as her technique was getting worse. I was amazed by the tragic magnificence of some fragments and said so. She went out in pouring rain, thought, as she said afterwards, that if she killed herself her verse would live instead of her. Went to the shore to jump in, then thought that she loved life and began to dance." The rest of Yeats's account is curiously perfunctory: "Next day she went to Barcelona and there went mad, climbing out of a window, falling through a baker's roof, breaking a kneecap, hiding in a ship's hold, singing her own poems most of the time" (Jeffares, *A New Commentary*, 366).

Ruddock's rejection of suicide in favor of a dance on the shore transforms the image of Cuchulain's battle against the sea from tragedy into a kind of gaiety. She loses the traditional meaning of heroic action in order to find its actual expression in a mad, winding border dance in which identity is both bound and unbound. At the end of *Fighting the Waves*, Yeats had similarly transformed Cuchulain into a dancer, but this transformation is only fully realized in the new Cuchulain of "A Crazed Girl":

> That crazed girl improvising her music,
> Her poetry, dancing upon the shore,
> Her soul in division from itself
> Climbing, falling she knew not where,
> Hiding amid the cargo of a steamship,
> Her knee-cap broken, that girl I declare
> A beautiful lofty thing, or a thing
> Heroically lost, heroically found.
>
> No matter what disaster occurred
> She stood in desperate music wound,
> Wound, wound, and she made in her triumph
> Where the bales and the baskets lay
> No common intelligible sound
> But sang, "O sea-starved, hungry sea."
> (Yeats, "A Crazed Girl," 1–14)

It is characteristic of Yeats's use of symbol that it functions as the means to transform not only the hero and his action, but the entire scene of heroism, the fight or dance, the hero's song, and the sea itself. In the girl's illogical, unintelligible song, the sea that is starved of itself not only marks the boundary which confines her, but echoes the division from self that is at once the mental split of her madness and the physical wound of her knee-cap which gives her dance an odd, syncopated rhythm: "in desperate music wound, / Wound, wound." The iconic value of heroism is lost, but its passion is found and expressed as Cuchulain's fight is made a winding form of writing, rather than a tragic memory. Like the picture of the gyres which Michael Robartes found written by dancers' feet on the sands of the desert, this bounded dance traces a writing of history in which heroism is not commemoratively represented but instead "takes fire in someone's imagination and becomes myth or passion."

In his first essay on Shelley, Yeats had written that, as a young man, he considered poetry the form of the only philosophy that endures; of this philosophy, Shelley's poetry was Yeats's greatest example. Yet he then adds, "I . . . am now certain that the imagination has some way of lighting on the truth that the reason has not, and that its commandments . . . are the most binding we can ever know" (Yeats, *Essays and Introductions*, 65). The image of Cuchulain "bound" to the sea is clearly one inaccessible to reason alone. It expresses an aestheticism that is illogical, imaginative, and yet absolutely "binding"; it concretizes the metaphorical state (in both senses) of Ireland by focusing on its boundary and its boundedness as the locus of a perpetual political and historical battle. The notion that Cuchulain dies a martyr to a past social order could not then be more mistaken.[27] What is evident is Cuchulain's lack of martyrdom, the causelessness which surrounds his death; and what is ultimately legible in Yeats's use of the Cuchulain myth is not his fidelity to a particular definition of national identity, but his recognition of the living complexity of that identity.

In becoming a martyr, in dying for a cause, the hero becomes, for Yeats, an image of stasis, a stone of identity that can function politically as a lethal ideal. For Yeats, national identity and freedom are not the result of fulfilling an imaged ideal but of passing through that lethal image to bring about the birth of a new self, one that is created in a moment and perpetually renewed. In the image of Cuchulain fighting the sea, then, Yeats's childhood wish to die on a beach joins with his desire, when old, to die "a foolish, passionate man" (Yeats, "A Prayer for Old Age," 12). However one reads the poetical hero's balletic battle, the image does not, ultimately, trace a sanctified vision of history, a commemorative evaluation of the authentic heroism of "Romantic Ireland"; Yeats's Cuchulain is not one of "those thoughts men think / In the mind alone" (Yeats, "A Prayer for Old Age," 1–2), but an instance of history-becoming-myth within a bounded historicism. The image of Cuchulain emerges not as an ideal reflection of true Irishness, but as the unbound poetical hero, "no hard bright mirror dawdling by the dry sticks of a hedge, but a swimmer, or rather the waves themselves" (Yeats, *Variorum Plays*, 569).

Yeats returns to figures like Cuchulain out of a commitment to a "counter-memorial" function in his work. These are structures that do not, primarily, index the past or its meanings, nor do they provide a point of access to history for a generalized reading public. Rather, their primary function is to confront the viewer/reader and, significantly, the writer precisely with the past's loss. Such structures serve Yeats as an artist for a number of different reasons, none of which have to do with what might be called a personal agenda with respect to Irish history and its meanings. To say this is to say that the poet is primarily a reader rather than a writer of history, and that his strategies of memorialization ought to be understood in that context. Put another way, Yeats writes as he does because he understands the past as an actively resistant text; he wants to preserve its capacity to resist for readers in the present. He also understands that the negotiation of this resistant text is an emotional and psychological undertaking, and not only a rational one. The desire to control the meanings of the past, while it serves, in different ways, the needs of the self for comfort and recognition and of the state for stability, identity, and power in the present, is a doomed effort which will only produce them as monuments in their turn. Recognizing that repetition makes all the difference, Yeats writes so as to extend to himself, and to his readers, the chance of continually returning to history.

CHAPTER 6

Joyce's erotics of memory: temporal anamorphosis *in* Finnegans Wake

> I beg you . . . not to try to understand too much of what I tell you.
> Sigmund Freud
> "The Dream-Work"
> *Introductory Lectures on Psycho-Analysis*

Among the most beguiling passages in *Finnegans Wake* is that in which the text relates its own myth of historical origin. A literary version of the paradigmatic chicken and egg conundrum, the passage recounts the discovery by an "original hen" of a letter which contains the *Wake* in microcosm and, implicitly therefore, the hen and her discovery as well. After some necessary distilling, the passage reads as follows:

> About that original hen. Midwinter . . . was in the offing and Premver a promise of a pril when . . . an iceclad shiverer . . . observed a cold fowl behaviourising strangely on that fatal midden . . . (dump for short) . . . . The bird in the case was Belinda of the Dorans . . . and what she was scratching at the hour of klokking twelve looked for all this zogzag world like a goodish-sized sheet of letterpaper. (Joyce, *FW*, 110.22–111.9)

The exhumed letter, fragments of which the passage goes on to quote, is, like the *Wake* itself, only partially legible; its content (something about a funeral) is ultimately obscure, as are the identities of both its addressee (one "Maggy") and its author (in place of a signature one finds only a tea stain: "affectionate largelooking tache of tch. The stain, and that a teastain . . . marked it off" [Joyce, *FW*, 111.15–18]).

Beyond its status as a narrative conceit, the text's paradoxical invocation of its own indeterminate origin is interesting because it places the *Wake* and our reading of it within a specifically historical frame of reference, a problematic comprised, however irresolvably, of pastness, presence, and the relation between the two. The recovery of the odd text from the refuse pile of history by an archaeologically-minded hen positions the *Wake* itself as a historical object, a sort of letter from the past.

Moreover, the hen's digging and scratching implicitly promises the efficacy of a similar, archaeological approach in deciphering Joyce's novel:
the reader who sifts patiently through the work's great mound of verbal
detritus will, apparently, be rewarded with fragmentary meanings, bits
of narrative, allusions, and references, all of which can then be pieced
together bit by bit to reveal the whole, restored to presence and fully
legible: "a genuine relique of ancient Irish pleasant pottery" (Joyce, *FW*,
III.22–23). The tale of the hen seems, in other words, to presage this
fragmentary text's eventual wholeness as a historical object, and to pre-
scribe a historical methodology of reading as the best possible means of
scratching its surface.

This historical paradigm appears indeed to have served Joyce's readers and commentators well. Many have approached reading the text as a
kind of hunt for buried treasure, mining its obscurity for bits of light and
sense in an attempt to expose the secrets of Joyce's "nonday diary" fully to
the daytime light of reason. At the same time, however, every such reader
has also discovered, sooner or later (and generally both), the *Wake*'s tendency to undermine the promise of completion which fuels such searches,
and indeed, its subversion of the integrity of the historical model itself.
This ambivalence is particularly clear in the text's own rather allusive
approach to historical representation. The *Wake*'s inherent interest in history beckons on every page: references to the Irish past abound (the 1916
Easter Rising, the life and death of Parnell, the Revolution of 1798, the
Potato Famine, and so on), as do allusions to world history more generally
(Napoleon, the Crimean War). One would be hard pressed, nonetheless,
to argue the *Wake*'s value as historiography – if, that is, that term is used
to mean the attempt at a faithful, or even simply coherent, representation of the past. Pursuit of a *Wakean* reference to Padraic Pearse's politics,
for instance, is as likely to lead the reader to a consideration of Humpty
Dumpty or to a rereading of Pascal's *Pensées* as it is to increase his or
her knowledge of events that occurred in Dublin during Easter Week,
1916. It is not that *Finnegans Wake* refuses its reader's attempts to access
its particular way of understanding the past, but that it continually in-
terrupts the progress and indeed the very hermeneutic integrity of that
endeavor. Every topic of seemingly discrete historical interest, precisely
in revealing itself as such, immediately offers a new beginning for other
interests that once seemed wholly unrelated. The attempt to negotiate
a discourse of history in *Finnegans Wake* is, like the attempt to decipher
Joyce's "book of the dark" (Joyce, *FW*, 251.24) itself, an undertaking with
which one is never finished, but only ever "phoenixed."[1]

In light of Joyce's emphasis on the paradoxes inherent in historical discourse's conventional hermeneutic of recovery, it is tempting to argue either that a meaningful engagement with history is entirely lacking in *Finnegans Wake* (that Joyce's text radically "denies" the past), or conversely, that the work's poly-vocal and non-linear style somehow activates a fuller, more dynamic, "ideal" historiography. In fact, the work of knowing the past is neither disabled nor perfected by the narrational and stylistic vagaries of Joyce's text. It would be more honest, as well as more accurate, to acknowledge at the outset that such judgments bear the notion of historical discourse before them like a scientifically calibrated measuring stick, a fixed and value-free benchmark against which the *Wake* can prove either equal or lacking. Our dominant fictions of knowing tend to insist on the objective fixity of the unknown, and on the process of gaining knowledge as a journey toward discrete, stable, and fundamentally passive objectives. That they do so is not a reflection of the truth of such objective fixity, however, but of the fact that the specification of the unknown as a discrete object serves a crucial purpose. The importance of the object's fixity in all forms of human knowing, scientific, literary, historical and otherwise, lies in its ability to determine the coherence of the journey itself. It is only when we are headed toward something already specified, though unknown, that our search, and the unknown's place within it, makes any sense. What the dominance of such fictions reveals, then, is not the reality of the historical truth's objective status but rather the strength of our investment in that objectivity, and in its tautologically insured result: the search disposes the object in such a way that its disposition will preserve and guarantee the integrity of the search.

Measuring the "status" of historical discourse in *Finnegans Wake* is always in this sense a foregone conclusion – it will be "one way or the other" – whereas the experience of reading that discourse itself is something else entirely: in making one's way through this bizarre "grand old historiorum" (Joyce, *FW*, 13.21), one is impressed, distressed, delighted, and disoriented by nothing so much as the volatility of one's "chosen" object. What is often referred to as the "illegibility" of *Finnegans Wake* can be traced to the experience, universal among readers of this text, of having one's object, and therefore one's path toward it, so often "reconstricted" (Joyce, *FW*, 36.9) by the text, and in such "returnally reproductive" (Joyce, *FW*, 298.17) ways: one can only predict in retrospect the text's productive reconstructions and reconstrictions of one's progress through it. Given the depth of most Western readers' schooling in empirical forms of knowing (forms which reveal their affinities with romantic and heroic modes of possession when their surfaces are scratched), such an experience can be profoundly disorienting. While it is necessary to select an initial anchoring point of some kind for one's reading of *Finnegans Wake*, to do so is also to find oneself repeatedly distracted from that goal, "chosen" by the text as it were for entirely different sorts of searches and experiences. The notorious "difficulty" of the *Wake* lies, then, in its destabilizing effect on the familiar roles underwritten by our working economies of knowledge. Instead of acting self-consciously and responsibly within that economy's predictably scripted system of exchange, subject and object are disposed as its effects, mutually determinative positions within a journey that is not so much incoherent as it is multiply coherent.

Put another way, the *Wake* makes its readers aware of precisely what culturally instilled notions about knowledge are designed to mask, namely that subjects and objects are jointly determined, and then only provisionally so, within an economy of desire. In broaching this latter term, I am aware of possibly resituating the matter of reading *Finnegans Wake*'s historical dimension within an even more ambiguous universe. Yet, since my use of this term denotes, first and foremost, a response to the indeterminacy of knowledge's object in *Finnegans Wake*, any attempt to define it at the outset (external to a reading of Joyce) would be disingenuous. To do so would simply be to place the entire question of desire within the continuum of unknown but specifiable objects of discovery – something that can no doubt be done, but is not my principal concern here. It must suffice for the moment to state, returning once again to the theoretical vocabulary employed in Chapter Three above, that unlike knowledge systems, the economy of "desire" is fundamentally one of non-relation.

Knowledge as I have been describing it (and especially historical knowledge when it is constrained by its dominant archaeological paradigm) is, clearly enough, a relational economy shared by stable subjects and objects. I have alluded to the fact that the stability of these members, and the coherence of their relation, is the result of their being specified as such within the economic universe of rational knowing; that their relation is in other words tautologically established. In the simplest terms, the non-relation of desire is not an alternative to this rational economy, but a remotivation of it, a reconsideration of the subject/object dyad highlighting the choices made rather than the facts discerned (the terms of investment and not of truth) in the structuring of their relation. From this "remotivated" point of view, the specification of a particular object of knowledge (a meaning discerned by a reader, for instance) reveals itself as an investment in the stability of subjectivity. Subject and object do not relate one-to-one through structures of perception and representation, but are themselves residual effects of a particular investment of desire. There are no stable positions of relation except those subtracted, as it were, from the economy of desire that motivates their formation.

This economy of non-relation can be clarified somewhat by returning to the terms of historical paradox defined for us in *Finnegans Wake* by the "strange behaviourising" of "that original hen." The objectification of the past as a letter to be deciphered, an artifact to be pieced together and known, is crucially and intimately implicated in the establishment of the subject because, in the perspective of the individual, the past is nothing other than the determining pre-text of identity, the subject's being-in-the-present. The object of historical knowledge projects itself in the present as, essentially, a temporally absent part of the subject. The attempt to know the past is fundamentally an attempt, then, to recover the self; what is lost of the past nonetheless remains linked to identity in the present through an economy of memory.

Memory, in these terms, is more than a faculty by which subjects recollect what happened in the past. It is the vital and processive modality of subjectivity itself, an activity in and through which the rememberer locates his or her own "self," not in the discrete confinement of a single "presence," but across all of history. As a discourse of desire, memory figures the subject in its temporally "stretched-out" modality:

Here, then, awaiting our study, lies man's authentic "being" – stretching the whole length of his past. Man is what has happened to him, what he has done. Other things might have happened to him or have been done by him, but what did in fact happen to him and was done by him, this constitutes a relentless trajectory of experiences that he carries on his back as the vagabond his bundle of all he possesses.[2]

This conception of the subject of memory as "stretched-out" across time and across particular acts of memory-work recalls a similar effect produced in the field of figural representation by the perspectival distortion of anamorphosis. The anamorphotic figure is one drawn or painted in such a way that it appears proportional and "realistic" only when regarded from precisely the right angle. Viewed from any other position, no figure is visible and the "stretched" picture itself appears entirely abstract and non-representational. Historically, the technique of anamorphosis was used in religious painting to counteract the spatial distortion characteristic of the cathedral setting. Because ceilings and walls were both high and curved, it was necessary to paint figures in a distorted fashion, so that from the pews below, such figures appeared proportionally accurate.

Subsequently, the technique came to be exploited precisely for its ability to distort, most notably by Hans Holbein in a famous painting titled "The Ambassadors" (1533). In this painting, a pair of realistically depicted figures confront one another in dialogue. The furniture and objects that surround them are richly symbolic of the enlightenment values of learning, science, exploration, and progress in which these figures' identities are invested. Stretched across the base of the painting, however, is an inexplicable smudge, a greyish stain on the otherwise coherent portrait. Viewed from a direct angle, the smudge is indecipherable. It is only as one turns away from the painting, catching a glimpse of it from an oblique angle that one perceives its anamorphotic effect. The smudge that appeared a moment previously to be a mistake at the center of the painting reveals, from this indirect perspective, a skull. A sort of visual punch line, the skull holds the symbolic meaning of "The Ambassadors" in abeyance until the last possible moment. It is only upon turning to leave – only upon abandoning our reading – that we realize that the depicted figures' ideology of clear-eyed empiricism (an ideology enacted by our own reading of the painting as "realistic") is predicated on a denial of death, the distorted skull in their midst.

In a well-known reading of Holbein's painting, Lacan related the anamorphotic effect in general, and the smudge in the foreground of "The Ambassadors" in particular, to the symbolic function of the phallus in psychoanalytic theory.[3] While Lacan cited the anamorphotic stretching of the skull figure as an echo of phallic tumescence and detumescence, his comparison is not fundamentally based on the stain's rough resemblance to the shape or physical properties of the phallic organ. What is "phallic" about the smudge is rather its symbolic status as a signifier of absence. A figural representation, the anamorphotic skull nonetheless refers by its very presence to its own absence as figure; a painted object, the smudge indexes (without representing) what in the painting is absent. In precisely the same way, the phallus operates within the discourse of the Symbolic as a locus of significance, a point at which the body "ends" for knowledge. Precisely by its presence, however, it refers to the absence which it masks, the "impossible Real" of a body that has not ended.

In precisely these terms, *Finnegans Wake* figures the remembering subject as a body that "has not ended." Meaning in the text is not obscure so much as it is "stretched out" across the whole of the text or, more accurately, across the temporality of our readings of it. In constructing such a text, Joyce proposes what amounts to a radical reconfiguration of the remembering subject. Looking "back," the rememberer confronts a temporal anamorphosis of the self, a body that, disfigured and rendered incoherent by time, is in need of recollection. I will return to this concept of temporal anamorphosis and its implications for reading *Finnegans Wake* below. For now, it is worth pointing out that what the *Wake* critiques, in these terms, is not the traditional disposition of subject and object in historical discourse, but their exclusive confinement to an economy of discrete relation. Historical knowledge exploits the past as the pre-text for identity: it is at once the narrative that makes the knower who he or she is, and it is the excuse, the convenient occasional truth that supports an identity in which that knower is deeply invested.

In announcing his famous dictum, "there is no sexual relation," Jacques Lacan sought to discount the sexual or, even more basically, the genital terms of exchange to which the matter of desire is so often reduced. Following Freud, who, while declaring that "the reality of the unconscious is sexual reality," insisted on an almost infinitely expansive and elastic definition of the sexual, Lacan sought to plumb the workings of desire beyond the boundaries of its received forms: sexual pleasure, biological reproduction, and so on. In Lacan's formulation, the perceived biological coherence of the sexual relation confines the function of desire within an exchange controlled and manipulated by fully integrated subjects and objects: the sexual relation, in other words, traces an economy of knowledge. In precisely the same way, I am suggesting that the traditional hermeneutic of recovery that dominates historical discourse imposes a relational economy of exchange on a situation that might best be described in a modification of our earlier paraphrase of Lacan: it is not only the case that "there is no textual relation," but also that "there is no historical relation." In underscoring history's disposition in a plane not of knowledge but of desire, *Finnegans Wake* neither disables the former model nor celebrates the exclusive "truth" of the latter, but reveals conventional historical discourse as the legible form of its own "returnally reprodictive" economy, its erotics of history.

BRIDGING LETHE, ABRIDGING HISTORY

In its conventional fictions, historical discourse offers itself as a bridge spanning the mutual alienation of the present and the past and measuring history itself in the gap between discrete subjects and objects of knowledge. The "gap" that is bridged by historical knowing is, within this metaphor, that forged by forgetfulness, the human capacity for which was indeed appropriately formalized by classical myth in the familiar image of the river Lethe. For Dante, as we have seen, crossing Lethe entails a total immersion in forgetfulness, rather than a bridging of it, and the poet's placement of Lethe at the border of Paradise aligns it with human life's final immersion in the oblivion of death. By "passing beyond" the river only with his eyes while "staying" with his feet, the pilgrim enables us to see the Lethean liminality as inscribed within the very notion of the historical moment. In the act of "remembering," subjects bypass the Lethean immersion continually, accessing the past, or portions of it, while remaining fixed and stable in the present. In this context, it is possible to see the extent to which historical discourse (and remembering itself) is conventionally understood as subjectivity's way of bridging oblivion: to remember is in effect to cross over the Lethean division without experiencing the passage's effects of forgetfulness. Remembering does not return us to the past itself, but allows us to continue to pass into a future in which (we imagine) the past is still present to us.

That such a bridging constitutes an abridgment of the past, rather than its re-acquisition, is of course acknowledged by even the most empirical approaches to historical discourse. The debates between literary theorists and historians aside, few practicing historians would suggest that their goal is to reproduce the past in its full objective truth. Still, the willingness to impute objective status to the past orients the project of history in general toward empirical systems of knowing. What is abridged by history's confinement to this plane of knowledge is not the reality of the past, but the matter of the knower's investment in that reality.

By troubling this relation, *Finnegans Wake* enables us to see that the pasts we occupy through memory as we pass into the future are in some sense willed pasts, histories which, in their abridged status, serve as pretexts for the identities in which we are deeply invested and which we would preserve at all costs. Here it becomes possible to see that historical representation's capacity both to present the past and to bury it within a single discursive instance has its corollary, at the level of subjective psychology, in a denial inscribed precisely within the conventional notion of memory itself. Remembering in some crucial sense embodies, and indeed carries out, the subject's fundamental denial of its historical passage toward death.

In their introduction to *Understanding Finnegans Wake*, Danis Rose and John O'Hanlon characterize the language of Joyce's last work as a "bridge" spanning "the mutual incomprehension of the conscious and the unconscious mind."⁴ In drawing such a figure, they declare their investment in reading scientifically, uncovering and bringing to light the secrets of the *Wake*. Such a characterization subscribes to a powerful historical scenario (one apparently supported by Joyce's characterization of *Finnegans Wake* as a letter exhumed from the midden heap of history), within which the text, or a reasonable approximation of it, can be ideally recovered in the present.

While it is perhaps one of the better examples of its kind, *Understanding Finnegans Wake* is, like all narrative reductions of Joyce's text, a better measure of its authors' own belief in this idea of history than it is of Joyce's desire to bridge this gap of incomprehension. Joyce seems bent, rather, on honoring the function of incomprehension, on underscoring the vital effect of what is missed, what is absent, what maintains silence, in producing what we call readings. History appears in Joyce's text not in the guise of positive, stable narratives or objectified events, but in the persistence of a constitutive split – a mutual incomprehensibility – between the perceptual power of memory and the radical absence of the past. For Joyce, the fact that history is radically Other to itself does not obviate the necessity of undertaking it; it may be that memory functions as a kind of bridge, although not necessarily one of comprehension and understanding.⁵

Joyce's respect for the role of blindness and incomprehension in constructing the text of history is shared, as we have seen, by Jochen Gerz, whose invisible monument might indeed serve as a rich and compelling introduction to the peculiar workings of historical discourse in *Finnegans Wake* on numerous levels. Just as many readers have judged the *Wake*'s most salient characteristic as literature to be its "illegibility," so "invisibility" seems, paradoxically enough, to be the most visible feature of *2,146 Stones* – a fact that might justify viewers' initial temptation to dismiss the work, as Oliver St. John Gogarty did Joyce's, as a "colossal leg-pull."⁶ Gerz's painstaking construction of a monument designed to remain permanently invisible recalls Joyce's own seventeen years spent willing his own literary monument into its notorious obscurity. Both projects employ textual media to throw the very notion of verbal or visual communication off balance, to strike at language's presumed practical utility as a vehicle for sense and meaning. Moreover, both works invite their viewers to confront their own expectations and motivations as readers, the former by saturating the field of signification, the latter by emptying it. Finally – and perhaps most crucially for the present discussion – both

works appropriate familiar formal paradigms of historical discourse in
order, seemingly, to betray them. While Joyce's text is not a work of
history in the traditional sense, it everywhere employs historiographical
conventions while broaching the questions of representational accuracy,
evidence, and interpretation that are implicit in every act of historical
writing.[7]

At the beginning of its "Nightlessons" episode (Joyce, *FW*, II.ii),
Finnegans Wake casts its own engagement with historical discourse as
a "probapossible prolegomena to ideareal history"; in direct parody of
knowledge's relational fiction, the text exploits the bridge image while
subverting its promise of connection:

Easy, calm your haste! Approach to lead our passage!	
This bridge is upper.	PROBA-
Cross.	POSSIBLE
Thus come to castle.	PROLEGO-
Knock.	MENA TO
A password, thanks.	IDEAREAL
Yes, pearse.	HISTORY.
Well, all be dumbed!	
O really?	

(Joyce, *FW*, 262.1–10; R1)

This discourse of passage does not offer a way to bridge Lethe without
abridging history. Instead, it emphasizes the convergence of denial and
affirmation in every effort to measure the gap between what, in Stephen
Dedalus's words, is "fabled by the daughters of memory" and what "was
in some way if not as memory fabled it" (Joyce, *Ulysses*, 2.7–8). The
principal mechanism by which this "bridge" to the "ideareal" past subverts the historical relation is an emphasis on the double significance of
the term "relation" itself, first as "telling" or "communication," and second as descriptive of the spatial disposition of subject and object. In this
passage the expected textual bridge to the past dissolves into what can
only be called an act of successful miscommunication, shared by subject
positions that are both internally unstable and mutually interchangeable.

Presented as a dialogue, the passage fails to deliver on any promise
of connection the reader may have inferred, instead emphasizing the
tenuousness of the relation itself: it is entirely unclear which interlocutor
is asking for the password and which is providing it, which is crossing
the bridge and which prohibited from crossing, which "yes, please"-
ing and which "thank you"-ing. The rhetoric of authoritative invitation
and assured passage into the seamless realm of "ideareal history" is first

thwarted by the fact that the means of communication, a drawbridge, appears to be up ("This bridge is upper"), then by the discovery, upon knocking at the castle door, that a password is apparently required for entry ("A password, thanks"). The problem here is not simply that the password is unknown. It is also that it is impossible to tell precisely who does not know it (and who does). The inversion of please ("pearse") and "thanks" renders unclear whether we as readers need the password or are being asked to supply it; meanwhile, the question as to whether either way the password will effectively pierce ("pearse") the silence of failed communication becomes moot, or at least mute ("all be dumbed!"). Finally, speaking mouth and listening ear are collapsed into a verbal identity ("O really?" yields both "orally," and *oreille* [Fr. ear]), and readers and interlocutors alike are left both dumb and dumbfounded at the whole situation.

The opening of "Nightlessons" thus figures the historical relation of discursive bridging and abridgment as an absence of relation in at least two senses: on the one hand, the passage depicts a failure of communication (relation as "telling"), and on the other, it presents subjective and objective positions which utterly refuse to remain discrete, separate, and stable (relation as "spatial disposition"). Joyce's subversion of the bridge of historical discourse here recalls his similar treatment of history in the "Nestor" episode of *Ulysses*. Discussing the battle of Asculum in 279 BC, Stephen Dedalus addresses his students concerning the battle's victorious general:

—You, Armstrong, Stephen said. What was the end of Pyrrhus?
—End of Pyrrhus, sir?
—I know, sir. Ask me, sir, Comyn said.
— Wait. You, Armstrong. Do you know anything about Pyrrhus?
   A bag of figrolls lay snugly in Armstrong's satchel. He curled them between his palms at whiles and swallowed them softly. Crumbs adhered to the tissue of his lips. A sweetened boy's breath. Welloff people, proud that their eldest son was in the navy. Vico road, Dalkey.
—Pyrrhus, sir? Pyrrhus, a pier.
   All laughed. Mirthless high malicious laughter. Armstrong looked round at his classmates, silly glee in profile. In a moment they will laugh more loudly, aware of my lack of rule and of the fees their papas pay. (Joyce, *Ulysses*, 2.18–29)

Stephen, trying in his capacity as history teacher to convey knowledge of the past, receives instead Armstrong's answer, an extreme example of historical discourse's ability to abridge the past. Asked to supply the details of Pyrrhus's end, Armstrong does so with admirable but unwitting economy by negative demonstration: he cuts off "Pyrrhus"'s end, leaving "Pyrrhus, a pier." The crumbs of fig adhering to Armstrong's lips and the details of his background ("Welloff people . . . Vico Road, Dalkey") bespeak the childishness and privileged laziness that are evident in this pun: Armstrong is not playing creatively with language, he is simply trying to evade both the question and the immediate consequences of his not knowing the answer. Armstrong's version of "historical discourse" would deny the past absolutely; his answer represents an unethical abandonment not only of the objective past, but of the entire economy of "recovery" (in both senses) which constitutes the historical.

While Armstrong is not even dimly aware of what he has done, Stephen understands the full implications of his student's (and his own) necessary detour to the past through language:

—Tell me now, Stephen said, poking the boy's shoulder with the book, what is a pier.
—A pier, sir, Armstrong said. A thing out in the water. A kind of a bridge. Kingstown pier, sir.
Some laughed again: mirthless but with meaning. Two in the back bench whispered. Yes. They knew: had never learned nor ever been innocent. All. With envy he watched their faces: Edith, Ethel, Gerty, Lily. Their likes: their breaths, too, sweetened with tea and jam, their bracelets tittering in the struggle.
—Kingstown pier, Stephen said. Yes, a disappointed bridge. (Joyce, *Ulysses*, 2.30–39)

Incongruous as the image of a disappointed Kingstown pier may seem in a discussion of Tarentine history, this passage represents for Stephen – and for the reader – a rearrival at the scene with which the novel began. It was Kingstown pier that sliced across Stephen's field of vision as, earlier on this morning, he gazed out from the parapet of the Martello tower to the ocean beyond. At that moment, with Buck Mulligan's aves to "our great sweet mother" the sea (Joyce, *Ulysses*, 1.77; 80) sounding in his ears, Stephen had brooded on his mother's recent death and the sea-like bowl of "green sluggish bile" she had vomited up before her death. A kind of return of the Real, the view from the tower takes on the complexion of Stephen's innermost thoughts, and suggests a convergence of subjective and objective experience that might be captured in the homophony (which Stephen's Francophone ear would surely appreciate) between the French *mer* [sea] and *mère* [mother]. Here in the classroom, the word "pier" suddenly "answers" Stephen's preoccupation again, returning him to the seascape he saw from the Martello tower, and adding to its maternal overtones those of the French "*père*," "father." For Stephen, in other words, the discussion of objective historical knowledge leads, inevitably, to the matter of his relation to his own historical others, his parents. Stephen's response to Armstrong shows that what is abridged by the latter's answer is not only the objective facts of the battle of Asculum, but our investments in particular pasts as parenting particular identities in us. For Stephen, then, Armstrong's mention of Kingstown pier figures the eruption of the question of subjective identity within that of objective history.[8]

The exchange between Stephen and Armstrong also explains why, in the passage from *Finnegans Wake* cited above, the parental figures of HCE and ALP stand guard at the beginning of every reader's bridging and abridging passage through the text: "**E**asy, **c**alm your **h**aste! **A**pproach to **l**ead our **p**assage!" The ability to access the past (the task of historical discourse) is associated here with the parental figures who are generative of the self; the self is an expression of historical non-relation to the extent that it is an abridged version of the parents. The question about an objective (and objectively distant) past is inseparable from – in its expression it is indeed flush with – the fact that because the past is the locus of identity's generation, historical discourse returns us to it as the knower's parental pre-text for identity.

Of *Finnegans Wake*'s seventeen chapters, the "Nightlessons" episode (Joyce, *FW*, II.ii) is at once the most easily identified – it is the most unusual, typographically speaking – and, as Joyce himself observed, the most difficult to decipher. Joyce described the chapter as "a reproduction of a schoolboy's (and schoolgirl's) old classbook complete with marginalia by the twins, who change sides at half time, footnotes by the girl (who doesn't), a Euclid diagram, funny drawings etc."[9] In other words, the text plays, in a parodic fashion, upon the conventional appurtenances of scholarly discourse. The outward signs of academic seriousness are present in abundance. A central block of text is surrounded by explanatory notes and marginal clarifications, emendations that promise to guide the wandering reader. Yet the footnotes and marginalia invariably betray the trust readers have come to place in such scholarly apparatus. While they connect with particular words and phrases from the main text, they do not illuminate or comment upon them in any direct way. Inverting a dominant cultural paradigm that would specify learning as problem-solving, the children seem to pick up particular loose ends of the text not to tie them up, but rather to extend them. The result is a discomfiting profusion of readerly questions, not the least of which are those customarily elided in normative economies of learning: Why, we begin to wonder, have we placed our trust in this textual structure in the first place? What does its promise ultimately deliver? As is the case with Jochen Gerz's invisible monument in Saarbrücken, the overall effect of the children's activity is to redirect our attention to the play of expectation and disappointment that we bring as readers to the text. As we read, we begin to notice the rigidity of our own textual paradigms and to question, perhaps for the first time, their efficacy: "**H**ave we **c**herished **e**xpectations? **A**re we for **l**iberty of **p**erusiveness?" (Joyce, *FW*, 614.23–24).

Indeed, the comparison with Gerz's *2,146 Stones* might be expressed in more literal terms. Like the artist and his students who accomplished their furtive work in a space designated as "public," the children of "Nightlessons" enter (discursively) a space of publication, a textual square designated as open to general access by its cultural and political codes. Once there, they turn up that text's blank "stones," its points of illegibility and opacity, in order to inscribe them with meaning. Like the cobblestones in Saarbrücken, however, these inscriptions remain more or less opaque to the general reader. In this way, the children's notes, though legible, serve as an index of the illegibility of "Nightlessons," as well as of *Finnegans Wake* as a whole.

Gerz's monument enacts its burial in order to emphasize the fact that normative textualizations of history in the present also bury, or more precisely "en-grave," the past as a dead body. In "Nightlessons," Joyce figures this burial of an abstract "past" in more concrete, or at least more familiarly human, terms: the dead body of "history" is realized in "Nightlessons" in the figures that represent the children's actual historical Others, their parents. Throughout the chapter, the figures of HCE and ALP remain in the pub downstairs, a grave-like space situated directly *below* the textual square in which the children pursue their own adult-eration by learning. That the children's notes effectively en-grave the historical Others in their midst is evident in the letter which they collectively address to their parents as the episode concludes:

NIGHTLETTER

With our best youlldied greedings to Pep and Memmy and the old folkers below and beyant, wishing them all very merry Incarnations in this land of the livvey and plenty of preprosperousness through their coming new yonks

from
jake, jack and little sousoucie
(the babes that mean too)

(Joyce, *FW*, 308.20–29)

Ultimately, this murder of the parental past is the effect of a scholarly discourse of knowledge, a discourse which, the reader must remember, is here an object of parody. The children's engagement with the body of the text engages normative forms of knowledge in order to derail them and, in the wake of such a derailing, to enact an alternative paradigm, one in which history is textualized as a discourse of desire. In this alternative paradigm, the textual body of history lies inert and seamless in the center of the page. Arrayed around it, the learners and seekers, Shem, Shaun, and Issy, come and go, taking the vital bits and pieces of this body as occasions for acts of verbal flight. The children's activity constitutes those parts of the text which they touch as significant, although without interring the textualized body itself within that significance. Their notes inform us only obliquely of the meaning of the body in their, and our, midst. Their processive knowing maintains the sameness of the body, while carrying out a transforming gesture upon it, a gesture through which the Real body becomes a Symbolic, that is textualized, one.

Put somewhat differently, the children's inscriptions on the textual square which they (and we) read are the residue of a non-relation in both senses: they do not relate – tell – anything, and they do not describe a subject-object relation. To this discursive residue we arrive as readers "too late," and thus find ourselves in a non-relation to this text, our understandings of which are then, in turn, residual accretions of a path that is only legible in retrospect. This retrospection is the crucial site of *Finnegans Wake*'s historical discourse. The text requires that one adopt a historical perspective in order to read it, that one "look back." But this looking back is not a mourning, not a burial, not a knowing commemoration of the past or of what the text ideally once was. It is an erotic non-relation shared by desiring readers and the living ("waking") body of history continually being re-covered in our midst.

What is being enacted in "Nightlessons" is, quite simply, the opposite of the daytime logic of education represented in "Nestor": here the children pursue a scholarship based not on knowledge and its acquisition, but on desire and its vicissitudes. Consequently, what this scholarship "recovers" are not the dead ends and endings of the past, accurate and adequate within the strict requirements of rational knowledge, but associative and contingent connections and disconnections with the Real text of history. This explains why in "Nightlessons," the education in history that the children are engaged in pursuing involves them in a circuitous exchange with the text in front of them. These children's learning – their discovery of the body of the past in their midst, the "paternity of history" so to speak – is a model for the reader's own adult-eration by the text of *Finnegans Wake*.

PYRRHUS, A PIER; PHALLUS, A FALL

The distinctive typography of "Nightlessons" serves to accentuate a reading and learning dynamic that is at work throughout the text of *Finnegans
Wake*. Indeed, in its engagement with historical discourse, the text as
a whole might be fairly characterized as a truly Dedal reformulation
of Stephen's question to Armstrong: in place of "What was the end of
Pyrrhus?" we have "What was the end of Finnegan?" The answer to
this question, "Finnegan fell," is clear enough when cast in terms commensurate with the narrative requirements of historical knowledge: "wan
warning Phill filt tippling full. His howd feeled heavy, his hoddit did shake.
(There was a wall of course in erection) Dimb! he stottered from the latter.
Damb! he was dud" (Joyce, *FW*, 6.7–10). But, of course, as suggested both
by Joyce's title and by the Irish-American ballad whose rhythms are audible in this passage – "Now Tim one mornin' got rather full, / His head
felt heavy, his hands did shake, / So he fell off the ladder and smash'd his
skull, / And his friends took home the corpse to wake" – Finnegan's fall
and his resulting death are anything but unambiguous. As is well known,
"The Ballad of Tim Finnegan's Wake" recounts the humorous story in
which Finnegan's death was precisely not his "end." In the lyrics of the
song, the mourners are drinking and dancing around the stretched-out
body of poor Tim, when a fight breaks out with unforeseen results:

> Thin Mickey Mulvany jist show'd his head,
> When Tim Donavan flung a full quart at him,
> It miss'd him, an' – fallin' on the bed,
> The liquor was spilt on the face of Tim;
> Now the sperrits new life gev the corpse, my joy!
> Tim jump'd like a Trojan from the bed,
> Cryin' whilst he wallop'd aitch girl an' boy –
> "Tare an' ages, yer sowls, d'ye think I'm dead?"[10]

The ballad's punch line, of course, contained within its title pun, is that
the mourning of Finnegan's death, the "wake," becomes literally the
occasion of his own "waking" from the dead.[11]

In Irish and other cultural traditions, the wake is an inherently ambiguous ritual, marking both the preparation of a body for burial and,
at the same time, the moment at which the memory-work of the living
begins in the telling of stories about the deceased. Just as the act of burial
lays to rest a physical body (and thus serves as a final confirmation of
that body's departure from life), so the weaving of history at the wake

lays to rest a life which, once present, is now identified as historically absent, or "past." It is the wake, in other words, that enacts in ritual terms the collapse of remembrance (discursive "recovery" of loss) and burial (discursive "re-covery" of historical "content" – a body) at the center of historical discourse.

What the ballad recounts as the mourners' humorous mistake, Joyce reformulates into an extended meditation on the mourning-work of historical discourse itself and on what happens when the object of historical knowledge refuses to stay dead. Joyce renders historical discourse's investment in the deadness of the past explicit by recasting the brawling mourners of "Tim Finnegan's Wake" as historians and, more specifically, as the authors of the *Annals of Irish History*. Anyone who has read the *Annals* will no doubt be convinced that their authors sought to fulfill their task as historians by weaving a discourse that definitively lays the past (and the reader of it) to rest. For this reason, they are remarkably suited as foils for Joyce's exploration of historical desire. Models of studiousness and pedantry, these "remembores" (Joyce, *FW*, 384.35; 387.17; 388.18; 390.34; 392.11) pursue the answer to the question of Finnegan's end with seriousness bordering on stupor. Revolving around the central historical event of the text, Finnegan's thunderous fall ("bababadalgharaghtakamminarronnkonnbronnton-nerronntuonnthunntrovarrhounawnskawntoohoohoordenenthurnuk!" [Joyce, *FW*, 3.15–17]), their discourse engages such issues as the circumstances leading up to the fall, the question of the deceased's guilt or innocence with respect to the commission of an unspecified crime, his reputation in the community, the precise time and cause of death, and so on. These and related queries resolve themselves, however, into a single, overarching concern about endings, a concern that is reflected in the ballad's rhetorical "Ora, why did ye die?" In the *Wake*, these Four Old Men constitute, collectively, a character whose effort to know the deceased is designed specifically to keep the corpse comfortably in its place.[12] Whenever Finnegan prepares to wake – "Anam muck an dhoul! Did ye drink me doornail?" (Joyce, *FW*, 24.15) – the four historians spring into action:

Now be aisy, good Mr Finnimore, sir. And take your laysure like a god on pension and don't be walking abroad... [L]et your ghost have no grievance. You're better off, sir, where you are... and have all you want, pouch, gloves, flask, bricket, kerchief, ring and amberulla, the whole treasure of the pyre, in the land of souls... And we'll be coming here, the ombre players, to rake your gravel

and bringing you presents, won't we, fenians? . . . There was never a warlord in
Great Erinnes and Brettland, no, nor in all Pike County like you, they say.
No, nor a king nor an ardking, bung king, sung king or hung king . . . Seven
times thereto we salute you! . . . Drop in your tracks, babe! Be not unrested!
The head boddylwatcher of the chempel of Isid, Totumcalmum, saith: I know
thee, metherjar, I know thee, salvation boat. For we have performed upon thee,
thou abramanation, who comest ever without being invoked, whose coming
is unknown, all the things which the company of the precentors and of the
grammarians of Christpatrick's ordered concerning thee in the matter of the
work of thy tombing. Howe of the shipmen, steep wall! (Joyce, *FW*, 24.16–26.24)

This passage is worth quoting at length because it makes clear the
many techniques by which historical discourse keeps the past at bay.
Memory's "discovery" of the objective past proceeds first by persuasion
("You're better off, sir, where you are"); then by flattery ("There was
never a warlord . . . like you"); and finally by an appeal to custom, according to which the one who prepares the body for burial (the "head
boddylwatcher" ["head and body washer"; also "body-watcher," "body-
snatcher," and "bottle-washer"], has decreed the discursive law concerning "the work of [history's] tombing," according to which dead bodies, as
everyone knows, must stay dead. Finnegan's waking (the coming of the
past "without being invoked") offends the order of historical knowledge
("I know thee . . . I know thee"), which is predicated on the deadness of its
object: "For we have performed upon thee . . . all the things . . . ordered
concerning . . . the matter of the work of thy tombing." Even Abraham,
progenitor of nations and embodiment of the past as origin, would be
regarded an abomination ("abramanation") if he were to so disregard
the orders of those whose knowledge is law: historians ("the company of
precentors" [presenters]), "grammarians," and the pillars of the church
in Ireland: Jesus Christ and St. Patrick. The implication here is once
again that the work of memory is invested as much in the past's covering
up as in its recovery; memory discerns its object only to the extent that
it disposes it as a dead body, the object of a "lethal history."

In the figures of the Four Old Men, undertakers as well as historians,
Joyce explicitly frames the effort to keep Finnegan down as the work
of historical discourse. But the *Wake*'s implicit question about the "end
of Finnegan" avails itself of another reading as well, one that is at once
implied in the language of historical knowing and opposed to its claims
to truth-value. Within this alternative reading the "end" of Finnegan
signifies not only the conclusion of his life, but also the physical extrem-
ities, or "ends" of his body:

The great fall of the offwall entailed at such short notice the pftjschute of Finnegan, erse solid man, that the humptyhillhead of humself promptly sends an unquiring one well to the west in quest of his tumptytumtoes: and their up-turnpikepointandplace is at the knock out in the park where oranges have been laid to rust upon the green since devlins first loved livvy. (Joyce, *FW*, 3.18–24)

In this passage, the precipitousness of the fall translates the "end" of Finnegan into bodily terms; the four historians "unquiring" into the matter of narrationally specified origins and endings becomes, literally, an attempt by the "knock[ed] out" Finnegan to locate the "ends" of his body, his "tumptytumtoes" and his "humptyhillhead." History's residuum is not simply a body *tout court*, but a bodily organization of meaning; the historical search for a dead body also "entails" the telling (counting) of toes, feet, hands, face, eyes, ears, and so on. Historical discourse "entails" both the recovery of a body that is mortally ended, and an "unquiring" process of mapping that body's physical ends, the specifiable, nameable parts that make the past over into a body of and for knowledge.[13]

Here the word "fall," given in answer to the question, "What was the end of Finnegan?" turns out to be a verbal truncation very like Armstrong's truncation of the word "Pyrrhus": "Phall if you but will, rise you must" (Joyce, *FW*, 4.15–16). In this version, the fall of Finnegan discovered by historical knowledge as his mortal end is joined verbally to that symbolically privileged end (the "phall," or phallus) around which Finnegan is configured as a body. Knowledge's perception of the moment of death is literally conflated with the constitution of knowledge's object in the form of a body, a body composed of symbolically significant "ends," or organs. What is striking is that this latter "end" figures the body's resistance to its own burial within knowledge. The end of the body is here the locus of its necessary and inevitable rising from the dead ("rise you must"). Within the humorous scenario of Finnegan's rising from the dead, then – his "waking" – a profound subversion of knowledge is at work, a declaration of that body's "returnally reproductive" excessiveness to knowing.

The prominence afforded the phallic term here suggests that this notion of the body as a field of potential and realized "ends" of meaning is a psychoanalytic rather than a biological one. The confusion surrounding the term itself in the history of psychoanalytic theory, while considerable, is ultimately instructive, since it enables us to distinguish on a basic level between the anatomical reality of the male organ and the symbolic meaning with which it is invested. The "phallic" ends of the body do not refer in psychoanalytic theory (nor do they in the present discussion) to actual bodily organs, but to the symbolic values which such "ends" bear in an economy of knowledge. It is the symbolic significance of such ends that allows the object of knowledge to come into its discursive being as a (buried) body; literally, it is these ends that organ-ize the body for knowledge. In this regard, any such "end" that acquires significance through an interpretive act of reading, whether or not it carries the properties typically associated with the male organ, might be considered "phallic."

In defining his concept of "erogenous zones," Freud went some distance toward acknowledging the essential malleability of bodily organs in terms of their symbolic, as opposed to biological, use. For Freud, such a zone was defined as simply any area of the body that could potentially become the receptive site of sexual stimulus. One of the most important results of Lacan's return to Freud was the extension of this notion beyond the sexual to include an explanation of language's role in thus delineating the body as a series of "erotic" zones. In Lacan's reading of Freud, the meaning of the erotic passes well beyond that of the sexual, or even the pleasurable. An "erotic zone" is simply any part of the bodily whole that can be designated, within Symbolic discourse, according to a perceived or actual use, a use for which it seems to be peculiarly made: the nose for smelling, the ear for hearing, and so on. The key factor is that the designation of such organs is held to be the result of knowledge's own limits and prominences rather than those of the natural body.[14]

This extension of Freud's implication is magnified in Lacan's rereading of the notion of the unconscious. While Freud insisted that "the reality of the unconscious is sexual reality" (a definition whose principal terms, "reality," "the unconscious," and "sexual" have all proven themselves susceptible to misreading), Lacan sought to distinguish the unspecifiability of the unconscious through uncompromising reference to what exceeds the symbolic coherence of sexuality, what Lacan called the Real. The unconscious, in as much as it is named, mapped, perceived, imagined, and specified by scientific, linguistic, poetic, or other means, is essentially an entity that coheres within the sphere of discursive intelligibility that Lacan named the Symbolic. On the plane of the Symbolic, the unconscious can exist as a zone of erasure or repression, the contents of which can at least be apprehended in a negative sense as what has not been (but could potentially be) translated. On the plane of the Real, on the other hand, the unconscious is anathema to speech, language, translation, apprehension, or comprehension; it is a zone (in the present description, we are still necessarily operating at the level of the Symbolic) of radical unknowing for which the mind-centered term, "unconscious," is inadequate; the Real of the unconscious exists at the level not of the mind, but of the human soma – a level of being not yet specifiably a body, an individual or even a subject. Freud's notion of an unconscious that expresses itself in a series of relations that the conscious mind understands as sexual is, like all concessions to the demands of rational economies of knowledge, a symptomatic compromise: it both reveals and buries the unconscious by specifying its "reality" as a sexual one.

The body of history in *Finnegans Wake* is certainly discernible in rational terms: it is a body that has been and will be sexually, historically, socially, and politically mapped by the symptomatic processes of readerly understanding to which it is subjected. At the same time, however, in a discursive movement that is flush with the very expression of this body's organization for knowledge, its "ends" elude all structures of Symbolic organization, be they sexual, historical, narrational, or otherwise. One way to visualize this coincidence of the Real and the Symbolic at the level of discourse is to remind oneself of the ways in which bodies themselves, in their very physicality, elude their own specification and organization as such. In addition to their many "parts" and "organs," bodies are of course rife with unmapped and unnamed areas, organizational "in-betweens" which might potentially be designated as zones as important in configuring recognizable bodies as the organs we know more familiarly: the boundaries between, for instance, thumb and forefinger, temple and forehead or, for that matter, tongue and cheek. These are points on the known body for which no linguistic designation exists because the body has not "ended" there for knowledge; at such points, visible on the corporal map (the Symbolic coherence of the body) but indexed there only as connective spaces, there is no end, no burial, and no discovery of meaning. At such points, the body might be said to elude or surpass its own reality, specified in the Symbolic as "sexual reality." It is at such points that the body emerges as an erotic body on the plane of the Real.

The fallen Finnegan's search "in quest of his tumptytumtoes" and "the humptyhillhead of humself" is, fundamentally, a search for the discursive ends and prominences of bodily meaning. This search is continually thwarted by the Real points at which that body is "phoenixed," the points at which it "rises up" to elude or surpass its own reality in the Symbolic. In this way, Finnegan's own quest exactly mirrors that undertaken by the reader of Joyce's text. Here again, the significance of the hen's archae-ological example comes to the fore. Reading *Finnegans Wake* as history text is not about restoring the shards of the past to their proper places in an organized, once and future narrative whole (the "truth"). It is the de-sire for the whole that determines how we as readers piece these shards together. To the question "what was the end of Finnegan," historical knowledge answers definitively, "he fell." *Finnegans Wake*, on the other hand, answers the question of Finnegan's end within a discourse of his-tory that acknowledges its own internal duplicity; in Joyce's "book of Doublends Jined" (Joyce, *FW*, 20.15–16) the double "ends" of history are joined textually, as the beginning and end of the book meet, so that the historical search for sense recovers a body (that of Dublin's giant) that is both upended and appended.

To say that reading engages an erotic, rather than sexual, discursive recovery of the body in *Finnegans Wake* is simply to acknowledge that read-ing discerns a body in Joyce's text "in the broadest way immarginable" (Joyce, *FW*, 4.19). The stretched-out corpse of HCE/Finnegan extends indefinitely toward its ends and endings for reading. As John Bishop has pointed out, Joyce recognized that Freud's psychoanalytic "science" made available a valuable model for such a body, though only in reduced form.[15] The more radical science, from Joyce's point of view, was that of Giambattista Vico, in whose *New Science* the body was apprehended as a field of "making" rather than of knowing.

Much attention has been paid to the cyclical structure of Vico's ideal history, and to Joyce's use of it as a "trellis" on which to structure *Finnegans Wake*. The core of Vico's *New Science*, however, concerns not historical repetition but the "Poetic Wisdom" of the originary, pre-rational ances-tors of the human race. According to Vico's familiar originary myth, the post-diluvial descendants of Noah's sons, Shem, Ham, and Japheth, spawned a race of giants who lived as nomads, wandering an earth devoid of society, cultivation, and culture. As the earth dried out, hot exhalations from its surface reacted with its upper atmosphere to produce lightning and thunder. At this unfamiliar sound from above, the frightened giants were driven into caves, where the domestic roots of social and cultural life began to germinate. What Vico stresses in this tale is the idea that the giants anthropomorphized the source of the thunder which they heard. Specifically, they saw the sky as the body of a powerful God, which came to be named Jupiter (Jove) or Zeus.[16] From that point, every other as-pect of experience was similarly embodied; knowing itself amounted to nothing other than the interment, or symbolization, of experience as a body. Thus, we needn't take Vico literally to believe him: the giants' entry into caves figures humanity's accession to a system of knowing that constitutes itself as both the revelation and burial of objective reality.

A further implication of this tale is that these giants, because they initially lacked the articulations and boundaries of Symbolic discourse, began the process of such knowing from a position, essentially, of bodilessness. Indeed, it is due to their originary lack of such boundaries, their somatic expansiveness, that Vico characterizes them as "giants" in the first place. Vico's point is that these beings lived wholly physically and emotionally, but without discerning their "life" and "activity" as being that of bodies. Rather, their entire experience consisted of making bodies of themselves and their surroundings. Through a proto-language of gesture, onomotopoeia and "song" (Vico's word), the giants produced not understanding of the world around them, but their own bodies as organizational structures: a gesture produced its "hand," looking produced its "eye," and so on. Moreover, Vico's rereadings of classical myths make it clear that such narratives are valuable not as analogical paradigms for our own historical experience, but as examples of this process by which desire creates bodies which can then be known. All of these mythic texts reveal the latent image of a body stretched across the plane of experience: Vico's originary giants made themselves and their world into bodies, and it is that made body that rationality and the economies of the symbolic continually re-examine, re-apportion, and re-organize.

Vico's emphasis on the convergence of experience and making in the lives of these "first poets" (from Greek, ποειυ, "to make") suggests, essentially, a convergence of the Symbolic and the Real at the level of the body. If we can say that sexual reality is an articulation of bodily experience based on knowledge, then we can begin to locate the erotic in Vico's more open-ended notion of experience as a vital re-membering that does not extend out from an existing body, but produces that body – its organ-ization and "ends" – as its own point of origin. Knowing (that is, knowledge in the form of the Symbolic: the "sexual") obeys the relational economy in which subjects and objects are discrete and separate; unknowing (knowledge in the form of the Real: the "erotic") pursues a course only of extension and becoming. In Vico's words, "man becomes all things by *not* understanding them . . . for when man understands, he extends his mind and takes in the things, but when he does not understand, he makes the things out of himself and becomes them by transforming himself into them" (Vico, *New Science*, 130). The core of *The New Science* lies not in the historical reality of humanity's origins in a race of beasts, but in the discovery that human knowing predicates itself on an ongoing experiential production of bodies.

Joyce's chief debt to Vico lies in the latter's formulation not of a principle of cyclical history, but of this erotic principle of human experience. Vico's emphasis on the tendency of human knowing to produce the corporal aspect in its objects can be read (as indeed it has been by prominent Joyce scholars[17]) as an innate tendency to anthropomorphism in human rationality; that would mean knowing is ultimately solipsistic or self-reflective. Everything known then would be nothing but a mimesis of a self already known, and humans would have no capacity to gain any access to anything as other. But Vico's entire undertaking is predicated on specifying the bases for experience prior to, or in the absence of, relational systems such as that of mimesis. At its origin, knowing, within Vico's system, is a poetic process of re-membering bodies; implicitly, therefore, all rational knowing has an erotic aspect, a production rather than a mimicking of experiential organ-izations and configurations. The body is never for Vico the prerequisite to erotic experience, but its result, an arrangement of organs invested by desire.

HIC CORPUS EST: HISTORY'S EROTIC BODY

Finnegans Wake poses the "question of history" as a problem not of memory but of re-membering; not of knowing how the past truthfully occurred but of specifying – creatively, continuously, poetically – "How it ends?" (Joyce, *FW*, 614.19). The body that historical knowledge knows does not exist originarily, objectively as a thing waiting to be discovered. Rather, it emerges suddenly in the midst of an erotic process of making, constituted there as a body to know. The manner of the bodily past's arrival for knowledge in *Finnegans Wake* is continually interruptive, as, for example, it is in a passage that appears immediately prior to "Nightlessons," at the conclusion of Book II, Chapter 1. This is the chapter of "play" in a double sense. In it the novel's principal characters appear as actors in a theatrical play, "The Mime of Mick, Nick and the Maggies" – Shem as "Glugg," Shaun as "Chuff," Issy (or "Miss Butys Pott") as "Izod," and so on – while at the same time these characters play at a series of traditional children's games. The most prominent example of this latter form of play is a game called "Angels and Devils" or "Colors," the rules of which Joyce recorded in a letter to Harriet Shaw Weaver: "The angels, girls, are grouped behind the Angel, Shawn, and the Devil has to come over three times and ask for a colour. If the colour he asks for has been chosen by any girl she has to run and he tries to catch her."[18] As the episode begins to conclude, Shem/Glugg (the "Devil") has just attempted and failed for the third time to guess the color of Izod's/Issy's underwear: "Evidentamcnt he has failed as tiercely as the deuce before for she is wearing none of the three" (Joyce, *FW*, 253.19–20). As the lassies shift about and laugh at Glugg/Shem, darkness rises and suddenly, in the midst of the whirling children, the paternal HCE appears to call them home: "Home all go. Halome" (Joyce, *FW*, 256.11).

HCE's arrival in this context seems to mark a simple and expedient resolution of the narrative by interruption. The children have played long enough it seems, and even though the object of their game has not been achieved (the correct color, "heliotrope," has not been guessed and the Devil has not captured his angel), the chapter too has gone on long enough; night is falling and it is time to end. As presented in the text, however, the relation between the progress of the game and its interruption by what is not only a figure of symbolic authority but a very physical, paternal body is less certain. Indeed, it is difficult to tell whether HCE's sudden arrival ends the game or whether the breakdown of the game itself in some way calls him into sudden, physical presence.

In the words of the text, Shem's failure to guess the correct color is described as "a hole in the ballet trough which the rest fell out" (Joyce, *FW*, 253.20–21). This phrase suggests that Shem's failure to know the correct color has also placed a "hole" in the male/female dance ("ballet") of sexual knowing that is implicit in the playing of the "Colors" game. Additionally, though, this reference to "a hole in the ballad" figures Shem's failure of knowledge explicitly as a moment of forgetting. As Roland McHugh (quoting P. W. Joyce) indicates, "When a person singing a song has to stop because he forgets the next verse, he says (mostly in joke) 'there's a hole in the ballad.'"[19] If the "ballad" in question here, as throughout the novel, is "The Ballad of Tim Finnegan's Wake," and if the narrative activity of mourning which takes place at this wake is a form of memory-work whose principal investment is in burying the body of the past, then this moment of memory's failure, this "hole in the ballad," figures another moment of forgetting (window of opportunity) in which Tim Finnegan himself rises up to speak.

What is at work in the playing of Devils and Angels is, in other words, a form of memory-work, an activity which predicates itself on the existence of a dead, buried body, that of the past in its status as truth. The denial by which the resurrected body appears is a "hole" in memory, necessary so that through it the "rest," a coherent historical narrative, can fall out.

The body of HCE which appears "amongst the brawlmiddle of this village childergarten" (Joyce, *FW*, 253.31–32) is in this sense connected
to Shem/Glugg's failure to guess (his failure to "know"; or, the "hole in
the ballad"). This connection cannot be construed as a straightforward
cause–effect relation, since narrationally the body's arrival is an interruption of the story. The body is rather in some sense the residual effect of
a denial, a moment of forgetting: "Because to explain why the residue is,
was, or will not be, according to the eighth axiom, proceeded with . . . one
must recken with the sudden and gigantesquesque appearance unwith-
standable . . . amongst the brawlmiddle of this village childergarten of
the largely longsuffering laird of Lucanhof" (Joyce, *FW*, 253.21–32).[20]
In other words, in order to understand the narrative residue or "textual
body" that memory posits as "history," it is necessary to account for the
appearance within that narrative of precisely what is excessive to it: the
presence of a living body of the past ("the largely longsuffering laird of
Lucanhof").[21]

    Finnegans Wake thus expresses historical knowledge's constitution of the
past as dead body in the repeated appearance of its protagonist, HCE,
that oddly inert "mounding's mass" (Joyce, *FW*, 8.1) who "cropse" up
(Joyce, *FW*, 55.8 [corpse; crops up]) repeatedly and ubiquitously, "in
various phases of scripture as in various poses of sepulture" (Joyce, *FW*,
254.27–28). Appearing under a variety of names (Humphrey Chimpden Earwicker, Here Comes Everybody, Haveth Childers Everywhere,
Homo Capite Erectus, Haroun Childeric Eggeberth), or simply as the
letters H, C, and E strewn in various acrostic combinations throughout
the text, this character assumes recognizable human dimensions "in the
broadest way immarginable" (Joyce, *FW*, 4.19), sometimes as an "over-
grown babeling" (Joyce, *FW*, 6.31), at others as an innkeeper, and at
still others (perhaps most often), as the corpse stretched out on its bier
at the novel's eponymous wake. Joyce himself cautioned against a too-
localized identification of this character, insisting that "there are, so to
say, no individual people in the book – it is as in a dream, the style gliding
and unreal as is the way in dreams. If one were to speak of a person in
the book, it would have to be of an old man, but even his relationship
to reality is doubtful" (quoted in Bishop, *Joyce's Book of the Dark*, 131).
Yet fifty-odd years of commentary have invested this supine form with
the coherence and status of a "protagonist" and "hero," thus enabling
readers to resolve its fundamental strangeness within the narrow confines
of narrative convention.

John Bishop's *Joyce's Book of the Dark* offers one of the finest readings of this textual body, arguing that if the *Wake* is Joyce's attempt to portray the unrepresentable world present only to the mind while asleep, HCE may reasonably be taken to be the sleeper himself. Within this reading, the *Wake*'s obscurity is rooted in the quotidian, human experience of being "dead to the world," the corpse-like inertia and unconsciousness from which sleepers eventually "wake." The origin of this supremely strange text is, then, a fictional but no less actual and specific human mind: "the sheer density of certain repeated details and concerns," Bishop writes, "allows us to know that [HCE] is a particular, real Dubliner . . . . Our hero seems to be an older Protestant male, of Scandinavian lineage, connected with the pubkeeping business somewhere in the neighborhood of Chapelizod, who has a wife, a daughter, and two sons" (Bishop, *Joyce's Book of the Dark*, 135).

I cite Bishop's well-known reading not to oppose it with an alternative vision of who HCE really is, but to suggest that, precisely because it is a particularly strong and rich reading, it offers a signal example of reading's investment in designating a body, a corpse which it both reveals and buries. Bishop's designation of this body as that of the sleeper situates HCE at the unconscious origin of this text; external to it, his sleeping mind produces it, and himself within it (another chicken and egg) as "HCE." Within this fictional metanarrative of the text's production, HCE has ceased to be a mere typographical cipher and has become human, the subject who acts to produce the text (even if it is only in sleep), and also the object within it, a "hero" that we come to know through reading. Bishop's reading maps a narrative economy of knowledge onto the text, bringing to light within it the presence of a discrete body, and thereby enabling subsequent readings (our readings) to gain direction and coherence. At the same time, Bishop's designation of this body also enacts its burial, laying to rest the question of HCE's identity (he sleeps; he is unconscious; he produces this text . . .) by specifying for us that identity's past as a narrative pre-text to the entire novel.

Bishop's reading is like those that would identify HCE as a Vichean giant; it localizes him as the likeness of a character, through which later readers can then come to understand the text. As strong as such likenesses may be, they effectively deny the experience of reading this textual body itself. In a pair of well-known graphics included in *Joyce's Book of the Dark*, Bishop has collected the textual "ends" of HCE's body, disposing them on the page so as to reveal that body in spatial terms.[22] Bishop's "relief maps" present remarkable graphic depictions of the textual body of HCE at rest, stretched out across the "langscape" (["landscape," "language-scape";] *FW* 595.04) of Dublin and the world. At the same time, they reveal the fact that that body does not exist objectively in the text, but is distilled, gradually, through long and repetitive acts of reading. In this connection, Bishop's "relief maps" are aptly named, since they convey not only the bumps and prominences of HCE's textual body, but also the relief that the less experienced reader feels upon seeing that this body can in fact be mapped – that indeed it has already been mapped – and that it has coherence and meaning. What Bishop's spatial embodiments of HCE's textual figure leave out is precisely the processive dimension of that figure, the capacity for resistance to discursive burial which it maintains in the face of its ongoing engraving by reading.

Bishop's engagement with the text demonstrates in this sense the way reading enacts a monumental gesture, a designation of the body that renders that body both legible (identified) and passively inert (dead or sleeping). Reading becomes a "murder of corpse" (Joyce, *FW*, 254.32: "matter of course"), a showing forth of evidence by logical, narrative means designed to mask the body's incommensurability with knowledge, its Real absence. Restored to their respective contexts in the *Wake* as a whole, the textual "ends" that Bishop has collected, while they do not cease to mark the ends of HCE's textual body, no longer reveal the coherent figure of a protagonist. This stretched-out HCE is at no point construable as being simply a character in the text; nor can "he" be pressed into service as a stable model of how we should organ-ize our own reading of the text. HCE is in this respect, rather, an irreducible, multiple instance of Joyce's text's erotic excessiveness to reading. While it is through its myriad textual instances that the textual quantity, HCE, comes to resolve itself as a discrete, legible body for reading, at the same time it is precisely these same textual instances that mark the insistent illegibility of this body, its resistance to endings, its tendency to wake and "phoenix."

The meaning of HCE/Finnegan's "waking" from the dead is legi-ble as this body's resistance to its own embodiment, its "ending" in an erotic sense. If the body's omnipresence in the text reflects Joyce's deep humanism, his desire to write about a particular, "real" man, that body also emerges only through its designation as such by reading; it appears "imparticular" (both "in particular" and "non-specific") under the name HCE, a name that en-graves it as any number of "imparticular" bodies: that of an aging Protestant publican, Napoleon, Parnell, and all the names in history. *Finnegans Wake* is a historical text because it concerns the disposition (discovery and burial) of a body by reading. Reading the historical text involves recognition of a body that has ended, gathering up the "hides and hints and misses in prints. Till ye finally (though not yet endlike) meet with the acquaintance of mister Typus" (Joyce, *FW*, 20.11–13). While the historical gaze would designate HCE as a body that has died, his disposition in the text is that of a body that is literally endless. HCE is, from the point of view of reading's attempt to locate a body, a body of infinite extension. His is a body that has not ended.

The crucial point to be made here is that the legible body of HCE coincides, verbally and textually, with the illegible one. What reading collects into an organized body of meaningful "ends" remains at the same time an uncollected series of erotic loose "ends" scattered through the text. This discovery that the *Wake*'s legibility is flush with its illegibility recalls once again the gesture of Jochen Gerz, whose invisible monument refuses to deny the necessity of remembering the past while drawing attention to the effective denial implicit in its own, and every, act of recollection. Gerz demonstrates that historical discourse, his own included, grounded in the experience of "lateness," inevitably takes the form of an indicative, memorial gesture, a "here lies the body" which infers the concrete objective status of the past in a double act both of presentation and burial. In precisely the same way, Joyce's text marks the act of burial at work in every critical discovery of an identity, a subject who relates to the objective world in fictive but human terms, beneath the letters HCE: "**H**ic **C**orpus **E**st." While the letters "HCE" designate the name of a hero, inscribed throughout a narrative universe which "he" coherently occupies, they also and at the same time describe the very textual gesture (en-graving) through which reading infers the presence (discovery and burial) of such a body; the hero's incorporation is only ever inferred by a discourse that both buries and re-covers him.

Joyce situates HCE in the text both as a man (Humphrey Chimpden Earwicker) whose body is to be buried, and as the discursive means (Hic Corpus Est) by which the historical gaze designates this body as already buried (dead, past). The body itself, nonetheless, continuously and inconveniently refuses to stay dead. It is precisely within historical discourse's designation of this body, therefore, that Joyce situates the past's resistance to being thus disposed as the dead, passive object of knowledge (HCE/Finnegan's "Tare an' ages, yer sowls, d'ye think I'm dead?"). The body that historical discourse "recovers," so far from being contained by its gaze as a finite, discrete, recognizable body, is one that resists such containment, a body of infinite extension, that is disposed as a body only "in the broadest way immarginable" (Joyce, *FW*, 4.19). The archaeological process by which readers piece together HCE's human character deserves reconsideration then: the effect of our readings in the most immediate sense, HCE's bodily presence is itself the processive path by which we maintain the coherence of our own memorial searches for a body of truth which (we imagine) the text promises. It is not Joyce's text in that sense that is monumental, but our interactions with it: it is reading that potentially en-graves the body of HCE/Finnegan within the text.

All of this implies that history, embodied in the figural stretched-out corpse of HCE, is not read so much as produced by readers of *Finnegans Wake*. This making of history differs in one crucial respect from that model, implicit in the tale of "that original hen" with which we began, by which knowledge re-makes the past as knowledge's original object. Understanding history is, according to this former model, simply a matter of finding the shards of what "has happened," and then piecing them together to reproduce a serviceable approximation of that original object. This is the method exemplified by Bishop's relief maps, a method which would reproduce the past like some great, colossal Humpty Dumpty, enlisting an army of readers ("all the king's horses and all the king's men") to recoup the effects of HCE/Finnegan's fall.

But the making of the historical body in *Finnegans Wake* is rather more like that process of "poetic making" invoked by Vico in *The New Science*. One of the powerful implications of Vico's argument is precisely that there is no original object for historical knowledge to reproduce; Vico's mythic giants possess no originary bodies from which they begin thinking rationally, but only those bodies that come into being as the residue of the process of their erotic (or in Vico's terms, "poetic") experience: it is indeed because this process produces their bodies "in the broadest way immarginable" that they appear in the myth as giants. The production of the body of history in *Finnegans Wake* suggests that while HCE, a Humpty Dumpty figure, is himself unrecoupable, his fall is the occasion of the making of Humpty Dumpty in another, bodily sense: "*Mon foie*, you wish to ave some homelette, yes, lady! Good, mein leber! Your hegg he must break himself. See, I crack, so, he sit in the poele, umbedimbt!" (Joyce, *FW*, 59.30–32). As Joyce's pun implies, the breaking of the egg makes possible the production not only of a homey breakfast omelette (home-lette), but also of a little man (*homme*-lette) who is, in the present terms, an erotic configuration of ends and endings: a body of history.

These two tales, the one focused on the hen's archaeological reconstitution of the past, the other on the egg's unrecoupable fall, sketch two approaches (both equally supported by the text because, in fact, they coincide verbally) available to the reader of the Wakean body of history. History greets us in this text unexpectedly, like a body suddenly appearing in our midst (whether dead or only sleeping we cannot be certain) and poses the question whether we will account for its appearance there as a thing recovered by reading, or as a thing produced in its original specificity by reading. If the former, we can follow Joyce's fable of "that original hen" toward a remotivation of history's archaeological paradigm, arriving, finally and ideally, at a reconstruction of the letter, of Humpty Dumpty's shell, and of the body of the past itself. If the latter, our reading will necessarily make, rather than remake the text of history, producing a textual body which indexes the Real loss of the past rather than commemorating it. The body of history in this case resembles not the shards of Humpty's shell, but the viscous, unrecoupable, liquid content of the broken egg itself: the historical subject in *Finnegans Wake* is above all a potential body, not one that is "split" (to borrow psychoanalytic parlance), but one that is *spilt* in a temporal sense, its "ends" extending "in the broadest way immarginable" across the ongoing history of its textualization by reading. The identity of HCE is not then localizable within a particular historical moment, a unitary space of reading, but spills itself across the space of a history that is mapped continually by readerly economies of knowledge.

The coincidence of the legible and the illegible in Joyce's text returns us, then, to the figure of the "stretched-out" or "spilt" anamorphotic subject of memory mentioned earlier.[23] In presenting the figure of HCE as both legible and illegible, Joyce reveals a textual, and therefore necessarily temporal, anamorphosis at work within historical discourse. Like anamorphotic distortion in the visual sphere, textual illegibility can be effectively exploited only when an ideology of visual perception is already in place: we are unable to see Holbein's skull, for example, precisely because we already "know how" to see. In a similar way, Joyce plays, in presenting the past, on the adeptness of the contemporary historical gaze, the ability of readers to discern the object of reading as a discrete, whole, proportional, and "ended" body. Like Holbein's skull, Joyce's historical body betrays readerly know-how, exceeding the gaze itself and confronting it at every point with its own incommensurability with knowledge.

What sets Joyce's textual anamorphosis apart from its figural cousin is that it effects its stretching out of representation not on the spatial plane but on the temporal one. HCE is not only stretched out across the spatial "langscape" of Joyce's text, but also across that text's history, a history charted by repetitious acts of reading. To the extent that HCE fills out the space of a discrete, organized body in the text, "he" is the monumental effect of our readerly processes of recovery, a stable, discrete, legible organ-ized, and en-graved body that results from the system of exchanges that take place between readers and the text over time. The body of HCE in *Finnegans Wake*, the legible/illegible body of a stretched-out corpse, is the result of a representation of the past in which the temporal extension of the body is deemphasized in order to reveal that body as a proportional, whole object. The temporally stretched-out figure is, unlike the spatially stretched-out one, never available as a figure to a single instance of reading; its meaningful "ends" are never collected into a single space of presence, and thus resist coalescing around a single, identified spatial figure. What is striking, however, is that these two HCEs, the spatial figure and the temporally stretched-out corpse, literally coincide at the immediate level of the words of the text. The legible body thus coincides with its own illegibility; the waking of the past as an erotic body incommensurate with knowledge occurs within the very moment of its constitution and burial by reading.

In historical terms, then, we might speak here of the "spilt" subject in *Finnegans Wake* as an effect of temporal anamorphosis. Specifying the body in the text in these terms, it is easy to see that its perception requires an erotic, rather than simply a rational basis for historical knowledge. The relational basis for historical knowing is not dissolved or disabled, but shown to be only the legible, resolved form of identity's stretching out across the exchanges of rational, narrational economies of knowing over time. Looking askance at this system of exchanges, emphasizing particular "ends" while eliding others, produces the image of a discrete, fixed bodily figure (a memorial "fixion") as the effect of a kind of temporal anamorphosis. The presence of this body in the text is the result of a kind of foreshortening, an anamorphotic effect of our readerly investments in identity.

Here the designation of the body by historical discourse, **h**ic **c**orpus **e**st, becomes an endlessly negotiable reconfiguration and re-organization: **h**istoriae **c**orpus **e**roticus, history's erotic body. To look "back," in an erotic sense, at a past that ultimately reflects one's identity as a present subject of history is to see the extension of that identity across time; the historical subject is never available to such a gaze as a discrete, bounded subject, but only as an unrecoupable spill. At the same time, it can be recouped and re-organ-ized "for the present," which is to say for consciousness and knowledge. In HCE, Joyce reveals the "spilt" rather than "split" subject of history; doing so, he suggests the ways in which identity, when it knows/buries the past as its own pre-text, is the result of a temporal anamorphosis, an illusion not only of wholeness but of stasis belied by the fact that we are constantly reorganizing our selves as histor- ical subjects. The historical body is not only a dead but an erotic body, one that we read in order to frame ourselves as self-identical, and also one that is configured and reconfigured by desire. Engaged as a discourse of desire in this way, history ceases to be a funeral and becomes instead, in the parlance of *Finnegans Wake*, a "funferal" (Joyce, *FW*, 120.10). At the "fun-for-all" of memory's wake, those who live to re-member are not identities who mourn (know and not-know; remember and forget), but desirers who joyfully recover, organ-izing and re-organ-izing that stretched-out body they continuously discover in their wake.

The ends of memory and the ex-sistence of Ireland

> What has gone? How it ends? Begin to forget it. It will remember itself from every sides, with all gestures, in each our word. Today's truth, tomorrow's trend. Forget, remember!
>
> James Joyce
> *Finnegans Wake*

In this book, as I have sketched the theoretical contours of an "erotics of memory," I have also sought to demonstrate the risks inherent in declaring Ireland a state that might ever be "no longer" what it was. The belief in a progressive historicism, in which the past is paradoxically known and revered precisely so as to be left behind, commits Irish culture to a myopic determinism, a selective perception of the past that results in the perpetual return of its "lethal histories." Such a historicism produces Irishness as a "dead" certainty, compensating the present for history's loss by granting it a stable, commemorative subjectivity. "To capitulate to such historicism," as David Lloyd has argued, "rather than continually opening the historical narrative to undeveloped possibilities, is to accept the reductive logic of domination" (Lloyd, *Anomalous States*, 10).

The erotic discourse of memory that I have described operating in *Finnegans Wake* and in other sites of Irish culture displaces the "ex-" of Fintan O'Toole's "ex-isle" metaphor in an alternative direction, that of Ireland's symptomatic and erotic "ex-sistence" in Lacan's sense. Rather than a condition of perpetual temporal partition, a divide across which the present obsessively confronts a dead past, history is Ireland's modality of ex-sistence, the site of its actual ceaseless unfolding in the field of what Lacan called the Real. The past "in-sists," in these terms, as a kind of symptom through which "Irishness" endlessly negotiates its relationship to that Real, constituting and reconstituting itself continuously. The field of possibilities is here neither reduced in the name of a uniquely Irish discourse of authenticity, nor restricted by the hegemonic demands of a colonialist, Other discourse. In the symptomatic reading of the past,

Ireland becomes an "Island off Britain" that expresses itself "in the broadest way immarginable": Irishness speaks in all languages and discourses, from the insistently local to the authentically ex-centric. Memory in this sense is not Ireland's special anomaly but its "own" discourse of infinite repetition and infinite variation, the erotics of its ex-sistence.

This configuration of Irishness as a series of discursively conditioned possibilities in the temporal register (what Deleuze and Guattari would call "becoming-Irish")[1] does not oppose in a simple binary structure Ireland's constitution through lethal discourses of historical knowing. Indeed, it is within Ireland's lethal histories that its ex-centric discourses of memory speak, and vice versa. In an erotic relation to the past, memory's aim is not to supplant an existing narrative with a more accurate and adequate one; neither is it to specify a preferred, revisionist version of events. In an erotics of memory, Irishness "occurs" (returning to Wilde's term) in the encounter with the past as unexpected eruption, exhibition, spectacle, actuality, attraction; in the rhythmic, material appearances and disappearances of the past as it "occurs" to the present in its memorial imagination.

Yeats's answer to Ireland's crisis of historical imagination was to "recite the past like a poetry lesson" until it acknowledged its rootedness in "the foul rag and bone shop of the heart." In Yeats's re-petitioning of the very monumental images that had rendered the poet a monument in his turn, in his expression of their ex-centric ex-sistence in figures like Crazy Jane, his labor of memory comes to resemble a "blossoming or dancing where / The body is not bruised to pleasure soul, / Nor beauty born out of its own despair, / Nor blear-eyed wisdom out of midnight oil" (Yeats, "Among School Children," 57–60). What Yeats appears intuitively to have understood is that lethal histories are always the products of a process in which forgetting and remembering are equal, positive forces, and that narrative acts of mourning, repeated often enough, are precisely what allow the past to occur to the present for the first time. History, for Yeats, is the responsibility not of the obsessive, controlling, and knowing subject, but of the passionate one: the past is the symptom that – willy nilly – structures the subject's erotic relation to being.

Joyce's response to the same cultural predicament was, in a way that is at once similar and different, not to attempt to awaken Ireland from its lethal histories but, on the contrary, to wake the past itself; that is, both to mourn it and to invite its textual, discursive awakening. Like Yeats, Joyce writes out of an awareness that the necessity of history is not to get the story straight, but to return to it continuously through narrative acts of mourning/morning (waking). Such acts enable a process of memory-work that, while always at some level invested in laying the past to rest, is also the very mechanism that releases the present from a too insistent history by giving the past its opportunity to "occur," suddenly, eruptively, and interruptively in the present.

Finnegans Wake, in these terms, is nothing other than Ireland's ex-sistent history. Joyce's text is "[o]ur wholemole millwheeling vicociclometer" (Joyce, *FW*, 614.27), a set of continuously repeating narratives in which the past occurs, over and over to us, the text's readers in the present: "We Irish." The act of reading *Finneagans Wake* is in its turn a process not of deciphering so much as of memory-work, through which the present tries to get the story straight, to give the past its adequate and accurate telling, but encounters in narrative's midst its own apprehensions of history. Reading the *Wake* is thus "symptomatic" in that it invites and necessitates two processes that appear opposed in their aims but are mutually implicated and indeed, complementary. The attempt to bestow narrative clarity on the *Wake*, to "understand" it, is precisely what allows the text to interrupt narrative, to break through memorial acts of knowing and to appear as spectacle, to "occur." At the same time, it is these very interruptions that prompt the continuous efforts of recovery and re-covery that make sense of the *Wake*.

Reading Yeats and Joyce, "We Irish" encounter Ireland's lethal histories not as stories to be disposed of, hidden or forgotten, but as spectacles told repeatedly, and with an end in sight. The "endnessnessessity" (Joyce, *FW*, 613.27) of history finds its purpose in an erotics of memory:

What has gone? How it ends? . . . [F]or the verypetpurpose of subsequent re-combination so that the heroticisms, catastrophes and eccentricities transmitted by the ancient legacy of the past, type by tope, letter from litter, word at ward, with sendence of sundance . . . all, anastomosically assimilated and preteriden-tified paraidiotically . . . may be there for you. (Joyce, *FW*, 614.19–615.8)

An erotics of memory is what brings Ireland continuously "into its own" in an endless play of connection to and disconnection from its exiled (and ex-isled) self. The human and profoundly ex-centric work of memory is what allows that which is excessive to narrative acts of mourning, the living body of the past, to sit up at the wake and announce its presence in the unfolding, erotic ex-sistence of Ireland.

Notes

INTRODUCTION

1 Fintan O'Toole, *The Ex-Isle of Erin* (Dublin: New Island Books, 1997), 11.
2 As a backdrop to the continuing struggles currently dogging the North's frag-
ile coalition government, Ireland's economic success seems only to highlight
the myriad political failures with which the country's past – and its present –
are riddled. The cease-fire that followed 1998's historic Good Friday Accords
may yet prove itself the historical anchor for a more permanent peace. For
now, though, it is worth noting that, in practice, the actuality of economic
opportunity has done little to soften old political identifications or to lessen
the prospects for violent conflict. Indeed, as I write these very words on
July 12, 2001, Catholic and Protestant factions in the North are marking the
memory of William of Orange's victory at the 1690 Battle of the Boyne with
the riots and violence that have become as traditional as marching season
itself.
3 E. Holt, *Protest under Arms: The Irish Troubles, 1916–23* (London: 1960), 258;
quoted in Oliver MacDonagh, *States of Mind: A Study of Anglo-Irish Conflict,
1780–1980* (London: George Allen & Unwin, 1983), 1.
4 Brian Friel, *Translations* (New York: Samuel French, Inc., 1981), 81.
5 David Lloyd, *Anomalous States: Irish Writing and the Post-Colonial Moment* (Dublin:
Lilliput Press, 1993), 10.
6 Foster has further suggested that the persistence of certain narrative strategies
in the telling of Irish history recalls Vladimir Propp's conclusions regarding
the structural elements of myth in *The Morphology of the Folk-tale*. See Roy
Foster, " 'The lovely magic of its dawn': Reading Irish History as a Story,"
Times Literary Supplement, 16 December 1994, 4–6. For other useful consid-
erations of Irish modernity and historical imagination, see Seamus Deane,
Strange Country: Modernity and Nationhood in Irish Writing since 1790 (Oxford:
Clarendon Press, 1997); Declan Kiberd, *Inventing Ireland* (Cambridge, MA:
Harvard University Press, 1996); and David Lloyd, *Ireland after History*
(Notre Dame, IN: University of Notre Dame Press, 1999).
7 Indeed, the partitioning of Ireland in 1921–22 may be taken as a kind of
concrete marker of the compromised nature of Ireland's effort to reconfigure
its knowledge of its past during this period. See especially Paul Bew, *Conflict*

and Conciliation in Ireland, 1898–1910: Parnellites and Radical Agrarians (New York: Oxford University Press, 1987), and F. S. L. Lyons, *Charles Stewart Parnell* (New York: Oxford University Press, 1977).

8 T. S. Eliot, "*Ulysses*, Order, and Myth," in *Selected Prose of T. S. Eliot*, ed. Frank Kermode (New York: Harcourt Brace Jovanovich, Publishers, 1975), 177.

9 See, for example, W. K. Wimsatt and Monroe C. Beardsley, "The Intentional Fallacy" (1946) and "The Affective Fallacy" (1949), in *Critical Theory Since Plato*, ed. Hazard Adams (New York: Harcourt Brace Jovanovich, Publishers, 1971), 1014–31; also, in the same volume, R. P. Blackmur, "A Critic's Job of Work" (1935), 891–904.

10 See Irving Howe, "The Idea of the Modern," in *Literary Modernism* (Greenwich, CT: Fawcett Publications, Inc., 1967), 15. In the same volume, see Lionel Trilling, "On the Modern Element in Modern Literature," 59–82, and David Jones, "Past and Present," 109–13.

11 Paul de Man, "Literary History and Literary Modernity," in *Blindness and Insight: Essays in the Rhetoric of Contemporary Criticism*, 2nd edn., Theory and History of Literature, vol. 7 (Minneapolis: University of Minnesota Press, 1983), 148. See also in the same volume, "The Rhetoric of Temporality," 187–228. Frank Lentricchia's *After the New Criticism* displaces modernism's disconnection from the past onto criticism itself, arguing that post-structuralism, in its American interpretations, is what denies history. See *After the New Criticism* (Chicago: University of Chicago Press, 1980).

12 For an interesting perspective on criticism's continued implication in modernism in the mid-1990s, see Steven Helming, "Modernism Now," in *The Sewanee Review* 102, no. 2 (spring 1994): 291–309.

13 The history of the critique of modernism is a field as rich, varied, and complex as it is vast. I do not mean to imply comprehensive treatment of that history through such a crude sketch, but merely to register a sameness of tone that unites otherwise broadly diverse theories and perspectives. See, for instance, Frank Kermode, *The Sense of an Ending* (New York: Oxford University Press, 1967); Charles Ferrall, *Modernist Writing and Reactionary Politics* (Cambridge: Cambridge University Press, 2001); Leon Surette, "Modernism, Postmodernism, Fascism, and Historicism," in *University of Toronto Quarterly* 60, no. 4 (summer 1991): 476–92; Paul Morrison, *The Poetics of Fascism: Ezra Pound, T. S. Eliot, Paul de Man* (New York: Oxford University Press, 1996). See also Michael Tratner, *Modernism and Mass Politics: Joyce, Woolf, Eliot, Yeats* (Stanford: Stanford University Press, 1995) and Jonathan Allison (ed.), *Yeat's Political Identities: Selected Essays* (Ann Arbor: The University of Michigan Press, 1996).

14 T. S. Eliot, "Tradition and the Individual Talent," in *The Sacred Wood: Essays on Poetry and Criticism* (New York: Routledge, 1989), 49.

15 See Marjorie Perloff's essay on "Modernist Studies," in *Redrawing the Boundaries: The Transformation of English and American Literary Studies*, ed. Stephen Greenblatt and Giles Gunn (New York: The Modern Language Association of America, 1992), 154–78.

16 In addition to David Lloyd's *Anomalous States*, cited above, see his discussion of "postcolonial" as a problematic term in "Regarding Ireland in a Postcolonial Frame," *Ireland after History*, 37–52). Also Terry Eagleton et al., *Nationalism, Colonialism and Literature* (Minneapolis: University of Minnesota Press, 1990) and David Bennett (ed.), *Multicultural States: Rethinking Difference and Identity* (New York: Routledge, 1998).

17 See Vincent J. Cheng, "Of Canons, Colonies, and Critics: The Ethics and Politics of Postcolonial Joyce Studies" in *Re: Joyce: Text, Culture, Politics*, ed. John Brannigan et al. (New York: St. Martin's Press, 1998), 224–45; and by the same author, *Joyce, Race, and Empire* (Cambridge; New York: Cambridge University Press, 1995). See also Judith Roof and Robyn Wiegman (eds.), *Who Can Speak? Authority and Critical Identity* (Urbana: University of Illinois Press, 1995); Luke Gibbons, *Transformations in Irish Culture*, Critical Conditions: Field Day Essays (Notre Dame, IN: University of Notre Dame Press, 1996); Emer Nolan, *James Joyce and Nationalism* (New York: Routledge, 1995); Enda Duffy, *The Subaltern Ulysses* (Minneapolis: University of Minnesota Press, 1994).

18 For a more frankly hostile view toward post-colonial approaches to modern Irish culture (one I do not share), see Denis Donoghue, "Fears for Irish Studies in an Age of Identity Politics," *The Chronical of Higher Education*, 21 November 1997, B4–B5.

19 Joep Leerssen has done much to complicate the standard post-colonial picture of Irish self-fashioning by broaching the question of an insistent past in relation to traditions of both romanticism and nationalism. For that, and for his exposition of the "pre-history of Irish national thought" before and after the Union of 1800, my own exploration of Irish memory in the modern period is indebted. See Joseph Th. Leerssen, *Mere Irish & Fíor-Ghael: Studies in the idea of Irish nationality, its development and literary expression prior to the nineteenth century*, Utrecht Publications in General and Comparative Literature, vol. 22 (Amsterdam/Philadelphia: John Benjamins Publishing Company, 1986) and *Remembrance and Imagination: Patterns in the Historical and Literary Representation of Ireland in the Nineteenth Century*, Critical Conditions: Field Day Monographs (Cork: Cork University Press, 1996), esp. 37–38. See also the essays contained in Joep Leerssen, et al. (eds.), *Forging in the Smithy: National Identity and Representation in Anglo-Irish Literary History*, The Literature of Politics, the Politics of Literature: Proceedings of the Leiden IASAIL Conference, vol. 1 (Amsterdam/Atlanta, GA: Editions Rodopi B. V., 1995).

20 Indeed, Joep Leersen has argued that the intractability of the "Irish problem" has been rooted, through centuries, in "a confusion in English policy as to whether the Irish situation should be confronted according to the modality of external or internal affairs." See Joep Leersen, "Law and Border (How and where we draw the line)," in *Irish Review* 24 (1999), 1–8. Central to this confusion is a pervasive doubt as to what is internal and external to Ireland itself. In *Remembrance and Imagination*, Leerssen traces the nineteenth-century historical and cultural underpinnings of an Ireland continually figured as strange, wild, alien, and so on. Such a tradition grounds a

historical tendency in Irish writing itself toward what Leerssen calls "auto-exoticism": "a mode of seeing, presenting and representing oneself in one's otherness" (*Remembrance and Imagination*, 37–38).

21 James Joyce, "The Dead," in *Dubliners* (New York: Viking, 1976), 189.

22 Oscar Wilde, "The Soul of Man Under Socialism," in *The Complete Works of Oscar Wilde* (New York: Harper and Row, Publishers, 1989), 1087.

23 See James Joyce, *Finnegans Wake* (New York: Viking Penguin, 1976 [1939]), 120.10; hereafter, passages from *Finnegans Wake* will be cited in the text in the form "Joyce, *FW*, [page number].[line number]."

1 LETHAL HISTORIES: MEMORY-WORK AND THE TEXT OF THE PAST

1 See Michael Gibson, "A Clandestine Warning of Grim History," in *The International Herald Tribune*, 2 December 1991, n.p.

2 The vote was won despite the walkout of the entire Christian Democratic delegation – about one-third of the total representation (see Gibson, "A Clandestine Warning").

3 In fact, the title is somewhat dynamic, since as more cemeteries are discovered, their names are added to the memorial. At present, the square contains approximately 2,160 inscribed stones.

4 James Joyce, *Ulysses*, ed. Hans Walter Gabler (New York: Random House, 1986), 3.1–4; hereafter, passages from *Ulysses* will be cited in the text in the form "Joyce, *Ulysses*, [episode number].[line number]."

5 In relating the narrative of the monument's construction, I have, of course, effectively repeated this textualizing gesture – a gesture repeated with greater economy by the Saarbrücken monument's plaque – in which an image that cannot be seen is nonetheless verbally rendered: a paradoxical ekphrasis of the invisible.

6 James E. Young, *The Texture of Memory: Holocaust Memorials and Meaning* (New Haven: Yale University Press, 1993).

7 *The Collected Poems of W. B. Yeats*, ed. Richard J. Finneran (New York: Collier Books, Macmillan Publishing Company, 1989), 347.31–32; all subsequent citations of Yeats's poetry are from this edition.

8 The planning and construction of the project, as Gerz pointed out, had little to do with art: "We were confronted with questions which had nothing to do with art. I am, in fact, frequently faced with these sorts of questions. We had no need for the studio. After a month, the school inquired what it was we were constructing and they were surprised when they discovered we were using the fax and the telephone, instead of wood or photographs." See Jacqueline Lichtenstein's and Gerard Wajeman's interview with Gerz in *Art Press* 179 (April, 1993), E4.

9 Such a replacement is not, however, unthinkable in the field of memorialization. Phonography, as Leopold Bloom muses in Glasnevin cemetery, offers an eminently practical, if overlooked, alternative to the customary inscriptions

on obelisks and granite slabs: "Besides how could you remember everybody? Eyes, walk, voice. Well, the voice, yes: gramophone. Have a gramophone in every grave or keep it in the house. After dinner on a Sunday. Put on poor old great-grandfather. Kraahraark! Hellohellohello amawfully glad kraark awfullygladaseeagain hellohello amawf krthsth. Remind you of the voice like the photograph reminds you of the face." See Joyce, *Ulysses*, 6.962–67.

10 See Lichtenstein, "Jochen Gerz," E3: "There will be nothing left one day, and this needs to be discussed openly. This necessity to talk is the souce [*sic*] of everything. We exist in time, so the trick generally consists in plucking the work of art from the ravages of time and lending it the durability that we mortals lack. I, however, would like to subject my work to the conditions of time, and confront myself with the lack, the absence of the work. In other words, I would like to take on the role of the work of art for myself, and be the element of durability. My aim has been to reverse the relationship between spectator and objects, cult objects, that is, or ones which arouse either fascination or rejection."

11 Young includes in his treatment of the monument photographs of its in-scribed surface, as well as a series of time-lapse images recording its decay and disappearance. See Young, *Texture of Memory*, 27–37.

12 In this regard, the pillar marks a certain detour, or hiatus, within the limited economy of memory which it ultimately respects. After its burial, it ceases to be a radical instrument of history, turning instead into nothing more than a traditional monument, a gravestone plaque commemorating a process of memory that took place in an increasingly distant past.

13 See Gerz's comment in Lichtenstein, "Jochen Gerz," E3: "Faced with Germany's past, a number of people of my age, even those too young to remember events, or born after the war, have always been aware of not knowing exactly how to behave. They exercise a sort of sublime repression of the past."

14 Jean-François Lyotard, *The Postmodern Condition: A Report on Knowledge*, trans. Geoff Bennington and Brian Massumi, Theory and History of Literature, vol. 10 (Minneapolis: University of Minnesota Press, 1984), 81.

15 An analogy might be made to Rene Magritte's painting, "Light Falls," in which shards of glass lie on the floor at the base of a broken window. Through the window a sunset can be seen, while below the window the pieces of glass reveal the same sunset in fragmented form. The habitual distinction between a "natural" sunset and a painted one is collapsed here, and the viewer's expectation that the window will present the former is thereby both revealed and frustrated.

2 A PISGAH SIGHT OF HISTORY: CRITICAL AUTHORITY AND THE PROMISE OF MEMORY

1 Ample evidence of the power of this linguistic conception of history exists in science fiction accounts of time travel. A signal example of such an account

from the modernist period in literature is, of course, H. G. Wells's *The Time Machine*. The coherence of Wells's novel – and the pleasure we derive as readers from its impossibility – is dependent on our having previously accepted the duplicitous notion of history I am describing. On one hand we must see history as a coherent, spatially organized system which we negotiate through the faculty of memory; on the other, we have to see our motion within this historical space as radically impossible: even though we conceive of history spatially, we cannot "travel" in time.

2 *Purgatorio* XXVIII.34. See Dante Alighieri, *The Divine Comedy*, 3 vols., trans. Charles S. Singleton, Bollingen Series 80 (Princeton: Princeton University Press, 1973), II, 304–05.

3 See Ovid, *Metamorphoses*, Book V, trans. Mary M. Innes (New York: Penguin Books, 1955), 126–30.

4 The pilgrim's attempt to recognize the young woman finds an interesting parallel in scholarly treatments of this passage. Dante does not reveal her name, "Matelda," until the end of this *cantica* (*Purg.* XXXIII.119), thus licensing a certain play in the literary and allusive memories of his readers. Scholars have "recognized" Matelda, in this sense, both as a reference to Guido Cavalcanti's *pastorella*, "In un boschetto trova' pasturella," and as an allegorical figure for "natural justice." Thus identified, however, the young woman becomes the object of an intense scholarly search for a historical analog, a search which has produced many candidates, but no definitive "Matelda." See Charles S. Singleton's note to *Purg.* XXXIII.119.

5 Cf. Virgil, *The Aeneid*, trans. Robert Fitzgerald (New York: Random House, 1983), 182–86.

6 The poet's removal of Lethe from the nether regions is startling enough for the pilgrim himself to have remarked it. While journeying through Hell, Dante had wondered why he did not see this particular river and was told that he would find it only after he had passed "out of this abyss" ["fuor di questa fossa"]. See *Inferno*, XIV.130–38.

7 *Deuteronomy* 3:23–27, in *The Jerusalem Bible* (New York: Doubleday & Company, Inc., 1966). See also *Deut.*, 32:48–52 and 34:1–12.

8 See *Purg.*, XXXI.91–105.

9 The homophony of these words, "lethal" and "Lethe," underscores obvious associations between death and oblivion here. Although the words are etymologically related, their confluence of sound and meaning is due more properly to usage than to a strict "genealogical" connection. "Lethal" stems from the Latin *let(h)um*, meaning "death," which in turn influenced English usage of the term "Lethe" (from the Greek $\lambda'\eta\theta\eta$) as a name for the mythological river. Cf. Shakespeare, *Julius Caesar*, III.i.206: "Heere was't thou bay'd, braue Hart, Heere did'st thou fall, and heere thy Hunters stand Sign'd in thy Spoyle, and Crimson'd in thy Lethee." See *Oxford English Dictionary*, at "Lethe."

10 See *Deuteronomy* 34:5–7: "There in the land of Moab, Moses the servant of Yahweh died as Yahweh decreed; he buried him in the valley, in the land

of Moab, opposite Beth-peor; but to this day no one has ever found his grave."

11 History, in these terms, is simply the systemic structure of conscious knowing. It is a system which appears to ground the subject only because its function within the system of consciousness is that of ground, context, support, and condition. It is the boundary which consciousness sets as its own internal limit. For classic structuralist articulations of the limit as internal to the system, see Althusser's "From *Capital* to Marx's Philosophy" (in *Reading* Capital, trans., Ben Brewster [New York: Verso, 1970], 13–69), in which a point of "blindness" is found to structure the field of vision; also Derrida's "Structure, Sign and Play in the Discourse of the Human Sciences" (in *Writing and Difference*, trans. Alan Bass [Chicago: University of Chicago Press, 1978], 278–93), in which the absence of a center organizes the field of knowledge as a whole.

12 The possibility of an alternative historiography, occasioned by this coincidence of knowledge and burial, is the subject of Chapter 6 below. The writing of history that is undertaken in *Finnegans Wake* posits the past as a body which knowledge – in this case, a visual "passing beyond" via reading – discovers "in various phases of scripture as in various poses of sepulture" (i.e., "sepulchre" or burial). Engaged through a process of historical knowing, such poses inevitably reveal the reader's own postures of interment. Cf. Joyce, *FW*, 254.27–28.

13 Matthew Arnold, "The Function of Criticism at the Present Time," in Hazard Adams (ed.), *Critical Theory Since Plato*, 595.

14 Indeed, education places the critic above even the poets in aesthetic expertise: "[T]he one thing wanting to make Wordsworth an even greater poet than he is," wrote Arnold in a memorable passage from the same essay, "was that he should have read more books" (Arnold, "Function," 585).

15 See Benjamin's analysis of Marinetti which concludes "The Work of Art in the Age of Mechanical Reproduction," in Walter Benjamin, *Illuminations*, ed. Hannah Arendt, trans. Harry Zohn (New York: Schocken Books, 1968) 241–42. Arnold, for his part, insists that criticism's true function is the exercise of "curiosity," which he defines, famously, as the "disinterested love of a free play of the mind on all subjects, for its own sake" (Arnold, "Function," 588). The notion that criticism is the occupation of the professionally curious highlights the proprietary or curatorial role which scholarship plays with respect to culture.

16 See Hannah Arendt's biographical introduction to the *Illuminations* volume of essays, 17–18. Arendt notes that Benjamin was mistaken in his fear of immediate arrest, and that the embargo on visas was lifted within a matter of weeks (Benjamin, *Illuminations*, 18).

17 For a sampling of the various issues at stake in this return to history, see Derek Attridge et al. (eds.), *Post-Structuralism and the Question of History* (Cambridge: Cambridge University Press, 1987); Jeffrey N. Cox and Larry J. Reynolds (eds.), *New Historical Literary Study* (Princeton: Princeton University Press,

1993); J. R. de J. Jackson, *Historical Criticism and the Meaning of Texts* (New York: Routledge, 1989); Jerome J. McGann (ed.), *Historical Studies and Literary Criticism* (Madison: University of Wisconsin Press, 1985); and H. Aram Veeser (ed.), *The New Historicism* (New York: Routledge, 1989).

18 Fredric Jameson, *The Political Unconscious* (Ithaca: Cornell University Press, 1981) 9.

19 In their introductory essay to *Post-Structuralism and the Question of History*, Geoff Bennington and Robert Young offer a useful review of this development with particular reference not to Jameson, but to Frank Lentricchia, who structured his history of modern criticism in *After the New Criticism* around the allegation of a "repeated and often extremely subtle denial of history by a variety of contemporary theorists." See Attridge, et al., *Post-Structuralism*, 4.

20 Chapter 3 below specifies the alternative to the narrative form that I am here proposing as that of the symptom. The symptom is at once textual in form and absolutely illegible (both Symbolic and Real); it is the sign of the subject's erotic relation to its own historical being.

21 "There is no possibility of explaining dreams as a psychical process, since to explain a thing means to trace it back to something already known." See Sigmund Freud, *The Interpretation of Dreams*, trans. and ed. James Strachey (New York: Avon Books, 1965 [1900]), 549.

22 See Chapter 6 "The Dream-Work," in Sigmund Freud, *The Interpretation of Dreams*, esp. 311–12.

23 The rhetorical figure of chiasmus (e.g., "the writing of history is the history of writing") is one example of discourse's capacity to resolve the historical question by reducing it to a system of suspended opposition. This form has emerged, not coincidentally, as a particular favorite among New Historicists seeking to articulate an alternative discourse of history. Compelling examples of the effort to move historical discourse beyond such rhetorical oppositions are found in the essays contained in Marjorie Levinson et al., *Rethinking Historicism: Critical Readings in Romantic History* (Oxford: Basil Blackwell, 1989).

24 Even more disingenuous than Jameson's reading of Althusser in this connection is his appropriation of the work of Deleuze and Guattari. It is after all Deleuze and Guattari who point out that the unconscious has nothing to do with meaning, that meaning is the work of the conscious and preconscious mind (the work therefore of fantasy, denial, projection, and so on). See Jameson, *The Political Unconscious*, 22 ff. Indeed, Deleuze and Guattari's real foe is not Freud's reduction of experience to the allegorical paradigm of the Oedipal family, but rather the support lent by this paradigm to the hegemony of the narrative dialectic itself, which Jameson uses to produce history as totality.

25 Hans Kellner, *Language and Historical Representation: Getting the Story Crooked* (Madison: The University of Wisconsin Press, 1989).

26 See in particular, Michel de Certeau, *The Writing of History*, trans. Tom Conley (New York: Columbia University Press, 1988).

27 See Louis Althusser, "Freud and Lacan," in *Lenin and Philosophy*, trans. Ben Brewster (New York: Monthly Review Press, 1971), 189–219. Althusser's

intended audience was in particular the members of the Parti communiste
français.

28 Cf. Bloom's marked coin in *Ulysses*, 17.987–88.

29 In this respect, Althusser's treatment of the unconscious recalls Nietzsche's
discussion of human memory at the beginning of "On the Uses and Disadvantages of History for Life": "Consider the cattle, grazing as they pass
you by: they do not know what is meant by yesterday or today . . ." See
Friedrich Nietzsche, "On the Uses and Disadvantages of History for Life,"
in *Untimely Meditations*, trans. R. J. Hollingdale (Cambridge: Cambridge
University Press, 1983), 60.

30 The unconscious might be said to "exist," in this sense, as a certain pregnancy
of consciousness, a kind of tumescence or swelling by which psychoanalysis
recognizes that the organism is "in the historical way" – in precisely the
sense that psychoanalysis usually refers to the subject as being, ideologically
as well as psychically, in "the family way."

31 The use of the term "unconscious" as a noun dates at least to Coleridge's
work on the imitative poetic faculty, although ideas about a capacity for
"unconscious activity" within the human mind are far older. See Samuel
Taylor Coleridge, "On Poesy or Art," in *English Essays: From Sir Philip Sidney
to Macaulay*, ed. Charles W. Eliot, The Harvard Classics, vol. 27 (New York:
P. F. Collier & Son, 1909–14).

32 W. H. Auden, "In Memory of Sigmund Freud," in *The Collected Poetry of
W. H. Auden* (New York: Random House, 1945), 165.

33 Freud caused a great deal of confusion by insisting on the presence of a death
"drive." Since the work of death is present in the disposition of the subject
as such, there would seem to be no need to project an end which the subject
consciously or unconsciously "wants."

3 A RESERVATION UNDER THE NAME OF JOYCE: ROSSELLINI'S *VIAGGIO IN ITALIA* AND THE SYMPTOM

1 Jacques Aubert (ed.), *Joyce avec Lacan*, Bibliothèque des Analytica (Paris:
Navarin Editeur, 1987), 21. In addition to Lacan's address to the 1975 International Joyce Conference, mentioned below, this volume contains two
excerpts from the seminar and four critical essays. All translations from this
text are my own.

2 See in particular "Desire and the Interpretation of Desire in *Hamlet*," in
Literature and Psychoanalysis: The Question of Reading: Otherwise, ed. Shoshana
Felman (Baltimore: The Johns Hopkins University Press, 1980), 11–52, and
"The Essence of Tragedy: A Commentary on Sophocles's *Antigone*," in *The
Ethics of Psychoanalysis*, book VII in *The Seminar of Jacques Lacan* (New York:
W. W. Norton & Co., 1992), 243–87.

3 In a much-revised version of his address to the Joyce community, published
with this name as title, Lacan wrote: "In formulating this title, 'Joyce le
symptôme,' I give to Joyce nothing less than his proper name, that under
which I believe he would be recognized in the dimension of nomination"

("Je donne à Joyce, en formulant ce titre, 'Joyce le symptôme,' rien de moins que son nom propre, celui où je crois qu'il serait reconnu dans la dimension de la nomination"). See Aubert, *Joyce avec Lacan*, 22.

4 At the conclusion of his Joyce seminar, Lacan re-emphasized the fact that for him, Joyce's symptomatic name marked the limit of reading for both literary analysis and psychoanalysis. Joyce was, he said, "the simplest consequence of a refusal – such a mental refusal! – of a psychoanalysis," and *Finnegans Wake* showed that Joyce was "désabonné à l'inconscient" – that he had "canceled his subscription" to the unconscious. See *The Four Fundamental Concepts of Psycho-Analysis* (New York: W. W. Norton & Co., 1981) ix, and Aubert, *Joyce avec Lacan*, 24 ff.

5 See Helena Schulz-Keil, "Psychoanalysis and Hystory," in *Hystoria*, special issue of *Lacan Study Notes*, nos. 6–9 (New York: The New York Lacan Study Group, 1988), 59.

6 See J. Laplanche and J.-B. Pontalis, *The Language of Psycho-Analysis*, trans. Donald Nicholson-Smith (New York: W. W. Norton & Co., 1973), at "Compromise-Formation."

7 See Sigmund Freud, "The Sense of Symptoms," and "The Paths to the Formation of Symptoms" in *Introductory Lectures on Psycho-Analysis*, trans. and ed. James Strachey (New York: W. W. Norton & Co., 1966). Also J. Laplanche and J.-B. Pontalis, *The Language of Psycho-Analysis*, at "Compromise-Formation."

8 See the seminar of 29 April 1964, in *The Four Fundamental Concepts of Psycho-analysis*, 150. This text represents Lacan's attempt to reconcile Freud's notion that the reality of the unconscious is sexual reality with his own dictum that the unconscious is structured like a language. In espousing his theory of the subject's determination by the "law of the signifier," Lacan sought to establish a model of subjectivity grounded not in the organic mysteries of sexual division and biological procreation, but in language. Yet from a certain point of view, this revolutionary theory of the symbolic subject seems merely to comply with the very discourses of naturalism and familialism which it initially tries to subvert: the symbolic reality of the subject is implicitly grounded, through the *nom du père*, in the biological legitimacy of generational continuity. Paternity thus comes to govern the determination of the subject not only as a matter of Oedipal identification or biological generation, but as a principle of symbolic descent as well. In the horizontal, connective, "matrimonial" function of the name, Lacan sought to locate a concrete refutation of these apparent sympathies with paternalism and biologism within his theory of Symbolic law.

9 In "The Function and Field of Speech and Language in Psychoanalysis" (the "Rome Discourse"), Lacan explained the subject's determination by language in terms of the fact that speech always "refers itself to the discourse of the other." Even if the interlocutor is silent, the subject's speech always puts itself in play as a way of specifying the reality from which the listener hears – as, in other words, a mode of naming: "you are my wife";

"you are my father"; "you are my master." Speech determines the subject in this fashion as being, in its very existence, *for* the other. It is through this law of linguistic communication, then, and not through cultural laws of social interchange, that the subject is constrained to existence in a familial mode: speech determines the subject as a son, a mother, a father, a wife, and so on. See *Écrits: A Selection*, 85. See also "The Direction of the Treatment and the Principles of Its Power," in the same volume, 269.

10 Quoted in James Naremore's review, "Return of the Living Dead," in *James Joyce Literary Supplement* (spring 1991): 16; my emphasis.

11 As scholars who followed or participated in the film's critical reception will no doubt attest, the "worthiness" of Huston's film emerges, for most viewers, in its self-conscious and studied concern with correctness of two main types: first, historical accuracy (period costumes and "ambiance"; songs that "would have been sung then," and so on); and second, faithfulness to the text – or more precisely, to the content of the text (Huston does not reproduce Joyce's punning style, his distant narration, and other formal aspects, so much as he does a familiar and indeed "classic" story of alienation at the heart of social and political politesse). To these two forms of correctness we must add Huston's faithfulness to his own vision, the purposefulness which clings everywhere to his film and allows it to speak, from an autobiographical standpoint, as the director's swan-song, his last and best, the film he always wanted, indeed needed, to make.

12 Significant exceptions to the film's rejection by critics are found in the contemporary reviews written by the theorists and filmmakers at *Cahiers du Cinéma*. *Viaggio in Italia* consistently appeared in that journal's annual top ten list of the best movies ever made. As for Joyce scholars, beyond Naremore's review, very few have bothered to record an opinion on the film one way or the other. This situation promises to be at least partly redressed by Kevin Barry's book, *The Dead* (Cork: Cork University Press, 2001). See also Luciana Bohne, "Rossellini's 'Viaggio in Italia': A Variation on a Theme by Joyce," in *Film Criticism* 3, no. 2 (winter 1979): 43–52. Laura Mulvey's more recent treatment of the film in *Sight and Sound* makes passing reference to Joyce, but focuses on the relationship between Rossellini's fictional narrative and the historical, geographical, and personal realities his film presents: "Fiction leads to reality, in this Rossellini movie," Mulvey writes, "rather than realism." See Laura Mulvey, "Satellites of Love," in *Sight and Sound* 10, no. 12 (Dec. 2000): 20–24.

13 Cf. Gabriel's response to Molly Ivors's needling nationalism in James Joyce, "The Dead," 189.

14 As Naremore points out, *Viaggio in Italia* is hardly an adaptation at all, but rather a wholly autonomous film which, for reasons of its own, plays with allusion and narrative strategy to orient its viewers toward Joyce and his story (Naremore, "Return of the Living Dead," 16).

15 Moreover, this insistence of the signifier is not the result of a willful authorial gesture, the repeated inscription of Joyce's name within the text. On the

contrary, the symptom betrays no self-regard; it speaks its subject precisely where it is least susceptible to a reading.

16 Lacan's neologism, "parlêtre," connotes the subject constituted as a being spoken by the unconscious.

17 See Peter Brunette, *Roberto Rossellini* (New York: Oxford University Press, 1987), 155 ff.

18 For extended descriptions of the adverse and unprofessional conditions under which he was forced to work, see George Sanders, *Memoirs of a Professional Cad* (London: The Scarecrow Press, 1992), 107 ff.

19 André Bazin, "In Defense of Rossellini," in *What is Cinema?* vol. 2, trans. Hugh Gray (Berkeley: University of California Press, 1971), 98 ff.

20 Cf. Slavoj Zizek, "How Real Is Reality?" Chap. 1 of *Looking Awry: An Introduction to Jacques Lacan through Popular Culture* (Cambridge, MA: MIT Press, 1991).

21 Cf. Jacques Lacan, *Écrits: A Selection*, 314 ff.

22 Ingrid Bergman and Alan Burgess, *Ingrid Bergman: My Story* (New York: Delacorte Press, 1980), 244–45.

23 Slavoj Zizek, "Rossellini: Woman as Symptom of Man," in *October* 54 (fall 1990): 19–44.

24 Zizek, "Rossellini," 20. Zizek does not speculate on what Bergman's thoughts might have been upon seeing her own name thus bifurcated in the director's double representation of evil. *Open City* was of course one of the two movies that initially inspired the actress to offer her acting services to Rossellini. Viewing the letter as her own response to the shock of discovering that she was, in a sense, already present in one of his films considerably complicates her letter's already ambiguous implications.

25 See Ellie Ragland-Sullivan, *Jacques Lacan and the Philosophy of Psychoanalysis* (Chicago: University of Illinois Press, 1987), 258. On this point it is interesting to note that the French newspaper, *Le Monde*, when reporting on Lacan's Joyce seminar, mistakenly printed its title as "Jacques le symbole," instead of "Joyce le symptôme." See Aubert, *Joyce avec Lacan*, 21.

26 Cf. *Oxford English Dictionary* at "Symptom." Lacan also emphasized an early spelling of the word, "sinthome," and punned on its French pronunciation in order to suggest that Joyce inscribed himself under the signifier as "saint-homme," the holy man of modern letters.

27 This image is also consistent with the literal meaning of "analysis," from the Greek, ἀναλυσιζ, meaning "to loosen" or "undo." See *OED* at "Analysis." Within the therapeutic scene, the borromean knot of the symptom constitutes the analysand's affective identity; it can be loosened by psychoanalysis, though never fully untied or dissolved.

28 In proposing the term *nom du mari*, I am not proposing a facile opposition to the "male" or "phallic" orientation of the signifier in Lacanian discourse. What the *nom du mari* signals, rather, is a more radical persistence of difference within what might be called the phallic strategies of signification itself. While the *nom du père* determines identity as repetition, the *nom du mari* reveals that

determination itself as a Symbolic suture of Real difference under a common name. These poles of the signifier's functioning, moreover, are not logically opposed, but reveal a conceptual asymmetry at work within the dimension of the Symbolic itself. Matrimony and patrimony are the perpendicular planes of the signifier's double agency, the dual coordinates by which the name pins the subject to the reality of its existence as an identity – a "legal fixion" – under symbolic law.

29 The symptom's prosthetic function is legible in other literary contexts as well. Melville's *Moby Dick* and Hitchcock's *Rear Window* come immediately to mind as texts that might form a symptomatic pair of much the same kind as that formed by *Viaggio in Italia* and "The Dead": each of these texts, of course, frames its central quest narrative around the circumstance of its hero's broken, or amputated, leg.

30 Full screenplays in both French and English are printed in *Hommage à Roberto Rossellini: Voyage en Italie*, a special issue of *L'Avant scène cinema*, no. 361 (June, 1987); for this passage, see 125 ff.

31 Richard Ellmann, *James Joyce* (New York: Oxford University Press, 1982), 243.

4 THE BIRTH OF A NATION: IRISH NATIONALISM AND THE TECHNOLOGY OF MEMORY, 1891–1921

1 *Irish Times*, Tuesday, 12 September 1916, microfilm held at National Library of Ireland, Dublin.

2 The poem with which Joyce concludes his story "Ivy Day in the Committee Room" bears witness, in its opening lines, to popular awareness of Parnell's unofficial title: "He is dead. Our Uncrowned King is dead. / O, Erin, mourn with grief and woe / For he lies dead whom the fell gang / Of modern hypocrites laid low." James Joyce, *Dubliners*, 134.

3 See Bew, *Conflict and Conciliation* and F. S. L. Lyons, *Charles Stewart Parnell*.

4 W. B. Yeats, *The Variorum Edition of the Plays of W. B. Yeats*, ed. Russell K. Alspach and Catharine C. Alspach (New York: The Macmillan Company, 1966), 568.

5 Walter Benjamin, "The Work of Art in the Age of Mechanical Reproduction," in *Illuminations*, 227 ff.

6 C. W. Ceram, *Archaeology of the Cinema* (New York: Harcourt, Brace & World, Inc., n.d.), 84.

7 That early audiences were aware of the artificiality of the image can be seen in the fact that several film-within-a-film parody shorts were made shortly after *Arrival of a Train*, in which a clown or "country bumpkin" figure watching the Lumieres' film runs away as the train approaches – to the delight and laughter of the real audience, of course.

8 Kevin Rockett et al., *Cinema and Ireland* (Syracuse: Syracuse University Press, 1987), 3–4. Rockett implies that "Arrival of a Train" was screened in Dublin on 29 October 1896, an impossibility according to Nathalie Morena, an

archivist at the Association frères Lumière in Paris. The Lumieres shot the film during the summer of 1897, and not, as almost universally reported, in 1896.

9 During the 19-teens, the Irish Events newsreel series brought the medium's documentary capabilities to bear on contemporary politics. Shown as preludes to feature-length narratives, such films included an Auxiliaries raid on Liberty Hall, the arrest of Arthur Griffith, a Peace conference in Dublin, horse-racing news, the funeral of the Lord Mayor of Cork, Terence MacSwiney, and images of the "elusive Mr. Michael Collins" speaking to crowds in Armagh and touring the ruins of a burned homestead.

10 See especially Luke Gibbons' essay, "Romanticism, Realism and Irish Cinema," in Rockett et al., *Cinema and Ireland*, 194–257. Valuable essays on film are also contained in Gibbons' *Transformations in Irish Culture*, Critical Conditions: Field Day Essays (Notre Dame, IN: University of Notre Dame Press, 1996).

11 *Memories in Focus*, a documentary on the development of film in Ireland, includes footage from an uncredited 1897 film, possibly one of the Lumieres', of firemen putting out a fire in Dublin's St. Stephen's Green. See Peter Canning (dir.), *Memories in Focus*, videorecording in six parts (60 minutes each; b/w), 1995 (Dublin: Irish Film Centre Archive).

12 See especially Tom Gunning, "The Cinema of Attractions: Early Film, Its Spectator and the Avant-Garde," in *Wide Angle* 8, nos. 3/4 (fall 1986). Reprinted in *Early Cinema: Space, Frame, Narrative*, ed. Thomas Elsaesser (London: BFI, 1990); also Miriam Hansen, "Benjamin, Cinema and Experience: The Blue Flower in the Land of Technology," *New German Critique* 40 (winter 1987), and *Babel and Babylon: Spectatorship in American Silent Film* (Cambridge, MA: Harvard University Press, 1991); Lynne Kirby, "Male Hysteria and Early Cinema," *Camera Obscura* 17 (May 1988).

13 Tom Gunning, "Now You See It, Now You Don't: The Temporality of the Cinema of Attractions," in *Silent Film* (New Brunswick: Rutgers University Press, 1996), 71. Interestingly, film began self-consciously to model itself on the theater, presenting famous players in adaptations of famous plays, for instance, only when the dominance of narrative was already well established. A fascinating case of cinema as a failed adaptation of Irish dramatic discourse is Hitchcock's early adaptation of Sean O'Casey's *Juno and the Paycock*. The film stars Sarah Allgood, of Abbey Theatre fame, and is the more interesting for having been made by the director later universally acknowledged as the master of cinema as a unique craft.

14 For Gunning, "cinema of attractions" refers backwards in time to the development of fairground and carnival entertainments such as those at Coney Island; at the same time it also refers forward to Eisenstein's codification of a "montage of attractions" as characteristic of his own film aesthetic's subversion of bourgeois realism. See Gunning, "An Aesthetic of Astonishment: Early Film and the (In)Credulous Spectator," in *Art and Text* 34 (spring 1989); reprinted in *Viewing Positions: Ways of Seeing Film*, ed. Linda Williams (New Brunswick: Rutgers University Press, 1995), 131, n. 13.

15 Reportedly, audiences were more intrigued by the spectacular effect of trees moving in the background than with such narrative concerns or with the family group at the center of the frame. See vol. 1: *"The Great Train Robbery and Other Primary Works,"* in *The Movies Begin,* a five-part series produced for video by David Shepard and Heather Stewart and by Film Preservation Associates and The British Film Institute (New York: Kino International, 1994).

16 See Janet Staiger, *"The Birth of a Nation:* Reconsidering Its Reception," in *The Birth of a Nation: D. W. Griffith, Director,* Films in Print, vol. 21, ed. Robert Lang (New Brunswick: Rutgers University Press, 1994).

17 Joseph Holloway, *Diaries, 1895 to 1944,* microfiche (Dublin: The National Library of Ireland).

18 R. F. Foster, *Modern Ireland: 1600–1972* (London: Allen Lane/The Penguin Press, 1988.) 484.

19 See L. Perry Curtis, Jr.'s well-known study, *Apes and Angels: The Irishman in Victorian Caricature,* rev. ed. (Washington, DC: Smithsonian Institution Press, 1997).

20 *The Critical Writings of James Joyce,* ed. Ellsworth Mason and Richard Ellmann (Ithaca: Cornell University Press, 1989), 228.

21 *Irish Limelight* (February 1918), n.p.

22 Maire and Conor Cruise O'Brien, *A Concise History of Ireland* (New York: Thames and Hudson, 1985), 141.

23 The emphasis is on "never *fully* apprehensible." Anne Crilly's documentary, *Mother Ireland,* contains some brief archival footage of the immediate aftermath of the Easter Rising. In the sense of "actualities" or "attractions," clips such as these make the historical event available through the visual grammar of the cinema.

5 FIGHTING THE WAVES: YEATS, CUCHULAIN, AND THE LETHAL HISTORIES OF "ROMANTIC IRELAND"

1 See especially *The Trembling of the Veil,* bk. 1, "Four Years: 1887–1891," in W. B. Yeats, *Autobiographies* (New York: The Macmillan Company, 1927) and "Magic," in *Essays and Introductions* (New York: Macmillan, 1961), 28–52. See also *A Vision,* Yeats's profoundly strange and inscrutable treatise on historical imagination, which the poet claimed was largely dictated to him and to his wife by spiritual familiars, or "communicators." In the introduction to this volume, Yeats describes his delight in his wife's experiments with automatic writing, and credits this "incredible experience" for the power of his poetry in *The Tower* and *The Winding Stair.* W. B. Yeats, *A Vision* (London: Macmillan & Co., 1937), 8–25.

2 See Patrick J. Keane, *Terrible Beauty: Yeats, Joyce, Ireland, and the Myth of the Devouring Female* (Columbia: University of Missouri Press, 1988), ix. Keane's "lethal mythology" focuses on female principles of destructiveness and death, such as the "Leanhaun Shee," the Morrigu, the Sheela-na-gig, Yeats's *Cathleen ni Houlihan,* and Joyce's "old sow that eats her farrow." For

Keane, Cuchulain remains an incidental but important term in this series of representations of Ireland as self-destructive or literally autophagous.

3 In fact, Cuchulain does not die on Baile's Strand, according to the legend, but only collapses after the three-day fight "from hunger and weakness." Yeats was not particularly faithful to the legend, at times treating the episode as the scene of Cuchulain's death, at others not. See Lady Augusta Gregory (trans.), *Cuchulain of Muirthemne* (Gerrards Cross, Buckinghamshire: Colin Smythe, Ltd., 1970), 237–41.

4 Denis Donoghue, "Romantic Ireland," in *We Irish: Essays on Irish Literature and Society* (New York: Knopf, 1986), 24–25.

5 See note 3 above.

6 Donoghue suggests that what gives "Romantic Ireland" the status of a myth, as opposed to that of a fiction, is that it constitutes a political quantity. It names a value for or against which one must *act*. By contrast, he defines fiction as "a means of being conscious without further responsibility." This useful distinction may require some qualification in the context of a discussion on Yeats, for whom consciousness and the unconscious are equally likely to incur political debts. As Yeats wrote in the epigraph to his volume, *Responsibilities*, "In dreams begins responsibility." See Donoghue, *We Irish*, 21–22.

7 In this connection, it is important to note the economics of producing a film like *The Field*, which suggest that the pathos of such figures serves a commercial as well as memorial function. Interestingly, Sheridan's film, while the top finisher at the Irish box office in 1990 and billed internationally as an "Irish film," was funded mainly by British and American investors.

8 Terence Brown, "Yeats, Joyce and the Irish Critical Debate," in Allison (ed.), *Yeats's Political Identities*, 279–92; see also Allison's introductory essay, "Fascism, Nationalism, Reception," 20.

9 Vicki Mahaffey, *States of Desire: Wilde, Yeats, Joyce and the Irish Experiment* (Oxford: Oxford University Press, 1998), 180–81; see also Alwyn and Brinley Rees, *Celtic Heritage: Ancient Tradition in Ireland and Wales* (London: Thames and Hudson, 1961), 53–69.

10 Apart from the early plays, Shelley's chief early influences on Yeats appear in *The Wind Among the Reeds*. The title of that volume suggests not only the harp as a national symbol of Ireland, but the metaphor of the lyre which Shelley used so often to suggest the natural and complex ease of poetic harmonization.

11 See William Butler Yeats, *"Prometheus Unbound,"* in *Essays and Introductions*, 424 ff.

12 George Bornstein, *Yeats and Shelley* (Chicago: University of Chicago Press, 1970), 123 ff.

13 See Stuart Sperry, *Shelley's Major Verse: The Narrative and Dramatic Poetry* (Cambridge, MA: Harvard University Press, 1988), 69.

14 What partly mitigates the potential boredom of this drama is the historicization of Prometheus's position. Shelley's metaphors tend to distract attention from the inevitability of Prometheus's – and the universe's – deliverance, by

emphasizing the excruciating slowness of plodding history, and therefore of his suffering. The image of the Titan being stabbed by "crawling glaciers" is an instance of the visceral power such metaphors can have.

15 Just as Prometheus's remembering of the curse led to his near submission to a despotic image of himself as a heroic Christ, so the remembrance of the Cuchulain saga leads to the commemoration and sanctification of the hero as a Christ figure. While the legends themselves are pre-Christian in origin, the earliest versions that remain are those transcribed by eighth- and ninth-century Christian monks in the *Book of the Dun Cow* and other manuscripts. Thus the tales were submitted to a process of redaction governed by a Christian value system that produced significant alterations. Such changes include, for example, redating the stories so that the heroes appear as contemporaries of Christ; the suppression of the doctrine of reincarnation; and, specifically, the addition to the Cuchulain cycle of a story in which the hero, after dying, rises up in a chariot to meet Christ. See Eleanor Hull (trans.), *The Cuchullin Saga in Irish Literature* (London: David Nutt, 1898).

16 See for instance, "Among School Children" and "Sailing to Byzantium." The term "monumentalism" here connotes the static nature of such images when used in political contexts, and not the monumental imagery – such as the tower – so common in Yeats's later poetry. The latter functions as a symbol, and thus, for Yeats, as an index or locus of the image's dynamism or movement.

17 See Norman Jeffares, *A New Commentary on the Poems of W. B. Yeats* (Stanford: Stanford University Press, 1984), 344. Parnell himself emerges as a Cuchulain figure for Yeats in "Parnell's Funeral," a poem that originally appeared as part of the "Introduction to Fighting the Waves," and in which the writing of passionate action is explicitly opposed to the binding force of the remembered image. See Jeffares, *A New Commentary*, 335.

18 Yeats's sense of responsibility is nowhere so evident as in "Man and Echo" where, in an often-quoted passage, he acknowledges responsibility for inspiring the revolutionaries with his play, "Cathleen ni Houlihan": "Did that play of mine send out / Certain men the English shot?"

19 Padraic Pearse, whose devotion to Cuchulain burned the brightest among the rebels, had said, "If I die it shall be out of excess of love I bear the Gael."

20 See Yeats's 1934 introduction to the prose version of *The Only Jealousy of Emer*, entitled "Fighting the Waves," in Alspach (ed.), *The Variorum Edition of the Plays of W. B. Yeats* (London: Macmillan, 1966), 567–68; my emphasis. Yeats further commented, "I wrote in blank verse, which I tried to bring as close to common speech as the subject permitted, a number of connected plays – *Deirdre, At the Hawk's Well, The Green Helmet, On Baile's Strand, The Only Jealousy of Emer*. I would have attempted the Battle of the Ford and the Death of Cuchulain, had not the mood of Ireland changed."

21 Phillip L. Marcus (ed.), *The Death of Cuchulain: Manuscript Materials Including the Author's Final Text*, (Ithaca: Cornell University Press, 1982), 14.

22 W. B. Yeats, *The Death of Cuchulain* in *Eleven Plays of William Butler Yeats* ed. A. Norman Jeffares (New York: Macmillan Publishing Company, 1964), 209.

23 Marcus has commented that the reference to the 1916 revolutionaries in the printed version of the poem is far less patriotic than in previous drafts. Indeed, the earliest draft that remains seems to idealize Cuchulain, along with Pearse, Connolly, and the others, as Ireland's true liberators: "When Perces boys began the fight / That set their country free / Cuchullain was so much in their thought / He seemed in their company." See Marcus, *Death of Cuchulain*, 117.

24 See Richard Ellmann, *The Identity of Yeats* (New York: Oxford University Press, 1964), 25.

25 See Richard Ellmann, *Yeats: The Man and the Masks* (New York: Macmillan, 1948), 261.

26 Compare the importance of boundaries in another Yeatsian metaphor of nationalism: "One can only reach out to the universe with a gloved hand; that glove is one's nation, the only thing one knows even a little of." See William Butler Yeats, *Letters to the New Island* (Cambridge, MA: Harvard University Press, 1934), 174.

27 See, for instance, Bornstein, *Yeats and Shelley*, 132.

6 JOYCE'S EROTICS OF MEMORY: TEMPORAL ANAMORPHOSIS IN *FINNEGANS WAKE*

1 Cf. ALP's monologue, which marks the closing of the book, and its reopening, in these terms: "It's Phoenix, dear . . . Let's our joornee sintomichael make it. Since the lausafire has lost and the book of the depth is. Closed. Come! Step out of your shell!" (*FW*, 621.1–4).

2 José Ortega y Gasset, *History as a System and Other Essays Toward a Philosophy of History* (New York: W. W. Norton & Co., Inc., 1961), 216.

3 Jacques Lacan, *The Ethics of Psychoanalysis*, bk. VII in *The Seminar of Jacques Lacan* (New York: W. W. Norton & Co., 1992), 135–40.

4 Danis Rose and John O'Hanlon, *Understanding Finnegans Wake: A Guide to the Narrative of James Joyce's Masterpiece* (New York: Garland Publishing, 1982), vii–viii.

5 Returning momentarily to the terms of Lacanian psychoanalytic theory, one might say that history is both (and at once) Real and Symbolic. The use of these terms merely underscores what is after all a common-sense distinction between representation and what is called reality; that is, between what we apprehend in discursive, textual terms as reality and that radically unattainable Other that is the historical past in its dimension of absence or loss.

6 See Oliver St. John Gogarty, review, *Observer* May 7, 1939, 4.

7 The "Quinet passage," a quotation from the seventeenth-century French philosopher of history, Edgar Quinet, which recurs in various forms at least half a dozen times in the *Wake*, is a prominent example of Joyce's borrowing of formal historiographical models. See Joyce, *FW*, 281.4–13 and variations of the passage at 14.35 ff., 117.11 ff., 236.19 ff., 354.22 ff., and

615.02 ff. Others include not only the ongoing mimicry of *The Annals of the Four Masters*, but parodies of Greek and Latin historical writers such as Caesar, Suetonius, Tacitus, and Thucydides.

8 Known under Viking occupation as "the town of the ford of the hurdles," the city of Dublin (from the Irish "dubh + linn," meaning "black pool") itself appears to have been nominally associated, from its earliest history, with this notion of difficult crossings, or "disappointed bridges."

9 Letter to Frank Budgen, dated end July 1939. See *Letters of James Joyce*, ed. Stuart Gilbert. (New York: The Viking Press, 1957), 405–06.

10 "Tim Finigan's Wake," words and music by John Durnal, in *Irish Songbook* (Miami Beach: Hansen House, n.d.).

11 The ballad turns, of course, on another pun as well. In his posthumous rising, Tim Finnegan resembles a spirit (ghost) awakened by spirits (liquor).

12 Their typical queries can be heard immediately before crossing the *Wake*'s disappointed bridge to ideareal history: "to speak broken heaventalk, is he? Who is he? Whose is he? Why is he? Howmuch is he? Which is he? When is he? Where is he? How is he? And what the decans is there about him anyway, the decemt man?" (*FW*, 261.27–62.1)

13 Indeed, the novel's question about "endings" is inscribed at the level of the work's very title (Fr. *fin* = "end"), as is the phoenixing process by which every reader engages it ("Finnegan" = *fin*-again, and "wake" = the corpse's Phoenix-like rising from the ashes of death).

14 An example of the way in which Joyce's text resists such traditional symbolic organizations of the body can be found in the conflation of mouth and ear in the phrase "O, really?" mentioned in reference to the passage cited earlier: orally = "mouth"; *oreille* = French, "ear."

15 See John Bishop, *Joyce's Book of the Dark* (Madison: University of Wisconsin Press, 1986), 17.

16 See Giambattista Vico, *The New Science*, 3rd edn. (1744), trans. Thomas Goddard Bergin and Max Harold Fisch (Ithaca: Cornell University Press, 1948), esp. 112–20.

17 See especially two classics of Joyce scholarship, James S. Atherton's *The Books at the Wake* (New York: Paul P. Appel, Publisher, 1974) and Clive Hart's *Structure and Motif in Finnegans Wake* (Chicago: Northwestern University Press, 1962). For a brilliant contrasting treatment, see Thomas Hofheinz, *Joyce and the Invention of Irish History* (Cambridge: Cambridge University Press, 1995). Hofheinz argues persuasively that the importance of Vico for Joyce's text is not, primarily, structural. While Vico's cyclical model of history provided a "trellis" for Joyce's work, Hofheinz suggests that Joyce found in Vico a model of the structures of paternal authority that govern much of Irish history, and that Joyce subverts those structures precisely in his references to Vico. The myth of the giants, Hofheinz argues, was Vico's way of reconciling God's establishment of paternity as the world's proper mode of authority with the adverse effects of that mode of authority.

18 Letter to Harriet Shaw Weaver, 22 November 1930. See *Letters*, 295.

19 Roland McHugh, *Annotations to* Finnegans Wake (Baltimore: The Johns Hopkins University Press, 1980), 253.

20 Vico's eighth axiom, mentioned in the passage cited above, states that "Giants, as we shall show by physical histories found in the Greek fables and by proofs both physical and moral drawn from civil histories, existed in nature among all the first gentile nations" (Vico, *The New Science*, 37). It is this axiom, in other words, that places the giants at the origin of Vico's human history.

21 A clear indication of the productive function of such forgetting exists in my own strategic placement of holes (ellipses) in the ballet of this *Wakean* sentence in order to make one sense of the passage more easily accessible.

22 See Bishop, *Joyce's Book of the Dark*, "Relief Map B" (34–35) and "Relief Map B′" (162–63).

23 Interestingly, Lacan described the anamorphotic smudge in Holbein's "The Ambassadors" as looking "roughly like fried eggs." See Lacan, *The Ethics of Psychoanalysis*, 135.

AFTERWORD

1 Gilles Deleuze and Felix Guattari, *Anti-Oedipus: Capitalism and Schizophrenia*, trans. Brian Massumi (Minneapolis: University of Minnesota Press, 1987), 18.

Bibliography

Adams, Hazard, ed. *Critical Theory Since Plato.* New York: Harcourt Brace Jovanovich, Publishers, 1971.

Allison, Jonathan, ed. *Yeats's Political Identities: Selected Essays.* Ann Arbor: The University of Michigan Press, 1996.

Althusser, Louis. *Lenin and Philosophy.* Trans. Ben Brewster. New York: Monthly Review Press, 1971.

Althusser, Louis and Etienne Balibar. *Reading* Capital. Trans. Ben Brewster. London: Verso, 1970.

Arnold, Matthew. "The Function of Criticism at the Present Time." In *Critical Theory Since Plato*, ed. Hazard Adams, 583–96. New York: Harcourt Brace Jovanovich, Publishers, 1971.

Atherton, James S. *The Books at the Wake.* New York: Paul P. Appel, Publisher, 1974.

Attridge, Derek, et al., eds. *Post-Structuralism and the Question of History.* Cambridge: Cambridge University Press, 1987.

Aubert, Jacques, ed. *Joyce avec Lacan.* Bibliothèque des Analytica. Paris: Navarin Editeur, 1987.

Auden, W. H. *The Collected Poetry of W. H. Auden.* New York: Random House, 1945.

Barry, Kevin. *The Dead.* Cork: Cork University Press, 2001.

Bazin, André. *What is Cinema?* 2 vols. Trans. Hugh Gray. Berkeley: University of California Press, 1967–71.

Benjamin, Walter. *Illuminations.* Ed. Hannah Arendt, trans. Harry Zohn. New York: Schocken Books, 1968.

  Reflections. Ed. Peter Demetz. New York: Schocken Books, 1978.

Bennett, David, ed. *Multicultural States: Rethinking Difference and Identity.* New York: Routledge, 1988.

Bergman, Ingrid, and Alan Burgess. *Ingrid Bergman: My Story.* New York: Delacorte Press, 1980.

Bergson, Henri. *Matter and Memory.* Trans. Nancy Margaret Paul and W. Scott Palmer. New York: Zone Books, 1991.

Bew, Paul. *Conflict and Conciliation in Ireland, 1898–1910: Parnellites and Radical Agrarians.* New York: Oxford University Press, 1987.

Bishop, John. *Joyce's Book of the Dark.* Madison: University of Wisconsin Press, 1986.

Bohne, Luciana. "Rossellini's 'Viaggio in Italia': A Variation on a Theme by Joyce." *Film Criticism* 3, no. 2 (winter 1979): 43–52.

Bornstein, George. *Yeats and Shelley.* Chicago: University of Chicago Press, 1970.

Brannigan, John, et al., eds. *Re:Joyce: Text, Culture, Politics.* New York: St. Martin's Press, 1998.

Brunette, Peter. *Roberto Rossellini.* New York: Oxford University Press, 1987.

Budgen, Frank. *James Joyce and the Making of* Ulysses. Bloomington: Indiana University Press, 1960.

Bürger, Peter. *The Decline of Modernism.* Trans. Nicholas Walker. University Park: The Pennsylvania State University Press, 1992.

Canning, Peter, dir. *Memories in Focus.* Six parts (60 minutes each, b/w). 1995. Dublin: Irish Film Centre Archive. Videorecording.

Ceram, C. W. *Archaeology of the Cinema.* New York: Harcourt, Brace & World, Inc., n.d.

Certeau, Michel de. *The Writing of History.* Trans. Tom Conley. New York: Columbia University Press, 1988.

Cheng, Vincent J. *Joyce, Race, and Empire.* Cambridge: Cambridge University Press, 1995.

Coleridge, Samuel Taylor. "On Poesy or Art." In *English Essays: From Sir Philip Sidney to Macaulay*, ed. Charles W. Eliot, The Harvard Classics, vol. 27, 267–77. New York: P. F. Collier & Son, 1909–14.

Cox, Jeffrey N., and Larry J. Reynolds, eds. *New Historical Literary Study.* Princeton: Princeton University Press, 1993.

Curtis, Jr., L. Perry. *Apes and Angels: The Irishman in Victorian Caricature.* Rev. edn. Washington, DC: Smithsonian Institution Press, 1997.

Dante Alighieri. *The Divine Comedy.* 3 vols. Trans. Charles S. Singleton. Bollingen Series 80. Princeton: Princeton University Press, 1973.

Danto, Arthur C. *Narration and Knowledge.* New York: Columbia University Press, 1985.

Deane, Seamus, ed. *Nationalism, Colonialism and Literature.* Minneapolis: University of Minnesota Press, 1990.

    Strange Country: Modernity and Nationhood in Irish Writing since 1790. Oxford: Clarendon Press, 1997.

Deleuze. Gilles, and Felix Guattari. *Anti-Oedipus: Capitalism and Schizophrenia.* Trans. Brian Massumi. Minneapolis: University of Minnesota Press, 1987.

    A Thousand Plateaus: Capitalism and Schizophrenia. Trans. Brian Massumi. Minneapolis: University of Minnesota Press, 1987.

de Man, Paul. *Blindness and Insight: Essays in the Rhetoric of Contemporary Criticism.* 2nd edn. Theory and History of Literature, vol. 7. Minneapolis: University of Minnesota Press, 1983.

Derrida, Jacques. *Writing and Difference.* Trans. Alan Bass. Chicago: University of Chicago Press, 1978.

Donoghue, Denis. "Fears for Irish Studies in an Age of Identity Politics." *The Chronicle of Higher Education*, 21 November 1997, B4–B5.

We Irish: Essays on Irish Literature and Society. New York: Knopf, 1986.

Duffy, Enda. *The Subaltern* Ulysses. Minneapolis: University of Minnesota Press, 1994.

Eliot, T. S. "Tradition and the Individual Talent." In *The Sacred Wood: Essays on Poetry and Criticism*, 47–59. New York: Routledge, 1989.

"*Ulysses*, Order, and Myth." In *Selected Prose of T. S. Eliot*, ed. Frank Kermode, 175–78. New York: Harcourt Brace Jovanovich, Publishers, 1975.

Ellmann, Richard. *The Identity of Yeats*. New York: Oxford University Press, 1964.

James Joyce. Rev. edn. New York: Oxford University Press, 1982.

Yeats: The Man and the Masks. New York: Macmillan, 1948.

Felman, Shoshana, ed. *Literature and Psychoanalysis: The Question of Reading: Otherwise*. Baltimore: The Johns Hopkins University Press, 1980.

Ferrall, Charles. *Modernist Writing and Reactionary Politics*. Cambridge: Cambridge University Press, 2001.

Fitzpatrick, David. *The Two Irelands: 1912–1939*. New York: Oxford University Press, 1998.

Foster, R. F. *Modern Ireland: 1600–1972*. London: Allen Lane/The Penguin Press, 1988.

Foster, Roy. "'The lovely magic of its dawn': Reading Irish History as a Story." *Times Literary Supplement*, 16 December 1994, 4–6.

Foucault, Michel. *Language, Counter-Memory, Practice*. Ed. Donald F. Bouchard, trans. Donald F. Bouchard and Sherry Simon. Ithaca: Cornell University Press, 1977.

Freud, Sigmund. *Inhibitions, Symptoms and Anxiety*. Ed. James Strachey, trans. Alix Strachey, Standard edn. New York: W. W. Norton & Co., 1959 (1926).

The Interpretation of Dreams. Trans. and ed. James Strachey. New York: Avon Books, 1965 (1900).

Introductory Lectures on Psycho-Analysis. Trans. and ed. James Strachey. New York: W. W. Norton & Co., 1966.

Friel, Brian. *Translations*. New York: Samuel French, Inc., 1981.

Gibbons, Luke. *Transformations in Irish Culture*. Critical Conditions: Field Day Essays. Notre Dame, IN: University of Notre Dame Press, 1996.

Gibson, Michael. "A Clandestine Warning of Grim History." *The International Herald Tribune*, 2 December 1991.

Gogarty, Oliver St. John. Review of *Finnegans Wake*. *Observer*, 7 May 1939. N.p.

Greenblatt, Stephen, and Giles Gunn, eds. *Redrawing the Boundaries: The Transformation of English and American Literary Studies*. New York: The Modern Language Association of America, 1992.

Gregory, Lady Augusta, trans. *Cuchulain of Muirthemne*. Gerrards Cross, Buckinghamshire: Colin Smythe, Ltd., 1970.

Gunning, Tom. "An Aesthetic of Astonishment: Early Film and the (In)Credulous Spectator." *Art and Text* 34 (spring 1989). Reprinted in

Viewing Positions: Ways of Seeing Film, ed. Linda Williams, 114–33. New Brunswick: Rutgers University Press, 1995.

"The Cinema of Attractions: Early Film, Its Spectator and the Avant-Garde." *Wide Angle* 8, nos. 3/4 (fall 1986). Reprinted in *Early Cinema: Space, Frame, Narrative*, ed. Thomas Elsaesser, 56–62. London: BFI, 1990.

"Now You See It, Now You Don't: The Temporality of the Cinema of Attractions." In *Silent Film*, 71–84. New Brunswick: Rutgers University Press, 1996.

Hansen, Miriam. *Babel and Babylon: Spectatorship in American Silent Film.* Cambridge, MA: Harvard University Press, 1991.

"Benjamin, Cinema and Experience: The Blue Flower in the Land of Technology." *New German Critique* 40 (winter 1987): 179–224.

Hart, Clive. *Structure and Motif in* Finnegans Wake. Chicago: Northwestern University Press, 1962.

Hegel, Georg Wilhelm Friedrich. *Lectures on the Philosophy of World History: Introduction: Reason in History.* Trans. H. B. Nisbet. Cambridge: Cambridge University Press, 1988.

Helming, Steven. "Modernism Now." *The Sewanee Review* 102, no. 2 (spring 1994): 291–309.

Hofheinz, Thomas C. *Joyce and the Invention of Irish History:* Finnegans Wake *in Context.* Cambridge: Cambridge University Press, 1995.

Holloway, Joseph. *Diaries, 1895 to 1944.* Dublin: The National Library of Ireland. Microfiche.

Hommage à Roberto Rossellini: Voyage en Italie. Special issue of *L'Avant scène cinema,* no. 361 (June 1987).

Howe, Irving, ed. *Literary Modernism.* Greenwich, CT: Fawcett Publications, Inc., 1967.

Hull, Eleanor, trans. *The Cuchullin Saga in Irish Literature.* London: David Nutt, 1898.

Iggers, Georg G. "Introduction: The Transformation of Historical Studies in Historical Perspective." In *International Handbook of Historical Studies: Contemporary Research and Theory*, ed. Georg G. Iggers and Harold T. Parker, 1–14. Westport, CT: Greenwood Press, 1979.

Jackson, J. R. de J. *Historical Criticism and the Meaning of Texts.* New York: Routledge, 1989.

Jameson, Fredric. *The Political Unconscious.* Ithaca: Cornell University Press, 1981.

Jeffares, Norman. *W. B. Yeats: Man and Poet.* London: Kyle Cathie Limited, 1996.

A New Commentary on the Poems of W. B. Yeats. Stanford: Stanford University Press, 1984.

The Jerusalem Bible. New York: Doubleday & Company, Inc., 1966.

Joyce, James. *The Critical Writings of James Joyce.* Ed. Ellsworth Mason and Richard Ellmann. Ithaca: Cornell University Press, 1989.

Dubliners. Ed. A. Walton Litz and Robert Scholes. The Viking Critical Library. New York: Penguin Books, 1976.

Finnegans Wake. New York: Viking Penguin, 1939.

Letters of James Joyce. Ed. Stuart Gilbert. New York: The Viking Press, 1957.

A Portrait of the Artist as a Young Man. Ed. Chester G. Anderson. Viking Critical Library. New York: Penguin Books, 1977.

Ulysses. Ed. Hans Walter Gabler. Vintage Books. New York: Random House, 1986.

Keane, Patrick J. *Terrible Beauty: Yeats, Joyce, Ireland, and the Myth of the Devouring Female*. Columbia: University of Missouri Press, 1988. Rev. edn. Washington, DC: Smithsonian Institution Press, 1997.

Kellner, Hans. *Language and Historical Representation: Getting the Story Crooked*. Madison: The University of Wisconsin Press, 1989.

Kermode, Frank. *The Sense of an Ending: Studies in the Theory of Fiction*. New York: Oxford University Press, 1967.

Kiberd, Declan. *Inventing Ireland*. Cambridge, MA: Harvard University Press, 1996.

Kirby, Lynne. "Male Hysteria and Early Cinema." *Camera Obscura* 17 (May 1988).

Lacan, Jacques. *Ecrits: A Selection*. Trans. Alan Sheridan. New York: W. W. Norton & Co., 1977.

The Ethics of Psychoanalysis. The Seminar of Jacques Lacan. Book VII. New York: W. W. Norton & Co., 1992.

The Four Fundamental Concepts of Psychoanalysis. Ed. Jacques-Alain Miller, trans. Alan Sheridan. New York: W. W. Norton & Co., 1981.

LaCapra, Dominick. *History and Criticism*. Ithaca: Cornell University Press, 1985.

Lang, Robert, ed. *The Birth of a Nation: D. W. Griffith, Director*. Films in Print, vol. 21. New Brunswick: Rutgers University Press, 1994.

Laplanche, J., and J.-B. Pontalis. *The Language of Psycho-Analysis*. Trans. Donald Nicholson-Smith. New York: W. W. Norton & Co., 1973.

Leerssen, Joseph Th. [Joep]. "Law and Border (How and where we draw the line)." *Irish Review* 24 (1999): 1–8.

Mere Irish & Fíor-Ghael: Studies in the idea of Irish nationality, its development and literary expression prior to the nineteenth century. Utrecht Publications in General and Comparative Literature, vol. 22. Amsterdam/Philadelphia: John Benjamins Publishing Company, 1986.

Remembrance and Imagination: Patterns in the Historical and Literary Representation of Ireland in the Nineteenth Century. Critical Conditions: Field Day Monographs. Cork: Cork University Press, 1996.

Leersen, Joep [Joseph] et al. *Forging in the Smithy: National Identity and Representation in Anglo-Irish History*. The Literature of Politics, the Politics of Literature: Proceedings of the Leiden IASAIL Conference, vol. 1. Amsterdam/Atlanta, GA: Editions Rodopi B. V., 1995.

Lentricchia, Frank. *After the New Criticism*. Chicago: The University of Chicago Press, 1980.

Leonard, Garry. "Joyce and Lacan: 'The Woman' as a Symptom of 'Masculinity' in 'The Dead'." *James Joyce Quarterly* 28, no. 1 (winter 1991): 451–72.

Levinson, Marjorie, et al. *Rethinking Historicism: Critical Readings in Romantic History*. Oxford: Basil Blackwell, 1989.

Lichtenstein, Jacqueline, and Gerard Wajeman. "Jochen Gerz: Invisible Monument." *Art Press* 179 (April 1993), E1–E11.

Lloyd, David. *Anomalous States: Irish Writing and the Post-Colonial Moment*. Dublin: Lilliput Press, 1993.

Ireland after History. Notre Dame, IN: University of Notre Dame Press, 1999.

Longenbach, James. *Modernist Poetics of History: Pound, Eliot, and the Sense of the Past*. Princeton: Princeton University Press, 1988.

Lyons, F. S. L. *Charles Stewart Parnell*. New York: Oxford University Press, 1977.

Lyotard, Jean-François. *The Postmodern Condition: A Report on Knowledge*. Trans. Geoff Bennington and Brian Massumi. Theory and History of Literature, vol. 10. Minneapolis: University of Minnesota Press, 1984.

MacDonagh, Oliver. *States of Mind: A Study of Anglo-Irish Conflict, 1780–1980*. London: George Allen & Unwin, 1983.

MacManus, Seumas. *The Story of the Irish Race: A Popular History of Ireland*. 2nd edn. New York: The Irish Publishing Co., 1921.

Mahaffey, Vicki. *Reauthorizing Joyce*. Cambridge: Cambridge University Press, 1988.

States of Desire: Wilde, Yeats, Joyce and the Irish Experiment. Oxford: Oxford University Press, 1998.

Marcus, Phillip L., ed. *The Death of Cuchulain: Manuscript Materials Including the Author's Final Text*. Ithaca: Cornell University Press, 1982.

McGann, Jerome J., ed. *Historical Studies and Literary Criticism*. Madison: University of Wisconsin Press, 1985.

McHugh, Roland. *Annotations to* Finnegans Wake. Baltimore: The Johns Hopkins University Press, 1980.

Mink, Louis O. *Historical Understanding*. Ithaca: Cornell University Press, 1987.

Moody, T. W., and F. X. Martin, eds. *The Course of Irish History*. Rev. edn. Cork: The Mercier Press, 1984.

Morrison, Paul. *The Poetics of Fascism: Ezra Pound, T. S. Eliot, Paul de Man*. New York: Oxford University Press, 1996.

Mulvey, Laura. "Satellites of Love." *Sight and Sound* 10, no. 12 (Dec. 2000): 20–24.

Naremore, James. "Return of the Living Dead." *James Joyce Literary Supplement* (spring 1991): 16.

Nietzsche, Friedrich. *On the Genealogy of Morals*. Trans. Walter Kauffman and R. J. Hollingdale. Vintage Books. New York: Random House, 1969.

"On the Uses and Disadvantages of History for Life." In *Untimely Meditations*, trans. R. J. Hollingdale, 57–124. Cambridge: Cambridge University Press, 1983.

Nolan, Emer. *James Joyce and Nationalism*. New York: Routledge, 1995.

O'Brien, Conor Cruise, and Maire O'Brien. *A Concise History of Ireland*. New York: Thames and Hudson, 1985.

"Passion and Cunning: An Essay on the Politics of W. B. Yeats." In *In Excited Reverie: A Centenary Tribute to William Bulter Yeats 1865–1939*, ed. A. Norman Jeffares and K. G. W. Cross, 207–78. New York: The Macmillan Company, 1965.

   States of Ireland. New York: Random House, 1972.

Ortega y Gasset, José. *History as a System and Other Essays Toward a Philosophy of History*. New York: W. W. Norton & Co., 1961.

O'Toole, Fintan. *Black Hole, Green Card: The Disappearance of Ireland*. Dublin: New Island Books, 1994.

   The Ex-Isle of Erin: Images of a Global Ireland. Dublin: New Island Books, 1997.

Ovid. *Metamorphoses*. Trans. Mary M. Innes. New York: Penguin Books, 1955.

Perloff, Marjorie. "Modernist Studies." In *Redrawing the Boundaries: The Transformation of English and American Literary Studies*, ed. Stephen Greenblatt and Giles Gunn. New York: The Modern Language Association of America 1992.

Plotnitsky, Arkady. *In the Shadow of Hegel: Complementarity, History, and the Unconscious*. Gainesville: University Press of Florida, 1993.

Popper, Karl R. *The Poverty of Historicism*. New York: Harper & Row, Publishers, 1961.

Propp, Vladimir. *Morphology of the Folk-tale*. Trans. Laurence Scott. Austin: University of Texas Press, 1968.

Rabaté, Jean-Michel. *The Ghosts of Modernity*. Gainesville: University Press of Florida, 1996.

   Jacques Lacan: Psychoanalysis and the Subject of Literature. New York: Palgrave, 2001.

Ragland-Sullivan, Ellie. *Jacques Lacan and the Philosophy of Psychoanalysis*. Chicago: University of Illinois Press, 1987.

   "Lacan's Seminars on James Joyce: Writing as Symptom and 'Singular Solution.'" In *Compromise Formations: Current Directions in Psychoanalytic Criticism*, ed. Vera J. Camden, 61–85. Kent, OH: Kent State University Press, 1989.

Rees, Alwyn, and Brinley. *Celtic Heritage: Ancient Tradition in Ireland and Wales*. London: Thames and Hudson, 1961.

Rickard, John. *Joyce's Book of Memory: The Mnemotechnic of Ulysses*. Durham, NC: Duke University Press, 1999.

Ricoeur, Paul. *The Reality of the Historical Past*. Milwaukee: Marquette University Press, 1984

   Time and Narrative. Trans. Kathleen McLaughlin and David Pellauer. Chicago: University of Chicago Press, 1984–88.

Rockett, Kevin, et al. *Cinema and Ireland*. Syracuse: Syracuse University Press, 1987.

   The Irish Filmography. Dublin: Red Mountain Media, 1996.

Roof, Judith, and Robyn Wiegman, eds. *Who Can Speak? Authority and Critical Identity*. Urbana: University of Illinois Press, 1995.

Rose, Danis, and John O'Hanlon. *Understanding Finnegans Wake: A Guide to the Narrative of James Joyce's Masterpiece*. New York: Garland Publishing, 1982.

Roudinesco, Elisabeth. *Jacques Lacan & Co.: A History of Psychoanalysis in France, 1925–1985*. Trans. Jeffrey Mehlman. Chicago: The University of Chicago Press, 1990.

Sanders, George. *Memoirs of a Professional Cad*. London: The Scarecrow Press, 1992.

Schulz-Keil, Helena. "Psychoanalysis and Hystory." *Hystoria*. Special issue of *Lacan Study Notes*, nos. 6–9, pp. 54–74. New York: The New York Lacan Study Group, 1988.

Shelley, Percy Bysshe. *Prometheus Unbound*. In *Shelley's Poetry and Prose: Authoritative Texts and Criticism*, ed. Donald H. Reiman and Sharon B. Powers. (New York: W. W. Norton & Co., 1977) 130–210.

Sperry, Stuart. *Shelley's Major Verse: The Narrative and Dramatic Poetry*. Cambridge, MA: Harvard University Press, 1988.

Spoo, Robert. *James Joyce and the Language of History: Dedalus's Nightmare*. New York: Oxford University Press, 1994.

Staiger, Janet. "*The Birth of a Nation*: Reconsidering Its Reception." In *The Birth of a Nation: D. W. Griffith, Director*, ed. Robert Lang. Films in Print, vol. 21, New Brunswick: Rutgers University Press, 1994.

Surette, Leon. "Modernism, Postmodernism, Fascism, and Historicism." *University of Toronto Quarterly* 60, no. 4 (summer 1991): 476–92.

Tratner, Michael. *Modernism and Mass Politics: Joyce, Woolf, Eliot, Yeats*. Stanford: Stanford University Press, 1995.

Veeser, H. Aram, ed. *The New Historicism*. New York: Routledge, 1989.

Vico, Giambattista. *The New Science*. 3rd edn. (1744). Trans. Thomas Goddard Bergin and Max Harold Fisch. Ithaca: Cornell University Press, 1948.

Virgil. *The Aeneid*. Trans. Robert Fitzgerald. New York: Random House, 1983.

Watson, G. J. *Irish Identity and the Literary Revival. Synge, Yeats. Joyce and O'Casey*. New York: Harper & Row Publishers. Inc., 1979.

Wells, H. G. *The Time Machine*. New York: Oxford University Press, 1996.

White, Hayden. *Tropics of Discourse: Essays in Cultural Criticism*. Baltimore: The Johns Hopkins University Press, 1978.

Wilde, Oscar. *The Complete Works of Oscar Wilde*. New York: Harper and Row, Publishers, 1989.

Yeats, William Butler. *Autobiographies*. New York: The Macmillan Company, 1927.

The Collected Poems of W. B. Yeats. Ed. Richard J. Finneran. New York: Collier Books, Macmillan Publishing Company, 1989.

The Death of Cuchulain. Ed. A. Norman Jeffares, 209–18. *Eleven Plays of William Butler Yeats*. New York: Macmillan Publishing Company, 1964.

Essays and Introductions. New York: Macmillan, 1961.

Letters to the New Island. Cambridge, MA: Harvard University Press, 1934.

The Letters of W. B. Yeats. Ed. Allan Wade. New York: Farrar, Straus and Giroux, 1980.

Mythologies. New York: Macmillan Publishing Company, 1969.

The Variorum Edition of the Plays of W. B. Yeats. Ed. Russell K. Alspach and Catharine C. Alspach. New York: The Macmillan Company, 1966.

A Vision. London: Macmillan & Co., Ltd., 1937.

Young, James E. *The Texture of Memory: Holocaust Memorials and Meaning.* New Haven: Yale University Press, 1993.

Young, Robert. *White Mythologies: Writing History and the West.* New York: Routledge, 1990.

Zizek, Slavoj. *Looking Awry: An Introduction to Jacques Lacan through Popular Culture.* Cambridge, MA: MIT Press, 1991.

"Rossellini: Woman as Symptom of Man." *October* 54 (fall 1990): 19–44.

Index